Maureen Pastine
Editor

Collection Development: Access in the Virtual Library

Collection Development: Access in the Virtual Library
has been co-published simultaneously as *Collection
Management,* Volume 22, Numbers 1/2 1997

*Pre-publication
REVIEWS,
COMMENTARIES,
EVALUATIONS . . .*

"**T**his anthology documents unequi-
vocably that collaboration–between library and customer, library and
vendor, and among libraries–is essential
for success in today's academic library.
From shared licensing agreements to
cooperative collection development, from
customer-driven service to providing a
space for community, fertile partnerships engender ongoing progress or
continued survival for institutions confronting the challenges of the evolving
information age. Each author addresses
the salient issues that shape the reality
of a shared digital library and presents
timely recommendations for reinventing
library service in that arena."

Kathryn Hammell Carpenter, MS
University Librarian,
Valparaiso University, Indiana

Collection Development:
Access in the Virtual Library

Collection Development: Access in the Virtual Library has been co-published simultaneously as *Collection Management*, Volume 22, Number 1/2 1997.

Collection Management Monographs/"Separates"

The State of Western European Studies: Implications for Collection Development, edited by Anthony M. Angiletta, Martha L. Brogan, Charles S. Fineman, and Clara M. Lovett

Collection Management for School Library Media Centers, edited by Brenda H. White

Reading and the Art of Librarianship: Selected Essays of John B. Nicholson, Jr., edited by Paul Z. DuBois and Dean H. Keller

International Conference on Research Library Cooperation, edited by The Research Libraries Group, Inc.

Euro-Librarianship: Shared Resources, Shared Responsibilities, edited by Assunta Pisani

Access Services in Libraries: New Solutions for Collection Management, edited by Gregg Sapp

Practical Issues in Collection Development and Collection Access, edited by Katina Strauch, Sally Somers, Susan Zappen, and Anne Jennings

Electronic Resources: Implications for Collection Management, edited by Genevieve S. Owens

Collection Development: Past and Future, edited by Maureen Pastine

Collection Development: Access in the Virtual Library, edited by Maureen Pastine

Collection Development: Access in the Virtual Library

Maureen Pastine
Editor

Collection Development: Access in the Virtual Library has been co-published simultaneously as *Collection Management*, Volume 22, Numbers 1/2 1997.

The Haworth Press, Inc.
New York • London

Collection Development: Access in the Virtual Library has been co-published simultaneously as *Collection Management*, Volume 22, Numbers 1/2 1997.

Cover design by Thomas J. Mayshock Jr.

Library of Congress Cataloging-in-Publication Data

Collection development : access in the virtual library / Maureen Pastine, editor.
    p. cm.
    "Has been co-published simultaneously as Collection management, volume 22, numbers 1/2."
    Includes bibliographical references and index.
    ISBN 0-7890-0385-6 (alk. paper)
    1. Libraries–United States–Special collections–Electronic information resources. 2. Digital libraries–United States. I. Pastine, Maureen.
Z692.C65C65 1997
025.2'84–dc21
                                                  97-38860
                                                   CIP

INDEXING & ABSTRACTING

Contributions to this publication are selectively indexed or abstracted in print, electronic, online, or CD-ROM version(s) of the reference tools and information services listed below. This list is current as of the copyright date of this publication. See the end of this section for additional notes.

- *Central Library & Documentation Bureau International Labour Office,* CH-1211 Geneva 22, Switzerland

- *CNPIEC Reference Guide: Chinese National Directory of Foreign Periodicals*, P.O. Box 88, Beijing, People's Republic of China

- *Combined Health Information Database (CHID)*, National Institutes of Health, 3 Information Way, Bethesda, MD 20892-3580

- *Current Awareness Abstracts,* Association for Information Management, Information House, 20-24 Old Street, London, EC1V 9AP, England

- *IBZ International Bibliography of Periodical Literature*, Zeller Verlag GmbH & Co., P.O.B. 1949, d-49009 Osnabruck, Germany

- *Index to Periodical Articles Related to Law,* University of Texas, 727 East 26th Street, Austin, TX 78705

- *Information Reports & Bibliographies,* Science Associates International, Inc., 6 Hastings Road, Marlboro, NJ 07746-1313

- *Information Science Abstracts,* Plenum Publishing Company, 233 Spring Street, New York, NY 10013-1578

- *Informed Librarian, The,* Infosources Publishing, 140 Norma Road, Teaneck, NJ 07666

(continued)

- *INTERNET ACCESS (& additional networks) Bulletin Board for Libraries ("BUBL") coverage of information resources on INTERNET, JANET, and other networks.*
  - <URL:http://bubl.ac.uk/>
  - The new locations will be found under <URL:http://bubl.ac.uk.link/>.
  - Any existing BUBL users who have problems finding information on the new service should contact the BUBL help line by sending e-mail to <bubl@bubl.ac.uk>.
  The Andersonian Library, Curran Building, 101 St. James Road, Glasgow G4 0NS, Scotland

- *Journal of Academic Librarianship: Guide to Professional Literature, The,* Grad School of Library & Information Science/Simmons College, 300 The Fenway, Boston, MA 02115-5898

- *Konyvtari Figyelo–Library Review*, National Szechenyi Library, Centre for Library and Information Science, H-1827 Budapest, Hungary

- *Library & Information Science Abstracts (LISA),* Bowker-Saur Limited, Maypole House, Maypole Road, East Grinstead, West Sussex, RH19 1HH, England

- *Library Hi Tech News,* Pierian Press, P.O. Box 1808, Ann Arbor, MI 48106

- *Library Literature,* The H.W. Wilson Company, 950 University Avenue, Bronx, NY 10452

- *OT BibSys,* American Occupational Therapy Foundation, P.O. Box 31220, Rockville, MD 20824-1220

- *PASCAL, c/o Institute de L'Information Scientifique et Technique. Cross-discipinary electronic database covering the fields of science, technology & medicine. Also available on CD-ROM, and can generate customized retrospective searches. For more information: INIST, Customer Desk, 2, alee du Parc de Brabois, F-54514 Vandoeuvre Cedex, France; http//www.inist.fr,* INIST/CNRS-Service Gestion des Documents Primaires, 2, allee du Parc de Brabois, F-54514 Vandoeuvre-les-Nancy, Cedex, France

(continued)

- ***Referativnyi Zhurnal (Abstracts Journal of the Institute of Scientific Information of the Republic of Russia),*** The Institute of Scientific Information, Baltijskaja ul., 14, Moscow, A-219, Republic of Russia

Book reviews are selectively excerpted by the Guide to Professional Literature of the Journal of Academic Librarianship.

SPECIAL BIBLIOGRAPHIC NOTES

related to special journal issues (separates) and indexing / abstracting

☐ indexing/abstracting services in this list will also cover material in any "separate" that is co-published simultaneously with Haworth's special thematic journal issue or DocuSerial. Indexing/abstracting usually covers material at the article/chapter level.

☐ monographic co-editions are intended for either non-subscribers or libraries which intend to purchase a second copy for their circulating collections.

☐ monographic co-editions are reported to all jobbers/wholesalers/approval plans. The source journal is listed as the "series" to assist the prevention of duplicate purchasing in the same manner utilized for books-in-series.

☐ to facilitate user/access services all indexing/abstracting services are encouraged to utilize the co-indexing entry note indicated at the bottom of the first page of each article/chapter/contribution.

☐ this is intended to assist a library user of any reference tool (whether print, electronic, online, or CD-ROM) to locate the monographic version if the library has purchased this version but not a subscription to the source journal.

☐ individual articles/chapters in any Haworth publication are also available through the Haworth Document Delivery Service (HDDS).

ABOUT THE EDITOR

Maureen Pastine is University Librarian, University Libraries, Paley Library, Temple University, Philadelphia, Pennsylvania. Previously, she was Central University Librarian, Central University Libraries, Southern Methodist University, in Dallas, Texas. She is responsible for administration and planning for libraries for humanities/social sciences, music/fine arts, science and engineering, geology/anthropology, special collections, and media and instructional technologies. Previous positions include Director of Libraries at Washington State University, 1985-89; University Librarian, San Jose State University, 1980-85; Head of Reference and Coordinator of Reference, Online Searching, and Bibliographic Instruction, University of Illinois at Urbana-Champaign, 1979-1980; Head of Undergraduate Library, University of Illinois at Urbana-Champaign, 1977-1979; and Head of Reference at the University of Nebraska at Omaha, 1974-1977.

Collection Development:
Access in the Virtual Library

CONTENTS

∞   ALL HAWORTH BOOKS AND JOURNALS
    ARE PRINTED ON CERTIFIED
    ACID-FREE PAPER

Introduction

Maureen Pastine

Brian Hawkins, Vice President for Academic Planning and Administration, Brown University, Providence, Rhode Island, presented a paper at the Stanford Forum for Higher Education Futures, The Aspen Institute, Aspen Meadows, Colorado, October 18, 1996, entitled *The Unsustainability of the Traditional Library and the Threat to Higher Education.* In the paper he predicted the demise of the university library as we know it, assuming that as we move "toward a cooperative strategy of electronic storage" we "will not only reduce problems associated with physical space, but will also address the critical problems of preservation of print materials that libraries are facing" (Hawkins, 1996, p. 10).

Unfortunately, there are many university administrators who believe that the major role of the librarian is to identify, collect, and organize the world's information. What they often fail to recognize, that is even more crucial, is that organizing methods to critically evaluate and use information is what libraries are all about. Technology has changed the way information can be stored, accessed, and used but it has also made it more difficult and complex for the end-user who needs even more help from the library staff so as not to be overwhelmed with too much irrelevant information. And, in doing this, libraries need adequate space to house the new information technology equipment and software for public access and to

Maureen Pastine, AB, MLS, is University Librarian, University Libraries, Paley Library, Temple University, Philadelphia, PA 19122.

[Haworth co-indexing entry note]: "Introduction." Pastine, Maureen. Co-published simultaneously in *Collection Management* (The Haworth Press, Inc.) Vol. 22, No. 1/2, 1997, pp. 1-8; and: *Collection Development: Access in the Virtual Library* (ed: Maureen Pastine) The Haworth Press, Inc., 1997, pp. 1-8. Single or multiple copies of this article are available for a fee from The Haworth Document Delivery Service [1-800-342-9678, 9:00 a.m. - 5:00 p.m. (EST). E-mail address: getinfo@haworth.com].

1

provide staff space, along with many of the more traditional print and non-print resources of the past. David Goding addresses some of these issues in his chapter on physical facilities/space in this volume.

The focus in academic libraries today may well be to "empower" the end-user, to turn libraries and users into self-service units, but if we truly understand the changes brought about by the new information technologies, we also understand that they are "enabling" technologies, not "replacement" for all of our resources, personnel, and other operations, nor are they the crucial element–libraries and librarians still remain as the most important elements in the research process. We do, of course, have many changing options for document delivery and some of those do replace past functions although most are just additional elements, adding to the library staff's already overwhelming workload. The crucial role for librarians remains as reference and research assistants who help library users find specific information and, even more importantly, teach the library user how to evaluate and use information in building upon their knowledge base. Our future remains doing what computers cannot do–i.e., instruction in teaching the user increasingly more sophisticated bibliographical retrieval and assessment methodologies.

Barbara Kemp's chapter in this volume is on the impact of change and shifting paradigms on public services staffing. She acknowledges the increasing complexity of educating both staff and user in both traditional information resources and the new information technologies. The "electronic publishing revolution" has not led to a decline in printed information resources. Indeed, the print information world has also experienced an "explosion." With scientific knowledge doubling every 15 to 17 years, and scientists expected to keep abreast of new knowledge in their fields, and humanists and social sciences becoming increasingly interdependent and interdisciplinary, library use has increased. And, use of the Internet and the World Wide Web continues to grow tremendously on a daily basis. The proportion of readings of articles from libraries has at least doubled, maybe even tripled, over the past 20 years (from 1977 to 1997)–partially, at least, because scientists have decreased personal subscriptions due to rising prices and because it is much easier to identify, locate, and retrieve journal articles through the expanding world of electronic access to citation and full-text databases. This has created a dramatic increase in use of interlibrary loan and new document delivery programs.

Some believe that publications of the future will be all electronic or all paper, online or CD-ROM. In fact, a combination of technologies and paper are likely to co-exist, each fulfilling a niche that satisfies specific information needs and requirements. There is, however, no doubt that electronic information is proliferating, along with network access capabilities to information stored at remote sites and/or added to local holdings capabilities via CD-ROM or digital databases stored in a library's online catalog. As David Goding explains in his chapter in this volume, the expanding Internet/World Wide Web have "significant technical, access, and content limitations which make it unlikely that they will replace the library as society's main source for information." As he notes, "librarians provide and maintain a place to select, collect, organize, manage and access information" but "what will change are tools and the details of facility design and implementation." He predicts that the "purely virtual digital library is a pipe dream," that the "library of the future will remain much as it exists now with some retrofitting, remodeling, and renovation to accommodate rapidly changing technologies and a growing interest in distributed learning/distance education."

Barbara Kemp notes that there will be "an increasing paradigm shift from local availability/ownership to access or delivery regardless of format or location, with increasingly more sophisticated library users with new demands for new technologies creating an environment of constant change, continual pressures/stress on staff for learning new complex hardware and software." She, too, sees a continuing need for physical space for libraries, and she notes that there will be "new costs in time to educate staff and users in the complexities of accessing and evaluating and using information resources in electronic format." Her discussion of the new "behind-the-scenes" costs points out how the "seductiveness of the computer" requires even greater time spent with library users.

In his chapter on the study of subject strengths using the OCLC/AMIGOS Collection Analysis CD and Alternatives to it in this volume, Curt Holleman notes that there are "increasingly complex measurements of collecting patterns" that librarians must become familiar with. He demonstrates how "the limitations inherent in the electronic data being collected" can create "errors of judgment in publication of seriously misleading data." But he also notes that these new alternatives for assessing strengths in collections will also be most valuable in working within consortia to reallocate resources and allow one or another library within a region to be the primary collector and distributor in one or another subject within that region, releasing other libraries' resources for further reallocation in order to both reduce local collecting costs and expand the universe of information and knowledge available to one's primary clientele.

"The rapid and relentless pace of change in information technology has exacted its toll in time," David Kohl explains in his chapter on the changing nature of library consortial partnerships in this volume. His statement that "we hardly have time to learn the new technology before it changes, or we spend so much time learning new technologies we have no time to plan for its effective use or how to teach it to others" leads us to rethink priorities to address these crucial problems. He notes that "the new electronic databases and the perceived need for these at the local level, where funds have declined or purchasing power has forced libraries to rely more on resource-sharing with other consortia members, has even created new demands for state-wide consortial development. His discussion of the OhioLINK consortium demonstrates how an excellent role model for other states and regions of the country can be developed. As he notes, most "academic libraries have cancelled many serials subscriptions and have begun to rely more heavily on purchasing only the needed articles." As libraries have initiated such efforts for cost reduction, they have found another benefit, i.e., release of funds for subsidizing electronic access and document delivery of specific journal articles to many more journals than any one library can afford to subscribe to with their limited funding. Kohl predicts that traditional interlibrary loan will change dramatically as they move into expanded and enhanced document delivery mechanisms, potentially growing from a small percentage of one library's circulation to a significant portion of circulation transactions. As he notes, a library's future "will be more reliant on document delivery of journal articles not held locally and more collecting by libraries in a limited number of subject areas." However, he does not believe that any library will be able to drop "core collecting" which is somewhat duplicative from one academic library to another because of the high use made of such materials. However, he does see some powerful cost-benefits to relying on consortial partnerships in site licenses to electronic, citation and full-text databases. In addition, there will be associated cost-benefits as the consortia share implementation and installation costs of hardware/software and networking access.

Kohl does feel that some physical space may be reallocated to other services or functions as the virtual library, or the 14" personal computer screen, assumes some of the former physical library space taken up in bound journals and even microforms. But, perhaps, even more importantly the "virtual library" offers incredible new enhancements and improvements in subject access by "enriching the online catalog with contents/index pages, links to book reviews, and links to relevant reference sources and Web sites." He also notes that a new and/or expanded role for the librarian will be in devotion of far more time to external relations with vendors, consortia, and other electronic networks, information agencies, and similar organizations in which our partnerships are growing by leaps and bounds. However, like the other contributors to this volume, Kohl also maintains that academic libraries will continue a significant amount of ownership along with the new electronic access information resources.

Robert Skinner takes the reader of this volume into another developing aspect of information delivery–i.e., collection management for the distributed learner/distance education site. He predicts that the exploding world of the remote learner will require greater reliance on the "virtual library." Like Peter Drucker, his prediction is that all of our universities are to become more dependent on learners who are not tied to the physical campus space, nor to the traditional classroom lecturer and library reserve book shelves, but rather to asynchronous and synchronous learning. He explains that "asynchronous" learning is a "store and forward" or "on-demand" instruction, more dependent on the "convenience of participants" than on the traditional classroom on-campus course scheduling. This type of learning will be more focused on the learner, rather than the teacher, moving "from lecturer to tutor/facilitator." He also discusses "synchronous" learning which is "real time," "face to face" or via electronic conferencing over a distance. Such educational programming often offered some distance from the traditional campus or over electronic networks will change the way our faculty teach and the way students learn, and along with that, place some new pressures on the libraries in provision of equivalent library services to students at a distance. Again, it will, undoubtedly, move the library into a more "virtual" or "electronic delivery" mode in the very near future.

James Kopp in his chapter on the politics of the virtual collection discusses many issues related to the developing "virtual library" of the future, from new competitors in the information storage and delivery world, to new partners that the libraries must work with in delivering information, helping library users to understand the complexities of access to electronic information storage, retrieval, and evaluation and use of that information. Along with traditional issues of student and faculty liaison, the librarian must also be aware of how to work with administrators and funding agents in provision of a balance between the traditional library resources and the new information technologies. They must work more closely in changing partnerships with other consortial members, vendors, booksellers, and other information agencies. In addition, they must become more knowledgeable about how to address bibliographical control of the chaos and maze of information, not all quality information, on the expanding Internet and the World Wide Web, as well as other developing electronic information storehouses and databases. Security issues are becoming more important and other problematic issues relate to copyright and whether or not universities and libraries should play a greater role in provision of intellectual property. Whether libraries should subsidize document delivery via telefacsimile or digital transmission of a journal article to the faculty or student desktop is another issue that warrants consideration in developing issues related to collection management in a "virtual library." And, then there is another issue gaining a great deal of discussion in library and higher education literature, and that is the "fee" vs. "free" debate with a new twist–should libraries subsidize the electronically delivered journal articles or make the user pay– and as the Internet/Web develops, will new charges for information services be required? Will users value information more if there is an associated case which they may be required to pay out of their own pockets, or will universities be able to subsidize not only the new technological equipment, software, and networking infrastructure but the "electronic information access" costs as well? If not, what will be given up or reallocated or not even considered in the library of the future?

Curt Holleman, in the chapter on the use of the OCLC/AMIGOS Collection Analysis CD, provides an excellent overview of the study of subject strengths' overlap and national collecting patterns in academic libraries. He notes that comparative quantitative volume counts are no longer adequate when analyzing subject strengths and weaknesses between two or more academic libraries. His chapter examines "three varieties of research into library collections: studies of subject strengths, studies of the overlap of collections, and studies of national collecting patterns." From the precursor to the National Shelflist count and the newer electronic analyses available, he details studies of subject strengths from 1973, from manual counts and measurement of shelflist cards to the current superior electronic products, especially the OCLC/AMIGOS Collection Analysis CD and other newer "sophisticated electronic engines for determining overlap."

As Holleman notes, the primary problem with the OCLC/AMIGOS product is that it "covers only eleven imprint years" but he still feels that this "restriction to eleven imprint years makes comparisons even more valid . . . [as] Libraries are very inconsistent in which older materials of theirs are represented on OCLC . . ." Holleman's critiques of the differing studies are thoughtful and insightful, adding to the vast literature on this topic. He points out errors, flaws, distortions, and exaggerations made in a few of the studies. He believes and justifies why "the restrictions of a comparison of subject strengths to imprint years" in the OCLC/AMIGOS CD product "allows for a more accurate electronic comparison than is possible without an imprint restriction." However, he cautions us in regard to "three weakness in the Collection Analysis CD's ability to do overlap studies . . ." As he mentions, "small errors can easily invalidate statistics when researchers use electronic products to compare and analyze collections . . . but should not . . . keep us from using excellent new products such as the OCLC/AMIGOS Collection Analysis CD." Endnotes for this chapter will assist others in evaluating and using the many different studies available for analyzing subject strengths in academic library collections.

There are two selective bibliographies at the end of this volume, one of U.K. sources by Jim Vickery and another of primarily U.S. sources by Maureen Pastine relating to many of the issues addressed in this volume, and even some not addressed in the chapters but closely related to the topics covered in this volume.

REFERENCES

Hawkins, Brian. *The Unsustainability of the Traditional Library and the Threat to Higher Education.*
(Stanford Forum for Higher Education Futures). The Aspen Institute, Aspen Meadows, Colorado, October 18, 1996. 18 pp. (Available from Brian L. Hawkins, Vice President for Academic Planning & Administration, Brown University, Providence, Rhode Island 02912.)

Chapter One:
The More Things Change, the More They Stay the Same: The Future of the Library and the Library Profession

David P. Goding

WHAT'S GOING ON HERE–SEEING THE ELEPHANT

During the American Civil War, soldiers in battle described their first glimpse of the approaching enemy army as "Seeing the Elephant," that moment of disorientation, anxiety and fear of the unknown that is felt in the pit of the stomach. Librarianship is "seeing the elephant" right now.

Electronic Library, Digital Library, Virtual Library, Information Manager, Systems Integrator, Intermediation, Disintermediation, Multimedia, Electronic Publishing, DVD, ISO 10162/10163, NII, Z39.50, Internet, World Wide Web, AI, Expert Systems, Robots, Avatars. It's enough to make one's head spin.

In only the last couple of years, digital technology has brought a deluge of new questions and concerns to the profession. Librarians have always been early adopters of new technology–on-line cata-

David P. Goding, MLS, is a library consultant in Iowa City, IA.

[Haworth co-indexing entry note]: "Chapter One: The More Things Change, the More They Stay the Same: The Future of the Library and the Library Profession." Goding, David P. Co-published simultaneously in *Collection Management* (The Haworth Press, Inc.) Vol. 22, No. 1/2, 1997, pp. 9-28; and: *Collection Development: Access in the Virtual Library* (ed: Maureen Pastine) The Haworth Press, Inc., 1997, pp. 9-28. Single or multiple copies of this article are available for a fee from The Haworth Document Delivery Service [1-800-342-9678, 9:00 a.m. - 5:00 p.m. (EST). E-mail address: getinfo@haworth.com].

loging, on-line searching, automated circulation, Microforms. However, digital technologies appear to affect the core of what we do,
how we do it, and where we do it. It's no wonder that disruption,
disorientation and uncertainty reign.

What's it all mean? Is librarianship rapidly becoming a dead-end
profession? Is the library devolving into a quaint anachronism? Will
the physical library as such cease to exist? It's clear that some form
of the Virtual Digital Library is in our professional future, its development inexorable, inevitable. What's not clear is the course of
developments or what the final picture will look like.

The literature is replete with articles by thoughtful professionals
trying to peer into the future and to chart a course for the profession.
Their efforts are commendable and useful. However, the fact is no
one really has the slightest idea what will happen.

Perhaps the situation is not as bad as it seems. A good place to
start, in fact the only place to start, is where we are right now. Let's
step back a bit and revisit some basic, fundamental concepts about
the profession. This will provide an overview or framework that
should bring some order and allow us more sensibly to make some
suggestions about the future.

BACK TO BASICS–LS 101

What is the larger environment within which librarians function
and what do they do within that environment? Simply put, librarians navigate an ocean of information. Information comes in all
shapes, sizes, forms and formats–information objects, if you will. In
accord with the specific aims of their institutions, librarians assume
intellectual and physical control of some of those information
objects. Within libraries, acquired information objects are "massaged"; value is added to them. Once massaged, the information
objects are made available to users–who go on to use it or to create
more information. That's it, that's the basic framework.

Information changes, information objects change, the ways
librarians massage information change, the way information is
served up to users changes. So what's new here? Not much really.
For example, we've progressed from papyri to inscribed books to
printed books to Microforms, to video/audio tape and now to digital

media in all its forms. Great advances–but it's all still just information.

Certainly, the information seeker, on his own, can always obtain information, in any of its forms. But the special role of the librarian is to make the process easier. Librarians do what an individual seeker can't or won't do. Librarians provide and maintain a place to select, collect, organize, manage and access information–the Library. These special functions and special places require money, large scale resources and expertise not available to the individual. Forms of information, tools, techniques, and modes of delivery change–always have, always will. The core functions of librarianship are not going to change.

Let's not forget our users. Library patrons can loosely be divided into casual and serious users. The term casual user is not pejorative but describes the person who drops into the library to read some magazines, review some A/V material, or perhaps browse the stacks to find a book to take home. Serious users come into the library with more specific information needs requiring specific materials containing the information they need in a variety of formats. User behavior is not going to change fundamentally. The library is and will continue to be a place for both kinds of users.

Form Follows Function–we've all heard that old design truism. In this case, the library building as a physical thing is designed and constructed to reflect and facilitate the functions and activities it houses. Library, Librarian and Library User are inextricably intertwined. The Library provides spaces and resources for librarians to collect, organize and maintain information–offices, workstations, bibliographic tools, etc. The Library provides spaces where information may be browsed or accessed by users–shelving, reading areas, Information Service/Reference Desks, A/V equipment, CD-ROM readers, computer terminals for Internet access, meeting rooms, etc. But this is not all the Library is.

The Library is also a public place. Architecturally, it reflects the priorities and values of the community and culture. The Library is a place for people in the community (town, university, school, company)–to gather, meet, study, research, learn, reflect and feel comfortable. The Library is a place of social interaction; it is a nice place to be.

As form follows function, since the core functions of the librarian have not and will not change, and user behaviors will not change, the basic form of the Library has not and will not change. What will change are tools and the details of facility design and implementation. All of which brings us to the Library Without Books–the Virtual Digital Library.

THE INTERNET/WORLD WIDE WEB–
WHAT TO DO WHEN THE ELEPHANT APPEARS

If nothing fundamental is going to change in the Library, what is all the hand wringing about? In one word, the Web. In two–over-used–words, the Information Superhighway. For years, the Internet was a place only the most adept techno-whizzes dared traverse. Slow modems, pokey CPUs, arcane UNIX commands, perverse communications protocols, obscure ftp sites, a text-based interface and similar obstacles rendered the Internet useful only to a rather select group of intrepid users, and even they used the Internet mainly for e-mail, newsgroups and exchange of scientific papers. Not much research was done. Fast modems, speedy CPUs, net browsers, HTML, graphical interface and the point and click ease of using the World Wide Web have forever transformed the Internet.

The unbelievable growth and potential of the Web are really what's gotten librarians worried. From some 130 Web sites in mid-1993, the Web grew to over 646,000 sites by January 1997, with an estimated net gain of 1200 sites being added each day! It is estimated that there are 35 million Web users now and that new users are logging on at the rate of almost 1 new user per second!

We all know what can be found on the Web–lots of stuff, lots of information. If all that information is out there being accessed by all those users, all by themselves, what use is a librarian, what need is there for a library?

Shall we hang on to our pensions until retirement and slink away? Shall we get out in front of the technology and make our-selves indispensable? Many believe that the profession should retrench, make do with even less money, share and pool scanty resources even more, cut back drastically on book acquisition and serial subscriptions, "flatten" organizational hierarchies, lay off even more staff. It is suggested that we use what funds we have to increase expenditures for technology–build new Hi-Tech libraries or retrofit old libraries to meet new technological standards, buy equipment, pay for on-line access fees, etc. The most pessimistic observers see even these adaptive measures as mere milestones on the road to the edificeless Virtual Digital Library.

It must be understood right off that there is no possibility of librarians getting ahead of the technology. Current developments in the profession are technology driven; we don't know exactly where technology is going. There is much evidence to indicate, however, that the Internet and specifically the World Wide Web will not replace the Library. The Library will continue its evolution to hi-tech gateway to information. Techno-heresy, you say. Well, perhaps. Let's take a closer look at the situation to see why this is how it will be.

A TRUE ADVENTURE–
CRAWLING THE WORLD WIDE WEB

In researching this article, the author wanted to find the most current estimate of total Web sites worldwide. With URL at hand, I fire up my computer, dial up my service provider, start up my Web browser and zip over to a site at MIT that purports to track Web growth–easy pickings. Hmm, it seems this site is being run by a student who tries to keep it up to date between classes and camping trips. It's a good effort on his part, but the information is six months old. No problem. After combining a few appropriate keywords using a cleverly formulated Boolean syntactical construction, I troll Alta Vista, Lycos, Excite and other search engines. I get tens of thousands of hits–too many citations. I narrow the search–thousands of hits. Well, better. I check out several citations and bingo, I find IDC, a company that issues reports on Web related topics. I hop to the site, conduct a search on it for "Web Growth" and get the message "Pipe Broken, Try Again Later." Huh? Now what? Back to the citation list. Another interesting citation and off I go. "404: URL Not Found." Mmm, a dropped link. Another citation. Hmm, a Web site about spiders. Guess not. Back to the citation list. Just as I find another possible site to view, the phone line to my service provider drops out. Grrr! I exit Netscape, exit the communications program, go get a glass of milk, re-open the communications program, re-connect to the service provider, start up Netscape, go back to Alta Vista and redo the search. Oh, oh, I can't remember the citation I was going to try before the line drop-out. I try IDC's site again–maybe that broken pipe's been fixed. I do a search for Web Growth and voila, a citation and brief abstract, alas, no information. I discover, however, that I can order the report on-line for the modest fee of $25.00! No thanks. Back to the citation list. After several more fruitless trips to promising sites, I finally find one with the information I want. Total time spent to find this one bit of information is about one hour. I may be a lousy cyberesearcher but this anecdote illustrates many of the problems with the Web as an information resource.

THE INFORMATION SUPERHIGHWAY AND THE WORLD WIDE WEB–HYPE AND REALITY

What are the myths and realities of the Information Superhighway as they pertain to the Library? What are the Web's technical, financial, content and access limitations?

It's no accident that the World Wide Web is often called the World Wide Wait. Using the Web can be excruciating. Busy signals, phone line dropouts, slow downloading of Web pages, browser freezes and crashes are everyday events. The Web is overused and overburdened. These problems are caused by technical limitations– slow analog phone lines, narrow bandwidth, too few and slow host servers, slow routers, buggy software, badly designed Web sites. The point is, all that information can't be accessed consistently and reliably, if the information delivery system is undependable. There are technical solutions to these technical problems; install more ISDN and fiber optic lines, increase bandwidth, add more, faster servers and routers, write better software, create better Web sites. Problems solved! Well, maybe not. First, all of these improvements will cost gobs of money. Who will pay for all this work and equipment? Further, there really is no quick fix. Even if mountains of money are found for upgrades and other improvements, actual implementation will take a long time. Finally, even after all this work has been done, past Web growth would suggest that the Web will become overloaded again. To put it succinctly: The volume of Web usage will increase in direct proportion to the increase in the Web's capacity to handle that volume.

It's been said that the Information Superhighway bypasses far more places than it connects. Not everyone owns or will ever own a computer or other digital device to access the Web. Outside of big cities, few places are wired for truly dependable local Internet access. Guess we'd better not shut the Library down just yet.

MONEY, MONEY–FEEDING THE BEAST

In the end, alas, most things in life come down to a question of money. How will implementing new technology get paid for? How will all the information now in print form get digitized, who will do it and who will pay for getting it done? If access to information is as good as or better than ownership, who will own digital information? What are the consequences of not owning information, how will access to it be paid for, by whom?

Beyond provider service charges, the Web is still largely a free ride for the user. It's a safe bet that situation will not last indefinitely. Providers are now looking into charging users for time and distance for each Internet site connection made rather than the current flat monthly fee for all access. There has even been talk of charging users "postage" for each e-mail message sent.

Not everyone can afford or will ever be able to afford to pay those monthly fees to Internet service providers. And when, as most assuredly they will, companies routinely charge even casual users to access information on their Web sites, not everyone will be able or willing to pay for this information. Will the technological "haves" increase their already substantial advantage over the technological "have-nots?" Will the "information poor" underclass grow? Can society ignore these people? What is it that's said about the necessity of a well-informed public in a democracy? The Public Library looks better and better.

It's expensive to set up and maintain a Web site. It is obvious that much of the growth of the Web has been driven by commercial interests. It is estimated that just over 50% of Web sites are now maintained by commercial interests–up from 1.5% in June 1993. Even the most casual Web user will notice that an ever increasing number of sites have advertising. A recent estimate predicts that 80% of sites will be commercial by 2000.

No doubt, the Web will be a commercial bonanza for many. However, boundless enthusiasm has been tempered by a dose of reality. Companies have assumed that their Web site costs would be met by digital advertising and/or by on-line sales. Recent developments challenge this assumption. Though the Web continues its growth, many commercial Web sites have ceased operation because they are money losers. Several sites, previously free, experienced huge drop-offs of usage once they started charging access fees. Many of these sites will likely disappear or turn into mere advertisements or digital mail-order catalogs. In fact, most commercial Web sites have been money losers so far. Ironically, on-line book sellers, like Amazon and Borders Books, are among the few commercial Web sites making any money. In any case, these commercial developments have consequences for libraries.

It's probable that the current setbacks to commerce on the Web are just temporary bumps in the road. The future of the Web is a Web dominated by commercial interests. There are many problems for libraries in this scenario. If, as is clear, only deep pockets will be able to digitize and maintain useful information on the Web, libraries, already strapped for money, will not be able to do it. In this eventuality, if commerce were to co-opt the role of the Librarian, the future of the Library would be very uncertain indeed. Who then decides what information makes the cut? Who controls the information? Who develops the search engines to access the information? Who will pay for the information? What about the privacy of persons accessing information? Can companies be counted on to ignore their self-interest in order better to serve the greater good of the community–not likely. Fortunately, as scary as this scenario sounds it's not going to happen–there's no money in it.

As budgets shrink, libraries nationwide have begun to champion the philosophy of access to information versus ownership of information. Sounds great doesn't it? Well, to carry this idea to its logical conclusion, let us assume that XYZ, Inc. has found ways to make a profit collecting, digitizing and selling the world's information resources at reasonable rates. Do we really want XYZ, Inc. owning and controlling access to electronic information? Perhaps not. Perhaps we'd better keep our collections intact.

If the private sector will not create and maintain an Internet Virtual Digital Library, perhaps government or the non-profit sector will do the job. Well, given its budget problems and the hostile social climate in the U.S. towards government, as well as the poor financial situation of most non-profit organizations, the possibility of these two sectors taking up the challenge may be dismissed without further discussion.

A recent interesting twist is the development of Intranets and Extranets. Intranets are subsets of the Internet. Intranets are created when companies reserve Internet information resources for their own internal and/or commercial purposes. It's probable that the owners of Intranets will treat them as private assets and make them inaccessible to the public. Extranets are subsets of Intranets to which companies permit public access for a fee. So much for unfettered access to the vast information resources of the Internet.

In a world increasingly driven by the profit motive, non-commercial information will not be digitized for or maintained on the Web unless someone can make money doing it. Other than in niche markets, commerce will never make any serious money purveying information on the Web.

The Web has wonderful potential as a source of vast amounts of information for the information seeker. Unfortunately, that potential will never be realized. There will always be a Web, but it won't have much more value as an information source than it does now. Librarians need not worry; the "Library without Books," the purely Virtual Digital Library, is a pipe dream.

WEB CONTENT–WHEN MORE IS REALLY LESS

The Web can be a wonderful thing. One can be entertained, amused, and distracted for hours at a time. Can one count on it as a comprehensive, reliable, accessible source of information? Well, that's another matter altogether. There are many reasons, related to content and access, why the Web will not replace the Library. Let's briefly examine a few of them.

Promoters of the Internet as the successor to libraries point out that the catalogs of more than fifty large libraries–including the Library of Congress with its 35 million entries–are accessible on-line. Wow, great, except for the fact that the actual books are not available in full-text on-line. The Library of Congress doesn't even lend its books out to the public. So much for the Library Without Books.

No full-text digital books available? No problem, digitize them all. It can be declared categorically; this is not going to happen. Project Gutenberg has, for decades, been involved in creating an on-line digital library of printed materials. Their work is very commendable. To date, they have actually digitized only a few hundred titles. Their current rate of digitization is about 120 titles per year. With over 51,000 new titles being printed each year in the US alone, they are falling behind at a spectacular rate. Furthermore, the Project is concentrating on titles that were printed after 1980 and which are in the public domain. What about the tens of millions of items printed before 1980? What about those materials not in the public domain?

The CMU Universal Library Repository on the Web appears to be a big site and boasts some 2800 full-text titles. Most of these, however, are duplications of titles from other sites, including the Gutenberg site. Big deal.

The Library of Congress has been microfilming and digitizing older parts of their collection for years to preserve the contents of books that are decaying. As it happens, the collection is decaying faster than the Preservation Staff can copy it. Given the slow pace of selective digitization, we come back to the question of who decides what small subset of titles gets digitized and who pays to do the work. Maybe the Librarian is still useful after all.

What about electronic publishing? Some serial and periodical titles are published electronically, why not publish the rest electronically? Publishers could bypass the Library altogether and put all their stuff on the Internet. A very interesting idea but for the problem of money–digitizing is expensive. Publishers must charge fees as high as several dollars per page to make a profit. As a consequence, out of the 165,000 or so serials, periodicals and newspapers published, only a couple thousand of these titles are published electronically. Even these are published for distribution to niche markets like doctors, and lawyers. These people can afford the high access/download fees; the rest of us can't. It's not likely that the economics of this will change soon. Libraries better not cancel all their subscriptions yet.

As for electronic publishing of books, apart from the high costs of digitizing, and the publisher's need to make a profit, it is a regrettable fact that the people who actually create things like books (and software, paintings, and music) want to be paid for their work also. There is simply no way, at present, to get around the complexities of copyright law, get authors paid and provide digital access to all books. The few pay-per-read schemes that have been tried have not worked. It's not likely that the economics of this will change soon. What's not on the Web? Nearly everything in print is not on the Web. Libraries better keep acquiring books for a while.

WEB INFORMATION ACCESS—
LIKE A NEEDLE IN A HAYSTACK

A wag has called the Internet a digital dumpster. In addition to on-line advertising, there's a vast amount of other junk on the Internet. Anyone with a little intelligence, authoring software, the proper equipment and much time can put up anything on the Web— and they do. With such a high signal-to-noise ratio, it's very difficult for even a skilled researcher to find information of value.

It can be difficult to sort through all the dross on the Web to get to those useful nuggets of information. For the casual user, the charm of the Web is that it's spontaneous, uncontrolled and unorganized, one can hop from link to link making serendipitous discoveries along the way. For the researcher, the curse of the Web is that it's spontaneous, uncontrolled and unorganized, one can slog from irrelevant link to irrelevant link finding nothing useful and wasting vast amounts of time. Fruitful information retrieval requires repositories of organized collections of information with indexing systems that ensure efficient retrieval. In the case of the Web, the digital repository is neither organized nor indexed.

To solve the access problem, information service providers like Alta Vista, Lycos, Yahoo, Excite and others have compiled databases and devised search engines to facilitate information retrieval on the Web. These services are now provided free of charge to the user (though there is some question how much longer they will remain free). Programs called Web crawlers troll the Web doing full-text searches and collecting abstracts to include in the data-bases–no human indexing is required. On the access side these services offer forms of Boolean Logic to retrieve information. Sounds great. Unfortunately none of it works very well.

The several databases contain different sets of overlapping citations and all the databases are very incomplete. Frequently, the citations are nothing more than a title, if there is a title, and the first few sentences of the page. If there's a graphic involved, all that is retrieved are a few lines of garbage characters. To compound the problem, Web pages are often mislabeled. A researcher must plow through all the databases to do the most complete search possible, even then much information will be overlooked. The hapless researcher never knows if his search has been thorough or shallow. He never knows if that essential article has been missed. Libraries have long since solved this problem with their effective, well-established methods of bibliographic control.

Web databases use no controlled indexing language. Consequently, any Web search is perforce unfocused, scattered. A search initiated using what seem like reasonably descriptive keywords often results in thousands of hits, most of which are completely irrelevant. Poor search technique? No, lousy control of the information at the source. Again, libraries have long since solved this problem with their effective, well-established methods of bibliographic control.

Each search service uses a slightly different, and very clumsy, Boolean syntax for its database search engine. What a pain to have to use several different sets of commands to do a thorough search. To overcome this problem, the researcher can perform searches automatically using clever little programs (called Robots or Avatars) on his own computer. Fantastic, but these programs only troll user specified Web sites to see what's changed on the site since their last search. If the user is not aware of other useful sites, he misses a lot.

It is true that attempts are being made to bring order out of the chaos of the Internet. Standards like Z39.50 are being developed and applied to ease access between on-line catalogs. Great, but just a drop in the ocean. In the fields of engineering and biology, researchers plan to impose established controlled vocabularies on their discipline's literature on the Web. These are good efforts but of little use to persons outside of those disciplines. Recently, the notion of concept searching has been suggested as the solution to Web access problems. The idea is that regardless of the special vocabulary used within each discipline, translation programs transparently will perform the job of vocabulary switching for the researcher so that he can do cross disciplinary research using familiar vocabulary. This is a good idea, too. Unfortunately, both solutions will require armies of indexers and abstracters to do the work retrospectively, as well as, to keep up with new Web pages as they appear. Who's going to pay for all these new people? Your friendly Librarian is already trained, experienced and is eager to help the researcher find relevant materials wherever they might be.

Web pages use hypertext links to facilitate movement from page to page. So, suppose, for example, the Web page you are reading provides a link to a footnoted article at another site you can jump over to that site at once and look at the referenced article. Neat stuff–sometimes. Hypertext links use Universal Resource Locators (URLs), which are Internet addresses to other pages on the site you are viewing or to different Internet sites altogether. The researcher can only jump to those URLs that are provided by the webmaster at the site he is currently accessing. No URL, no link. For a variety of reasons, URLs change all the time, so if the webmaster does not regularly update the URLs on his site the links are useless.

Another problem with hypertext searching is that the researcher is always looking at information through blinders, one Web page at a time. It's fairly easy to get confused and off the track particularly if webmasters have not constructed their Web pages well. Again, the researcher can only go where a Web site's URLs point him. This tends to result in myopic, shallow searching. In contrast, good old fashioned browsing in the stacks still has much to recommend it. The researcher finds his subject area, and because of the way library collections are organized, he is sure to find more material related to his search interests within the space of a few feet of shelving.

VIRTUAL HEAVEN

Let us imagine that all technical, financial, content and access problems with the Web are resolved. On-line Internet connections are fast and reliable, everyone who submits and supports Web content is paid, everything that ever has been published and ever will be published is available at reasonable cost, AI and other Expert Systems compile and index the information superbly, using a desktop computer, laptop computer, PDA or other device users can access and retrieve relevant information efficiently. Virtual Heaven has been achieved. The Library is history. Well, not so fast, maybe it won't happen.

People dislike inconvenience and discomfort. Desktop computers, wonderful though they may be, are not portable. They are heavy; they require electrical and communications connections. Frequent, repeated, lengthy sessions at computer screens can be unbearably tedious and tiring. Imagine reading *War and Peace* at your desktop computer.

Laptops and PDAs are portable. With the blessings of portability, however, come the limits of media. It's going to be a long time, if ever, until reliable, wireless digital communication links are established for a portable device that will serve as a full-text reader. Until then, we must carry device compatible, limited capacity media for information access. This is fine as long as the user doesn't mind carrying around his portable digital reading thingie and has just the DVD disk he needs with him always. To date, every attempt to market and sell full-text books on CD-ROM for use in hand held readers has failed miserably.

Electronic devices are expensive; they are fragile; they fail, get broken, are stolen, require electricity, quickly become obsolete; they are inconvenient. People like books; they like to curl up in a comfy chair or in bed to read a book. People like to come into the library, be there, see other people, socialize, browse through the stacks, find books to read, check them out and take them home–like treasures. Books are convenient and comfortable to use. It's not likely that libraries or librarians will disappear any time soon.

The Information Superhighway, which is now an Information Freeway, will become an Information Toll Road. It will become so plastered with digital billboards that it will be impossible for the user to view the scenery. The Internet will become a vast arm of the commercial world, a place where businesses can conduct business, a place where limited information of use for non-business purposes will be available only on a pay-as-you-go basis to those few who can afford it. This Internet is no threat to libraries.

LIBRARY OF THE FUTURE–A QUICK TOUR

Despite all that's been said here about the Internet and Web, there is a Digital Virtual Library in our future. What then will this Digital Virtual Library of the future look like? Though the Library will benefit from the application of improved automation technology to do the drudge work and benefit from the addition of new tools for information access, it will probably look very much as it does today. There will be shelves with books and serials on them, as well as other storage areas with a variety of multimedia information resources. As more information becomes available on-line, however, collections will become leaner and more focused. Libraries will have local, core collections in a variety of formats while serving also as nodes or gateways to digital information elsewhere. Libraries will have areas for reading, for study and for meetings. Public libraries will have areas for children's activities like the story hour. University and college libraries will have areas for classes, areas for traditional bibliographic instruction and areas for instruction in the use of new information technologies. Special libraries will look much as they do today though with even more tightly focused core collections and access to their local Intranet. Libraries will have Information/Reference Desks staffed by Librarians who will have reliable old printed tools and wonderful new tools for accessing information for users. There will be areas with equipment for users to access in-house digital media such as CD, DVD, and formats not yet invented. There will be areas with terminals where users can access the Internet and other on-line resources. Users will be able to access the Virtual Public Library from home. In addition to the catalog, the Virtual Public Library will allow on-line access to as much of the collection as has been digitized. In universities and colleges, students enrolled in distance education programs will access the Virtual Library to view the catalog, to view materials in the collection that have been digitized, and to order materials in non-digitized formats that can be faxed or otherwise delivered to them off campus.

LIBRARY OF THE FUTURE–
GENERAL CONSIDERATIONS

Though most of the long-established principles of library design and construction will remain valid in future building efforts, new technologies require that new design and construction considerations be included as well.

As a result of shrinking funds, the future won't include many new library buildings. The Library of the Future is most likely to be an old library that has been retrofitted, remodeled or renovated.

Since it is the least expensive way to go, and because it is quite a satisfactory solution, in most cases, many libraries will undergo retrofitting. Essentially, this means keeping the interior of the physical structure intact while modernizing HVAC systems, installing up-to-date communications cable, buying and installing new equipment, while moving functions, furnishings and equipment around within the old space.

Remodeling projects will be required where an old building is basically adequate but where out-of-date design of interior spaces severely hampers functioning. Remodeling could include everything involved in a retrofit but would also include actual removal of interior walls, placement of new walls, and more extensive refurbishing of the interior spaces.

Renovation is the closest thing to building a new library but cheaper. Renovation would involve the gutting of a library's interior and starting anew. Regardless of the scale of a library building project, a few key design concepts must be integrated into the plan.

LIBRARY OF THE FUTURE–DESIGN CONSIDERATIONS

Libraries should be designed modularly. Modularity, an old planning concept, is based on the simple idea of standardized, recurring units of measure such as: one length of shelving, one study table, one carrel, one unit of free space for traffic flow, or one computer workstation. Once the size of the modular unit is set, the interior configuration of load-bearing walls, columns and similar immovable objects, can then be planned to accommodate the modular movable objects. If this is done correctly, changing space requirements would allow, for example, 5 lengths of shelving to be replaced by 3 computer workstations and two units of free space. The beauty of modularity is that it maximizes flexibility.

Future library design must allow for maximum flexibility. We know what technologies we must accommodate in library buildings now but no one knows what new technologies will mean for future accommodation. Hence, there is an absolute requirement that building design allow for as great a degree of flexibility as possible to incorporate appropriate new technologies.

For the foreseeable future, essential to the Virtual Digital Library are physical digital connections. Until reasonably priced, reliable wireless digital communications systems able to broadcast to inexpensive, lightweight, portable receivers become a reality, library design must allow for communications cables to connect local area networks, networks within the larger organization and external networks. Planning for this can be tricky. Modes of data transmission change with annoying frequency. In the early days, networked devices could be hard-wired or connected by means of telephone lines. Then, just a few years ago, most networks were changed over to faster Ethernet cabling. Now, libraries are faced with another conversion, this time to fiber optic cabling. What's next, who knows? All planners can do is ensure that the library is designed to accommodate the inevitable future changes.

LIBRARY OF THE FUTURE– FUNCTIONAL CONSIDERATIONS

Besides general design considerations, libraries must be planned to accommodate some new functions. Space must be provided for the ever-changing variety of devices required to access digital information on-site, locally within the parent organization and remotely. Although views differ as to whether it is better to place these equipments in the midst of all the other library resources or to place them in separate areas, some accommodation for them must be made. Since librarians will be playing an increasing role in helping users get the most out of new technologies it may a good idea to have an area set aside in the library specifically for instruction in electronic research skills.

In universities and colleges, distance education will probably increase in importance. It's rather ironic that an area must be set aside in the library where the Virtual Library can be "housed." Here, staff will create and maintain Web pages and otherwise provide for the electronic access of on-site resources by off-campus students. An area should also be set aside and staffed specifically to meet the information retrieval needs of off-campus students. This area should be wired and equipped to facilitate the processing of requests and the delivery of library materials via mail, fax, e-mail or other appropriate means to off-campus students.

LIBRARY OF THE FUTURE–EQUIPMENT

In addition to paying fees to providers for access to on-line information, the Library of the Future must own or lease whatever digital media and compatible equipment is currently available for information storage and retrieval. While having the "latest thing" is unavoidable, a big note of caution is in order. Just as libraries must plan for the obsolescence of network cabling hardware, they must plan also for the inevitable obsolescence of digital media hardware and software.

Just a few years ago, CD-ROM appeared. With its huge storage capacity and relatively speedy access times, entire backfiles of indexes and abstracts were suddenly available on one or two tiny discs. This was a fantastic development. Many libraries bought CD-ROMs along with computers or single purpose readers to access them. Space was saved, subscriptions were canceled, staff was cut, budgets were cut. Great. Here's the problem–in the very near future, libraries will have to decide what to do about the newest digital format DVD, with its storage capacity many times greater than that of CD-ROM. Just over the horizon is crystal storage that utilizes the almost limitless number of internal facets of crystals to store data. After crystals, what new format will be next? The implications for libraries are obvious.

Are libraries, with smaller budgets and less staff going to replace their entire collections of digital media and the equipment to read them every decade or so? Certainly, libraries can hold onto the media for as long as it lasts physically but what happens when the media deteriorates? What happens when the equipment required to read the media wears out? How long will manufacturers support the old formats? Who will fix the readers? Where will they get parts? Anyone who's tried to get an old 386 based PC fixed will immediately see the problem—you're told to throw it out and get a new computer. Recall some other obsolete formats: 78 RPM records, computer punch cards and paper tape, 8mm home movie film, 8 track cartridges, Betamax tapes, 5 1/2 inch floppy disks, etc. Obsolescence is unavoidable. Libraries must plan for it.

LIBRARY OF THE FUTURE–
THE ELEPHANT TURNS OUT TO BE SOMETHING ELSE

What should Librarians do right now? Nothing that we aren't doing, is the answer. We should maintain our traditional knowledge and skills and continue to perform our core functions as good professionals: to make users aware of information; to offer users the best tools and techniques we can to access information; to educate and assist them in the use of these tools and techniques. To prepare for the Library of the Future, we should continue to embrace and master new tools, technologies and techniques as they come along. We would do these things in any event. We really must do more, however.

Librarians are aiding and abetting in their own extinction. We have bought into the hype about the Internet and the digital future. We must champion our own cause better. Technology is not a threat to the profession—inadequate support and misdirected funding are the threat. It is very depressing to walk into a library today and see dirty floors, flickering lights, battered furniture, unshelved materials lying about, and not a librarian in sight. This happens because money that used to be spent on even these basic maintenance activities is now being spent on the latest gizmo.

We must, in the end, come back to the distasteful subject of money. All of this wonderful, useful new technology costs money. New, retrofitted or renovated library buildings are expensive. Internet access must be paid for, on-line publication and database access must be paid for. Equipment must be paid for, digital media must be paid for. Maintenance and repairs are expensive. Librarians have not sufficiently resisted the belief that money spent on new technologies can be robbed from funds for books, subscriptions, upkeep and staff without consequence.

Librarians must disabuse themselves of any notion that they are a dying breed, that libraries are obsolete. Librarians must resist the common perception that new technology means the end of the Library. If librarians believe there is merit in the points raised here, they must take the case to funding authorities; they must demonstrate that new technology and the Information Superhighway do not obviate the need for libraries. Librarians must make the case that steadily diminishing budgets, shrinking staff, the slow bleeding off of vital resources to feed the technology beast, will surely kill off the Library. The process that finishes off the Library won't be like an elephant crashing in, trampling all underfoot. It's clear even now–the process that will leave the Library a hollow shell or finish it off altogether will be more like the slow gnawing of mice from the inside.

Chapter Two:
May You Live in Interesting Times:
The Impact of Revolutions
and Shifting Paradigms
on Public Services Staff

Barbara E. Kemp

"May you live in interesting times." This oft-quoted saying can be viewed as either a blessing or a curse, depending on one's outlook and attitude toward change and upheaval. It might also serve as a slogan for academic library staff in the 1990s. The new words and phrases describing the current environment of libraries and librarians are many and well-known. Who has not heard of the "virtual library" existing in "cyberspace?" Are we librarians (or "cyberians") experiencing a "paradigm shift" between access and ownership or riding the waves of the "digital revolution" as we "surf the 'Net?" No matter the terminology used, it seems clear that *change* has become a constant factor in our lives. It is, perhaps, one of the few constants remaining to us. Of course, libraries and librarians, like all of society, have been experiencing change over

Barbara E. Kemp is Assistant Director for the Governor Thomas E. Dewey Library for Public Affairs and Policy, University Libraries, The University at Albany, State University of New York, 135 Western Avenue, Albany, NY 12222 (email: phantom@cnsvax.albany.edu).

[Haworth co-indexing entry note]: "Chapter Two: May You Live in Interesting Times: The Impact of Revolutions and Shifting Paradigms on Public Services Staff." Kemp, Barbara E. Co-published simultaneously in *Collection Management* (The Haworth Press, Inc.) Vol. 22, No. 1/2, 1997, pp. 29-41; and: *Collection Development: Access in the Virtual Library* (ed: Maureen Pastine) The Haworth Press, Inc., 1997, pp. 29-41. Single or multiple copies of this article are available for a fee from The Haworth Document Delivery Service [1-800-342-9678, 9:00 a.m. - 5:00 p.m. (EST). E-mail address: getinfo@haworth.com].

© 1997 by The Haworth Press, Inc. All rights reserved.

many decades, even centuries. It is the rate of change and the resulting confusion, uncertainty, and anxiety that really call attention to this particular era and give it its ambiguous distinction as an "interesting time."

The literature of many fields abounds with analyses of how we have reached this point and what the future might look like as current trends develop and play out. There is much exciting speculation about what libraries and library services of the future will look like and the opportunities we have to create them. Articles and presentations about experiments and pilot projects already undertaken to test and shape the future invigorate, challenge, and encourage others to adapt, extend, or create still more projects. Much of this activity centers on improving the user's access to information. In fact, one of the most common themes describing the transformation of libraries has been "access vs. ownership."

ACCESS, OWNERSHIP, AND USERS

Ownership has not been a difficult concept to define, generally being used to indicate the purchase of physical items of information and their on-site housing and control. This definition is being stretched, however, with the introduction of more and more licensing agreements by which materials might be held on-site only for a specified period of time before being returned to the vendor. In essence, libraries are renting such resources rather than truly owning them. Such agreements frequently add another dimension to "ownership" by dictating the conditions under which the product may be used or the population that is permitted to do so.

Access, on the other hand, has always been much less clearly defined, meaning different things to different people. To some, the term is narrowly equated with the bibliographic identification of physical items, regardless of their physical locations, with the actual delivery of the item being a separate consideration. To others, access is very broadly defined as the provision of information, regardless of format or location. Between these extremes, lies a wide range of variations on these definitions.

For the majority of this century, academic and research librarians have followed the ownership model for their collections. Having an item on-site was considered to be the best, most cost-effective method of providing information. This model has been supported and reinforced by both internal and external forces. Certainly, academic faculty and administrators have strongly encouraged local acquisition of materials. Our professional associations, which have emphasized holdings as a ranking measure for libraries, have also supported the ownership model. Another force emphasizing ownership, which is often overlooked, has been the auditing practices of parent institutions and governmental agencies, which often demand that expenditures be linked to physical items purchased.

In the ownership model, access, in the sense of availability, is generally assumed because the item is locally held. In reality, however, this is often not the case. Ownership guarantees only the possibility of access, not actual delivery. As any user knows, finding an item in the catalog can often be an extremely frustrating experience. The chances that the item is checked out, in the library but off the shelf, or simply missing are often very high. When the desired item is an issue of a serial, the frustration level can be raised even higher as the user wends his or her way laboriously through all the steps in identifying and locating an item, only to find that the desired issue or pages are missing. Frustration often peaks when the user is told that an item owned by the library cannot be requested through interlibrary loan even though it is checked out or not on the shelf. The often lengthy processes of recalling or searching an item hardly seem like "access" to information for someone under the pressure of a deadline. It also seems illogical to be told that an item owned by the library is not as readily available as might be an item the library has not purchased.

The ownership model for collections has been under pressure from different quarters. The static or declining nature of budgets, the increasing volume of materials being published, and the increased variety of formats available have all combined to strain acquisitions budgets to the limit. At the same time, the success of CD-ROM and online services, including the Internet, have made users more aware of the vast amount and array of information available somewhere in the "knowledge universe." The success of automated systems is also their curse. Proliferating services and transparent interfaces have helped librarians and users identify materials never before "accessible," but expectations have now been raised that such items should actually be delivered.

This broadening of the concept of access to mean the provision of information regardless of format or location probably fits more closely the average user's wants and needs. Add in the concept of timely delivery of that information and the situation approaches Nirvana. This information paradise appears to be the ideal toward which libraries are now working. Unfortunately, much of the literature, and therefore, much of the open public discussion tends to cast this movement in an either/or, often adversarial, light. Certainly a common theme is *"access versus ownership,"* implying at least some level of mutual exclusivity. An underlying assumption in this debate also seems to be that *access* should be interpreted as *electronic access*. Taken to the extreme, this could be interpreted to mean that no local holdings are required at all as long as information can be identified and delivered in a timely fashion. Of course, few librarians would argue for such a radical interpretation of the paradigm at this time. In fact, *access* should also include well-maintained local collections, consortial agreements for collaborative collection development, and traditional interlibrary loan. Whatever definition of access is used, however, it seems likely that some level of local collections will continue to be the norm for most libraries. Given the reality that the literatures of the various disciplines currently have differential availability in electronic formats and that all existing print materials are unlikely to be digitized in the near future, libraries will be working with both print and electronic formats for many years to come. The mix of formats will undoubtedly vary from library to library and will change over time, but the formats themselves are not mutually exclusive. Instead they will continue to complement one another.

Most academic librarians are fully appreciative of the extraordinary improvements in access that new technologies have made possible, yet these improvements are not without costs. It is sometimes hard not to yearn for quieter, less momentous times, or even to resent the technologies causing the often wrenching changes in our lives. The advent of the electronic library has brought about changes in virtually every aspect of operations in academic libraries. All library staff have been impacted by these changes and can feel the stresses in their everyday situations. Public services staff have their share of the benefits, problems, and challenges brought about by the introduction of new technologies. These are compounded by their role as interface between the library and its users, who themselves are challenged and sometimes confused by the major changes taking place.

DEFINING PUBLIC SERVICES

There has always been some debate as to what constitutes "public services" in libraries. Philosophically speaking, one might argue that everyone who works in a library is there to serve the public, and thus, all positions fall within public service units. Even the standard indexing tool, *Library Literature*, does not use the term "public services" as a subject heading, although "technical services" is accorded that status. Traditionally, however, *public services* have been identified as or associated with those departments or units having direct contact with the public. Reference is one of the units most commonly associated with public services. User education and interlibrary loan, often parts of the reference department, are usually included, too. Circulation and its "sister" service, reserves, also rank within public service units. Beyond these departments, identification of public service units depends largely on the organization of individual libraries. Collection development is somewhat problematic. Often it is simply one area of responsibility assigned to librarians, usually reference librarians. In some libraries collection development is separately organized, being a division in itself, equal to but separate from public and technical services. In others, selection is considered linked to acquisitions and is thus included in technical services. In still others, collection development is carried out in a matrix organization, with selectors or bibliographers having other assignments such as reference or cataloging with separate, distinct reporting lines. No matter the organization, however, there is no denying the connection between a library's collections and its users.

Technology has played a major role in breaking down traditional barriers between functional areas in libraries and caused many libraries to re-examine their organizational design, especially as integrated systems change the way we work. In the past, circulation was almost always included within public services, but with the advent of integrated library systems circulation is now seen as having a strong systems or technical component and is sometimes aligned with the library systems or technical services department. In some libraries, "access services" departments have been created by the merging of circulation/reserves with interlibrary loan and document delivery services. Other forms of organization will undoubtedly appear as libraries try to become more responsive to user needs and demands and to move from a traditional hierarchy organized around functions or tasks to what is now called a client- or user-centered organization.

Although library organizations are changing, for the purposes of this article, public services will be defined in a broad, traditional way as collection development, interlibrary loan, circulation/reserves, reference, and user education.

CHANGING REALITIES, SHIFTING ROLES

For much of the past, public services staff have worked pretty much unilaterally. That is, they have had control of the resources and services offered with little else to challenge or compete for their clientele. There might have been complaints about the types or levels of services or the lack of resources, but most users were grateful for any information or assistance they could find. Few had any other services with which they could compare those offered by the library. Now, however, users are becoming increasingly more sophisticated in their knowledge and demands. Most students coming from high school have had at least some exposure to computers and the Internet. Thanks to the media, there are probably few people in the United States who have not heard of the "information superhighway" and the riches it promises. Services such as *America Online* and *Compuserve* are heavily marketed, leading many people to believe that everything is easily available on the Internet or the World Wide Web. This belief is often brought to the library since for many people the library is still their only Internet/Web access. Unfortunately, the result can be some very disappointed or unhappy users when they learn that *everything* is not really on the 'Net and that what is there is not always easily found. The reality is that for every truly sophisticated user coming to the library, there are many more who have only a surface knowledge, or more likely, have unreasonable expectations based on media hype.

Academic administrators, like the users, have high expectations for the new technologies, and increasingly, high hopes that they might be used to solve other problems. Thus, staff and resources budgets are cut on the premise that computers reduce the need for staff and that shared resources will save money. Similarly, existing library space might be claimed for other purposes since many believe that the virtual library is here and that it does not require physical space. Needless to say, this is far from the case. The new technologies have added new layers of work to existing jobs and created the need for new positions to install and maintain hardware and software and create useable interfaces for users. As systems proliferate, so does the complexity of existing work. Costs for electronic resources, especially for distributed access, are not as easily predictable as are the costs for less volatile formats. Most librarians have experienced or know of widely varying prices depending on negotiations with producers and vendors. The need for physical space remains much the same in most libraries. Print collections are still growing and will continue to do so. On top of the need to house these volumes is the need to create space for an increasing number of computer workstations, often with a concomitant need to retrofit older buildings for additional electrical wiring and telecommunication cabling. A third cost for increased access, often overlooked by administrators, is the need for regular maintenance and upgrades of existing hardware and software. As the number of workstations multiplies, this figure will become an increasingly large and important part of any library's budget. These infrastructure costs have been a rude awakening for many college or university administrators who had been used to policies of deferred maintenance and libraries as academic units with relatively low, stable equipment needs.

REFERENCE SERVICES

Of all the public service units, reference has possibly reaped the most immediate and visible benefits of the new technologies and the resulting improved access to information. Dealing directly with users, reference librarians are the "wizards" who can tap into a seemingly limitless world of information to supply needed information. For some time now, reference librarians have either performed or assisted users in performing online database searches. Now, they can open up the worlds of CD-ROM, the Internet, and the World Wide Web. Of course, librarians have been assisting users in finding information and answers to questions all along, but slogging through countless print sources, following leads, has little of the flash and dash of sitting at a computer terminal and bringing things up on a screen for the users to see. Because of the direct patron contact, it is the reference librarian who has the immediate gratification of the user's thanks and appreciation, sometimes even a formal written acknowledgment of services rendered, which can go into a personnel file. For many reference librarians, there is a challenge in finding the desired information and a certain amount of thrill and perhaps pride in being able to manipulate the many available systems to retrieve it.

There are costs in this situation, however. As previously mentioned, many users come to the library with high, sometimes unreasonable, expectations of the technologies, and it is the reference librarian who bears the brunt of such encounters. In some cases, the library simply might not subscribe to a service the user knows exists or even has used in other libraries. In others, there might be limitations on use of a product according to the license agreement. In both cases, the reference librarian must be able to explain the situation and suggest alternatives. Of course, most academic librarians have had the experience with users, especially students, who are willing to wait in line to use a computer terminal when a print source would serve their needs quite nicely, perhaps even more appropriately. The seductiveness of the computer has, to a certain extent, interfered with the educational mission of the library.

If on the one hand there are users who expect too much of the technologies and want only to use a computer, there are still users who want nothing to do with anything that has been automated. There have been some highly publicized protests against the demise of the card catalog, but there are other, less well-known protests as well. Some people refuse to use a computer terminal at all and expect the reference librarian to do all of their searching for them, even in the OPAC. This can be very time-consuming or lead to unpleasant encounters with irate users. Even when a reluctant user tries his or her hand at searching, there is likely to be much more time spent in point-of-use instruction.

In addition to the costs in time spent on additional or extended user interactions, there are many other, "behind-the-scenes" costs. Perhaps chief of these is the stress induced by the need to know an increasing number of sophisticated, unique systems. As these products multiply more and more rapidly, reference librarians have less and less time to really learn the systems they are supposed to be able to manipulate as experts and even teach to the users. Along the same lines, in most libraries, reference librarians are now expected to be able to troubleshoot at least basic problems with the hardware. This technical expectation is something for which many librarians have not been trained. It is certainly an additional duty that takes away from the primary responsibility of reference work, yet it is hard to ignore. This becomes even more difficult when the questions come from a remote user who might have any kind of computer hardware and telecommunications software. The explosion of equipment in reference areas can also lead to a decline in the working environment in terms of noise. Even with baffled housing, the constant hum of computers and clatter of printers can eat away at one's nerves.

USER EDUCATION

Many of the problems and challenges faced by reference librarians are also faced by librarians providing user education. The multiplicity of systems alone is a challenge to teach. The guest lecture spot or an hour-long training session still seem to be the norm for most instructional sessions. If that length of time was not sufficient to teach complex topics before, it is woefully inadequate to teach the same topics with the layer of technology added on. If anything, computers have discouraged many users from employing critical thinking in the research process. With a widespread belief that the computer does it all, they feel that learning which buttons to push is all that is required. In addition to an increase in the number of resources that users might need to learn, training for new user groups is also a challenge. Certainly, there is more need for internal staff training than ever before and this on an almost constant basis. Remote users offer a unique challenge, whether they be faculty in offices, students in dormitories and apartments, or distance learners spread far away from the central campus. Even within a library building, there is likely to be a need for a greater range of instructional modes, including programmed learning and hands-on instruction. The latter can be a problem since the creation of an appropriately equipped teaching facility is costly in terms of equipment, cabling and space.

ACCESS SERVICES: CIRCULATION, RESERVES, INTERLIBRARY LOAN

Circulation services were likely to have been the first automated services publicly visible in many academic libraries. As such, circulation staff have been living with the impact of technology for a long time. The benefits of improved record and account keeping have been obvious. As users became familiar with automated circulation, they began to expect more convenience. Among such improvements have been the ability of users to check their own circulation records through an OPAC, automatic renewal lists, self-check units, and online requests for various circulation services through the use of electronic forms.

The display of the status of materials in online catalogs has put pressure on circulation staff for better and better stack maintenance and inventory control. Users quite reasonably expect that an item shown as being in the library should actually be available on the shelf, yet that is often not the case. Of course, there are many reasons why an item might not be available, but the burden of searches and user complaints falls on the circulation staff.

Reserve services can be divided into two parts: circulation and processing. Automation of reserve circulation has led to much the same benefits as have accrued in automating regular circulation routines. The behind-the-scenes work of processing reserve materials is another matter. Many libraries have created local systems or tailored turn-key systems to meet their needs. In some cases, manual processing would actually be more efficient, but automated processing is done in order to create machine-readable records to display in an online catalog. One of the brightest promises for reserves is the ability to scan materials and make readings available electronically. This will be especially important in providing support for distance learners. Issues relating to copyright and quality of scanned images are among those remaining to be solved.

Interlibrary loan units are among those most heavily impacted by new technologies. The bibliographic utilities have long made it easier to verify and locate materials, and new technologies, such as Ariel, make rapid delivery of higher quality copies available. The development of document delivery services has also made rapid delivery of materials more feasible, although costs for the latter can really drain a budget. This in turn can lead to policy questions of passing some or all costs of such services on to the user as fees for "value-added" service.

Although bibliographic utilities have made an interlibrary loan unit's work easier in one sense, by providing rapid identification of sources for loans, the converse is also true. It is now easier for other libraries to find out what *you* have, thus increasing your interlibrary loan unit's workload. User expectations have also risen. It is difficult for many to understand why actual delivery of some materials, most particularly monographs, still takes so long when verification and identification of locations has become so efficient.

Another technological trend impacting on interlibrary loan is the increase in the number of resources available electronically. While this makes it easier to supply some materials, identifying those items available can be very time-consuming, especially if the library has chosen not to create cataloging records for items available through various subscription services (*Westlaw, Lexis/Nexis, Dialog*, etc.) or the Internet and World Wide Web.

COLLECTION DEVELOPMENT

Collection development librarians are at the heart of the access/ ownership equation. As noted earlier, this is not an either/or situation for libraries. Rather, it is a dynamic process with ownership and access being spread over a wide continuum that varies from library to library. Given this situation, it is no longer sufficient for selectors to know the academic departments for which they are responsible and competent in the literatures of one or more subject areas. Now they must also be familiar with various technologies in order to make informed judgments about the most appropriate format for the purchase of materials available in multiple formats: print, CD-ROM, online databases. For electronic resources, there are also issues of access: stand alone CD-ROM, local or wide area networks, tape loading on a local mainframe, Internet or Web access, etc. Obviously, such decisions cannot be made in isolation, but selectors are usually the individuals who identify, analyze, and recommend purchase/lease of or subscription to materials. This in itself can be a large added workload, multiplied by the number of subject areas for which the selector is responsible.

Many academic librarians now create their own homepages for the World Wide Web, and selectors have often been in the forefront of such activity. Homepages provide excellent communication tools with academic departments and general users interested in specific subject areas. If the homepages are used to provide links to appropriate subject-related sites, the work of the selector becomes even more complex. Locating and evaluating sites, then maintaining correct links is extremely time-consuming given the exponential growth of Web-based resources and the volatile nature of the environment.

CONCLUSION

In addition to the present impacts of technology, there are, of course, implications for the future. Organizational structures of libraries will continue to evolve, adding to feelings of insecurity among staff. The current fascination with computers and electronic resources has serious implications for life-long learning and information literacy. One might wonder if the educational role of the library is changing to one of training. The full impact of the new technologies on library education is yet to be seen. Will the emphasis on technology weaken training in traditional print reference sources? If so, there could be serious implications for library services and collections in the future since solid knowledge of print sources is necessary for both reference and collection development.

There is no denying that new technologies have drastically changed the environment of academic libraries, and it is likely that libraries will continue to be affected by rapid change. Both the work being done and the way it is performed are being transformed. Changes have already brought unprecedented improvements in access to information and many efficiencies in work processes and procedures. These changes have not been without costs, however. Aside from the obvious financial costs of equipment, telecommunications, and software, there are human costs as well. Already burdened staff can now feel overwhelmed by the new and often unfamiliar tasks and responsibilities being assigned to them. Many long-term staff, who were never trained for such a technical environment and never expected to work in such a situation, can feel particularly threatened. Morale can suffer and the working environment grow tense if staff feel that some individuals are not "pulling their weight" or certain skills are more highly valued than others. A bad situation can deteriorate even more if staff feel that administrators are not aware of or are uncaring about their plight.

Each person and each library respond differently to the changes occurring in their worlds. Most staff probably feel torn, and their responses can vary from situation to situation and even day to day. Reactions will doubtless range from enthusiasm to reluctance and even outright hostility, sometimes from the same individual. Administrators must acknowledge the stresses these changes cause and take them into account when planning and introducing new programs and services. Library staff, however, also bear a responsibility to themselves and their colleagues to alleviate stress in the workplace to the best of their abilities. Much of how one responds depends on one's outlook. Keeping a positive attitude can be difficult, but it is essential. Similarly, supporting and encouraging one another can ease tension and make changes more bearable.

Many can agree with a paraphrase of Charles Dickens, writing about another revolution in *A Tale of Two Cities*, "It is the best of times. It is the worst of times." It is clear that the new technologies and their eventual upgrades or replacements are here to stay with us. It is up to us to determine whether we view them as a blessing or curse.

Chapter Three:
Had We but World Enough, and Time . . .

David F. Kohl

Andrew Marvell's classic, and possibly these days not quite politically correct, poem about the perils of delay and indecision in a world where time is short, may resonate more strongly with today's stressed out employees of the information age than the Elizabethan audience for whom it was intended. While the computer may have given us infinitely more power and convenience in dealing with the world of information, the rapid and relentless pace of change in information technology has exacted its toll in time. We hardly have time to learn the new technology before it changes, or we spend so much time learning new technologies we have no time to plan for its effective use or how to teach it to others. We seem to have made a Faustian bargain–the power of the computer at the price of our time.

But Marvell's poem is not just a lament about the limited temporal span allotted to each of us. It is a poem of seduction, and so it is also a call to action. The second line (following the line that serves as the title of this article) runs "This coyness, Lady, were no crime," and it is hardly necessary to read to the end of the poem to figure out what kind of action Marvell has in mind. While the library's agenda may be rather different than Marvell's, his poem suggests

---

David F. Kohl is Dean and University Librarian at the University of Cincinnati, Cincinnati, OH 45221-0033.

[Haworth co-indexing entry note]: "Chapter Three: Had We but World Enough, and Time . . ." Kohl, David F. Co-published simultaneously in *Collection Management* (The Haworth Press, Inc.) Vol. 22, No. 1/2, 1997, pp. 43-55; and: *Collection Development: Access in the Virtual Library* (ed: Maureen Pastine) The Haworth Press, Inc., 1997, pp. 43-55. Single or multiple copies of this article are available for a fee from The Haworth Document Delivery Service [1-800-342-9678, 9:00 a.m. - 5:00 p.m. (EST). E-mail address: getinfo@haworth.com].

both an interesting parallel between the Elizabethan era and our own "time" and reminds us of an important truth. Both the Elizabethan Age and present times represent periods of rapid and, at times, chaotic change and that in such an environment coyness may be less of value than the decision to act.

And act we must. In the library world collection development, even after almost a decade of discussing access rather than ownership, has proved remarkably resistant to change at the operational level. The size of local, on-site collections continues to be a major factor in ARL rankings, national status, and faculty regard. And yet almost every librarian, as well as thoughtful university administrators and concerned faculty members, realizes that the ownership model requires fundamental restructuring. The well-documented problems of serials inflation, the vastly increased demand for research and instructional resources due to the proliferation of bibliographic databases, the growth of interdisciplinary studies and the increased specialization of faculty research, all combined with an almost universal reduction in library allocations have made it impossible for any local collection or institution to seriously attempt to purchase and house all needed materials. While a few voices continue to argue for the traditional model, asserting that the key problem is just a matter of more funding (reminiscent of General Westmorland arguing that the Viet Nam War could be won if he could only have more troops and supplies), a number of experiments are underway in libraries and library consortia to begin to identify the elements of a new collection development model more closely attuned to the realities and possibilities of today's funding and automation environment. Although it is far too early for there to be universal consensus on all the details of this emerging model, there are a number of promising developments which allow us to begin to act now in positive and productive ways.

BUYING BY THE DRINK

Libraries have traditionally felt that the best way to provide access to the article literature was to subscribe to as many journals as possible. This is such an accepted practice that it seems to have occurred to few people that subscribing to a journal is really an amazing act of faith. The library pays money in advance and the publisher promises that they will provide a year's worth of articles relevant and important to the library's patrons. While some journals may be of the stature and reliability to guarantee that most of their articles are a worthwhile purchase for a given library, a wide range of citation studies suggests that many academic articles are in fact not read, or at least not referenced in subsequent literature. The obvious conclusion is that for many journal titles the most efficient strategy is to "unbundle" the journals and purchase only the needed articles when they are needed.

Several years ago when the University of Cincinnati was forced by budgetary pressures to cut $200,000 worth of journals subscriptions, staff there discovered that approximately half of the titles (in terms of dollar amount) were available on an article-by-article basis through UnCover. By providing the articles for all UnCover titles not held at UC free of charge through the UnCover service to all faculty (approximately 2,000) and graduate students (approximately 5,000), we found our annual costs in the subsequent two years running just over $20,000 for the faculty alone and around $30,000 for faculty and graduate students combined. Not only were we saving approximately $70,000 a year but the 18,000 journal titles whose articles were available in UnCover almost doubled the number of journal titles our faculty and graduate students had access to. In short, somewhat to our amazement we reduced costs and increased access by the simple expedient of buying journal articles individually as needed from relatively low-use journals, rather than by subscription to the whole journal.

Adopting such a strategy is not entirely straight-forward, however. A key point in selling such a strategy to patrons is turnaround time. If patrons compare a document delivery service to traditional ILL, they will probably easily accept the three-to-five-day lapse between request and delivery and absolutely be astounded by the not infrequent two-hour delivery. On the other hand, the turnaround time compared to going directly to the stacks and getting the article (assuming the journal is not being bound, has not been lost, or the article razored or mutilated) may be disappointing. Faculty and student acceptance of article document delivery has been universally enthusiastic at Cincinnati, however, since it was seen as thwarting a major serials cut and a short delay was preferable to the delays of ILL or no access at all.

A second key issue is the degree to control the library retains over the process of ordering articles via commercial document delivery. At Cincinnati, although the UnCover articles were provided at no cost to faculty and graduate students, the service was mediated by branch librarians or bibliographers in order to provide some control, or at least early warning, over expenditures. Colorado State University, however, has pioneered in providing the UnCover article service without mediation to its faculty. While they do require that patrons request articles from library terminals (requests from offices or home are not allowed), the patron does so directly and without cost to themselves. Although it is still early days, their experience over the last couple of years suggests that their costs for providing the service are roughly the same as Cincinnati's more cautious mediated service. Recent reports from other academic libraries following CSU's lead seem to confirm that direct patron requesting is not, or at least not yet, being abused.

ENHANCING CONSORTIAL INTEGRATION

It is hard to conceive of a library which does not have consortial ties in this day and age. Consequently the problem for most libraries is not finding or forming a consortium, but transforming already existing consortial arrangements to meet new needs. Historically most libraries have co-operated with other libraries only in limited and fringe ways. Interlibrary loan is a perfect example. Although the rich ILL web which developed after WWII is one of the U.S. library profession's great success stories, it is increasingly unable to deal with today's reality without major transformation. Particularly among academic libraries, the information demands of increased research pressures combined with an explosive growth in bibliographic databases which allow faculty and students to know about remote resources have overwhelmed the traditional ILL system. It is simply too costly and logistically cumbersome to handle high volume traffic. This is not surprising since it evolved primarily to serve the exceptional, occasional need.

If libraries are to seriously move towards the access model for supplying more than a minuscule fraction of their patrons' materials needs, ILL must become more like circulation. Specifically, ILL must become as fast, inexpensive, convenient and reliable as circulation if ILL transactions are to change from 1/10th of 1% of a library's circulation to something as high as 10% or more of its circulation. The expense and cumbersome logistics of ILL come primarily in two areas–determining the correct and precise bibliographic identity of a desired item and discovering who can and will loan it. The consequent need for skilled, often professional, staff to solve these problems accounts for much of the average $30.00 cost of the requesting/loaning process. Circulation, on the other hand, involves known items (identified in the catalog), in known locations (call numbers) which the patrons retrieve themselves (non-mediated and as fast as they wish). Transforming ILL into circulation is both a possible and an extremely important goal for a consortium; and in Ohio, the OhioLINK consortium has shown how this can work.

For all practical purposes, all Ohio academic libraries–both public and private–belong to OhioLINK (OL). Operating on a common hardware platform with identical software, any OL patron can search the holdings of any OL library. If a desired item is found, the patron simply enters his/her name, ID, and the library location they would like the material delivered to. A pull slip is generated in the holding library circulation unit, a student retrieves the item from the shelf and puts it with the request slip into a delivery pouch. A commercial delivery service makes daily stops at each library to pick up and deliver materials. Fifty percent of the items requested are delivered within 2 days of request while 75% are delivered within 3 days of request. Since the patrons search for and identify the desired items themselves and student workers handle the rest, the cost is no more than that of a local, closed stack circulation operation. The commercial delivery adds an additional 50 cents per item per round trip. The system is obviously fast, cheap, reliable (the main problem encountered is when an identified item is not on the shelf where the library's catalog says it should be, a problem independent of the system and one which a local patron would encounter as well) and convenient. In fact, in the area of convenience the OL system is arguably more convenient for patrons than actually going to the stacks since they may request materials from their homes, their offices or while traveling (location independent) as well as 7 days a week, 24 hours a day (time independent).

A second key area where consortial integration needs to be enhanced is in the realm of co-ordinated collection development. The different nature of books and journals requires somewhat different approaches. In both cases the OhioLINK model may be instructive.

In the case of books, two important lessons have been learned. The first is that it is important to demonstrate a viable locating and delivery system before talking to the faculty, students and administration about co-ordinated collection development. Without such a demonstration, the only model most patrons have for a delivery system is ILL–a system with too many negatives to convince most faculty that they can rely on other consortial partners for crucial materials. Even with a convincing delivery demonstration, there is a historical prejudice for wanting key materials held locally. A phenomenon not likely to surprise many experienced librarians.

The second lesson, whose details OL libraries are still figuring out, is that collections that historically have been thought of as independent and stand-alone must be transformed into effective components of a much larger whole. This really requires thinking of the collection in a very different way but results in considerable advantages. Instead of spreading limited resources over a thinly covered waterfront, it allows individual libraries to focus on collecting in a limited number of areas in great strength–knowing that reciprocal in-depth collecting is going on in other institutions. Especially important is the potential for reducing unnecessary duplication. Although the number of unique materials held in the various OL collections is surprising (57.7% of OL member monograph titles are unique to one OL library), there clearly is unnecessary duplication (23.8% of the requests for an item show there are 6 or more identical items available at the time of request). What seems increasingly clear at this point is that heavily used core materials should probably be widely duplicated and that the focus for collection coordination should be at what the ARL conspectus identifies as the research or comprehensive level or involving local specialties such as Wright State University's Wright Brothers collection. The use of the ARL conspectus appears to be most useful for its subject and collecting level categories. Using it to determine historical strengths is too expensive in terms of staff time and there is an increasing suspicion that historical strength is less an indication of future commitment to an area than written agreements supported by Provosts or Presidents. And of course, it will come as no surprise that OL libraries are finding that establishing coordinated collection development at a highly integrated level is a very complex and politically complicated process.

In the case of serials, a different approach has been taken by OL libraries. After considerable struggle to try to find ways to more efficiently and cheaply exchange articles already held in print subscriptions in member libraries and finding great frustrations in both the technological and the legal arena, OL libraries have begun to focus primarily on electronic, fulltext journal articles. The key strategy here has been to use the buying power of the consortium to arrange favorable deals on what is essentially a state-wide basis. The most important advantage consortial purchase provides to both publishers and libraries is a huge win-win possibility. Publishers can stabilize or even increase their revenue stream and the consortial members can lower per capita costs as well as gain other advantages. For example, ILL among OL libraries for consortially purchased materials is unnecessary since the publisher is providing the access to all. Consortial purchase also allows libraries to spread implementation and installation costs over a large number of purchasers so that these costs are reduced as well. While over 50 bibliographic databases have been purchased on a consortial basis, there have been two major journal fulltext experiments.

The first OL experiment with the delivery with article fulltext was with UMI using massive CD jukeboxes (with hundreds of CDs per jukebox) to deliver what is now called ProQuest Direct. Providing the full text of articles for over 600 journal titles, this is an extremely popular service even though at this point it can only be used in the library itself. In our busy Winter quarter patrons print off upwards of 1,000 articles a day. UMI is what has now become known as an "aggregator" in that they make arrangements with a large number of publishers to offer to libraries a bundled group of journal titles in electronic form. The cost to the libraries is not bad with the page costs for content running 10-12 cents, the equipment costs in the 3-4 cents/page range and the paper and toner costs adding 2-3 cents/page. When subscription, processing, claiming, binding, vandalism/theft replacement and storage costs of paper copies are considered, the expense of providing UMI electronic articles seems roughly comparable. Convenient and useful as such aggregator services are, however, there is some evidence that they may be losing out to direct publisher offerings.

OL's second experiment is with direct publisher offerings or what might be called vertical versions of electronic journals, i.e., where a publisher makes available all their journals in electronic format (in contrast to the horizontal offerings of an aggregator). Recently, OL was the first consortium in North America to sign an agreement with Academic Press for what is a state-wide contract for all 175 AP titles in electronic format. From a collection development point of view, a number of collections problems were addressed in this agreement.

Probably the first issue to come to a librarian's mind is how the library maintains its preservation role when dealing with electronic journals. Particularly if they are provided from a central, non-library location, the guaranteed, continued access to electronic journals over time seems problematic. OL dealt with this problem on two levels. The first was to provide contract language guaranteeing permanent future access to any electronic journal issues published during the contract period. Even if OL does not continue a relationship with AP, those journals published during the contract period will continue to be available in perpetuity to OL libraries. The second point was to insist that an archival tape (or disk) of the electronic journals published during the contract period would be held in escrow or by OL so that if, at a future point, the contract were discontinued or disaster struck AP, a "physical" copy of the electronic journals would be available. An even better solution should soon be available when OCLC announces its Electronic Collections Online (ECO) service. Among other features, this will provide an OCLC guarantee of ongoing library access to the contracted-for electronic journals–a critical service to member libraries which OCLC is uniquely equipped to provide.

Less likely to come to mind immediately for collection development officers who have not already been talking with publishers about electronic journals are ILL implications. The Academic Press talks, both with OhioLINK and other groups, almost came to grief on this issue. Publishers are very nervous about allowing libraries with access to electronic journals to forward electronic copies of articles to other libraries even under standard Fair Use provisions. The ease with which they feel this can be done (yes, they are pretty naive) raises fears in their minds that this ability would be too easily abused and would encourage further library serials cancellations. Libraries, on the other hand, absolutely depend on their ILL relationships to provide reasonable access to low use materials and would face serious complications in the ILL relationships if they were not able to reciprocate as a growing number of their serial titles are represented by electronic journals. The compromise Ohio-LINK eventually worked out with AP with regard to ILL agreements with non-OL libraries, was that OL libraries could continue ILL relationships with non-OL libraries with respect to AP titles as long as articles were provided in print, rather than electronic, format. And, of course, only within the limits provided by the CONTU guidelines.

Much more positive was the agreement on ILL between OL libraries. On the one hand it is no longer necessary to provide ILL services to each other for AP titles since everyone in OL has a subscription. In addition, it was also agreed that OL libraries could share unlimited numbers of articles from AP titles with each other from the already existing print backfiles held in member collections. While no one expects this to be a large number (almost certainly no more than allowed under CONTU guidelines), it relieves the OL libraries from the burden of tracking use and collecting statistics for in-state use of AP articles. Although the number of titles involved in the AP agreement is relatively modest in comparison to most OL library's serials collections, OL libraries think that the AP agreement represents an important first step in reducing the local ILL workload while still improving service.

A third important solution of interest to collection development officers is that the AP agreement allows OL libraries the freedom to use AP articles for legitimate classroom, reserves, and coursepack use. The complicated and time-consuming process of getting permissions or trying to determine just what is allowed under CONTU guidelines is simply bypassed.

IMPROVING THE VIRTUAL ENVIRONMENT

Although seemingly outside of the collection development officer's purview, the issue of the virtual environment is important to the creation and success of the new CD model based on access rather than ownership. While infrastructure–equipment, software and connectivity–is important, there are at least two areas closer to home for the collection development officer to be concerned about.

The first is the development of good electronic presentation design. In earlier days when the virtual library meant moving the card catalog to an online version, determining how the electronic version would be presented to the user in a helpful and intuitively obvious manner was, in retrospect, relatively straight-forward. In the last twenty years, however, with the addition of reference and fulltext information to the original catalog of bibliographic records in conjunction with hypertext, gopher and WEB links, we have a richness which is chaotic in its possibilities. Developing coherent and intuitive ways of organizing and presenting the available electronic resources represents an important agenda item of concern to collection development officers. Simply adding more electronic resources to this heady mixture without giving thought to how these resources will be integrated into a larger and overall information design, is like giving more saltwater to a castaway in a lifeboat.

One of the dawning realizations of the OL libraries is that the creation of a virtual library is not just putting resources in electronic form, but a much larger task. It is the re-creation through the means of a 14-inch screen of a whole physical library with all its attendant visual and spacial cues for assisting patrons to understand how to find and use the resources they need. This is a massive task of translation and clearly an effort which requires, among others, the imaginative gifts of those entrusted with selecting the content of the virtual library.

The second, and more prosaic but probably more practical, area is the importance of enhancing the virtual environment by enriching the catalog record. Assuming that for the foreseeable future a key mission for any library will continue to be identifying and locating print materials, it is important that we not fall into the trap of paving the cowpaths. Limitations which were necessary to the card catalog are increasingly dissolving in the online environment. A prime example is browsing the stacks. One of the most often heard arguments from faculty opposing the virtual library is that it does not allow them to browse the stacks. When pressed, however, for details why this is important, it is clear that they are not attracted to dimly lit stacks open to them only limited hours and lined with dusty books. What they invariably answer is that they want to pull a book off the shelf, check the Table of Contents and Index and maybe skim a few chapters. Accepting the limitations of the bibliographic record they have divided their search for relevant materials into two parts: a search in the catalog supplemented by a physical trip to the stacks. In other words, much of the value of browsing comes from the inadequacies of the bibliographic record.

For the virtual library to equal (or surpass) the advantages of a bibliographic record supplemented by a trip to the local holdings, it is obviously necessary to enhance the traditional bibliographic record. The OL libraries have already begun this task by adding Table of Contents information to the bibliographic record on a regular basis and there is individual consideration of such further enrichments as Index information (from Chadwyck-Healy), links to book reviews (Choice) and links to relevant reference sources (e.g., Encyclopedia Britannica) and even WEB sites. A substantially enriched bibliographic record combined with 7 day/24 hour access to a huge consortial database such as OL's 20 million volumes should make browsing a limited local collection an increasingly unsatisfactory enterprise. If done properly, browsing the stacks in the 21st century, like horseback riding in the 20th, will turn from a necessity, to an activity undertaken for pleasure or whim.

ESTABLISHING A NEW ROLE FOR BIBLIOGRAPHERS

A final action item is the need for bibliographers to both define a new role for themselves and rethink their collection development policies. The central change in terms of their role is the substantial focus of time and energy which must be devoted outside of the institution. While developing the traditional, local onsite collection required primarily an internal focus, in a consortial, virtual library environment a major part of the bibliographer's focus must now be external. An access strategy which depends on materials being "out there" requires someone to make sure that the "out there" is actually out there. This is what bibliographers now must do. In particular, they must now be actively involved with their peers throughout the consortium to work out the mechanisms and agreements for sharing resources, they must work with consortial peers to define and allocate reciprocal collection areas, they must work with vendors to develop new resources and define the agreements which allow their use in libraries, and they need to take the lead in working with departmental faculty committees to interpret to the faculty the opportunities and advantages of this new environment. Obviously, the bibliographer's role has become not only more externally focused but more complex and demanding as well.

Since the context for collection development policies has also changed, the policies themselves must change as well. It is no longer a sufficient job description for a bibliographer to accommodate faculty purchase requests, review approval program materials, scan publisher blurbs and materials reviews and make sure that all the money gets spent. In fact, as libraries move away from the view that they must own it all in order to provide access, a much more comprehensive possibility begins to emerge for support of college and university instruction and research.

Rather than the bibliographer starting with the budget and then seeing how far that will go in buying needed materials for the collection, the 21st century bibliographer can start with the information and resource needs of the students and faculty and then design a strategy which will provide access to needed materials from a wide range of sources. In other words, instead of collection building–a single strategy–the bibliographer needs to focus on collection mapping–a complex strategy.

Collection mapping is not unlike the way librarians have traditionally talked about reference librarians–it's not necessary to know all the answers, just where the answers can be found. So with materials, it's not necessary to own them all, just to identify how they can all be made available. Through mapping, the bibliographer specifically determines how each needed element will be supplied–via ILL, regional consortia, commercial vendor, local purchase/ownership, etc. It is important to note that local purchase continues to be a significant means of access. The change is that local ownership is no longer the exclusive or even necessarily the central element in providing access to the materials needed by faculty and students for research and instruction. Buying materials for the local collection becomes simply one strategy among many for providing access to materials. The development of such a virtual collection, or collection map, focuses not on staying within the budget (and the limitations that implies), but on using multiple sources to provide vastly increased access to needed materials. Collection mapping, which provides a cost-effective way to provide access to a huge range of low-use materials for the library patron in contrast to the increasingly unaffordable traditional collection development, fundamentally changes the mission of the bibliographer and the nature of the collection development policy.

CONCLUSION

The primary reality facing bibliographers today, is that every year they continue to spend more to acquire less. The traditional model of independent libraries providing access to research and instructional materials primarily through locally purchased collections is clearly a doomed strategy for the 21st century. While the new directions are by no means clear or certain, the elements mentioned above–buying by the drink, enhancing consortial integration, improving the virtual environment and establishing a new role for bibliographers–do suggest methods by which a number of pioneering libraries are beginning to sketch out a new strategy for thinking about and dealing with collections issues in tomorrow's world. We need to continue to experiment, to discuss and report, and above all, to act. As Marvell cautions:

But at my back I always hear
Time's wingèd chariot hurrying near.

Chapter Four:
The Study of Subject Strengths, Overlap, and National Collecting Patterns: The Uses of the OCLC/AMIGOS Collection Analysis CD and Alternatives to It

Curt Holleman

In the days when electronic coverage of library collections was primitive, librarians bravely attempted to compare their collections quantitatively. Total volume counts for collections were compiled in countless libraries and published in a wide range of resources, such as R. R. Bowker's *American Library Directory* and the Association of Research Libraries' *ARL Statistics*, both of which continue to publish these statistics today. As time has passed, collection managers and other academic and library administrators have wanted more sophisticated measurements to compare library collections. Early on, through the Herculean efforts of librarians and groups of librarians, fairly sophisticated collection studies took place at a great cost of time and hard work. With the advent of computerized

Curt Holleman, MLS, is Director of Central University Libraries Collection Development and Management, Fondren Library, Southern Methodist University, Dallas, TX 75275.

[Haworth co-indexing entry note]: "Chapter Four: The Study of Subject Strengths, Overlap, and National Collecting Patterns: The Uses of the OCLC/AMIGOS Collection Analysis CD and Alternatives to It." Holleman, Curt. Co-published simultaneously in *Collection Management* (The Haworth Press, Inc.) Vol. 22, No. 1/2, 1997, pp. 57-69; and: *Collection Development: Access in the Virtual Library* (ed: Maureen Pastine) The Haworth Press, Inc., 1997, pp. 57-69. Single or multiple copies of this article are available for a fee from The Haworth Document Delivery Service [1-800-342-9678, 9:00 a.m. - 5:00 p.m. (EST). E-mail address: getinfo@haworth.com].

57

cataloging and such products as the OCLC/AMIGOS Collection Analysis CD, it has become possible almost instantaneously to obtain data that formerly took many hours of labor.

Here we will examine three varieties of research into library collections: studies of subject strengths, studies of the overlap of collections, and studies of national collecting patterns. In the course of our examination of these types of studies, we will assess the relative merits of the old and new ways of conducting research into collections, and we will recommend the best means for doing so in the future.

STUDIES OF SUBJECT STRENGTHS

The year 1973 saw the birth of the first major quantitative attempt to study the subject strengths of some of the nation's most important academic libraries. Pioneered by Leroy D. Ortopan of the University of California at Berkeley and the Chief Collection Development Officers of Large Research Libraries Discussion Group, the precursor to the National Shelflist count was published.[1] Two years later, the number of participating libraries had grown from sixteen to twenty-five, and the National Shelflist Count was born.[2] Ortopan has described the methods used to compile the early counts, methods which can only seem painful and imprecise to us today. Shelflists (library catalog cards filed in call number order) were studied to determine how many cards fit per centimeter and then carefully chosen call number ranges were measured. Because some libraries used Library of Congress classifications for their books and others the Dewey Decimal, Ortopan also had to construct a conversion table from Dewey to Library of Congress classifications.[3] Librarians who struggled with the methodology and their fears of incomparibility among libraries were rewarded with an interesting product that was, however, maligned for its inaccuracies. As Ortopan said in the Shelflist's defense, ". . . it is undoubtedly better to know something about a subject than to know nothing about it simply because that something is incomplete or inexact."[4]

Arguments will persist about the relative merits of electronic and paper products for readers and libraries, but there can be no doubt about the superiority of electronic products for comparing the subject strengths of libraries. The foremost electronic tool available today that allows a library to compare its collecting strength in academic subjects with other libraries of its choosing is the OCLC/ AMIGOS Collection Analysis CD. Tom Nisonger has described the origin of the Collection Analysis CD. In 1982 a group of librarians meeting in Dallas sought to compare the subject strengths of libraries in their consortium, the Association for Higher Education in North Texas.[5] They chose to combine the subject breakdown of the RLG (Research Libraries Group) Conspectus with the SUNY/ OCLC approach, which offered ingenious tables for comparing libraries' holdings but with a primitive and broad-based subject approach. Nisonger describes how these librarians worked with the RLG Conspectus until they had divided it into 53 major categories and 2,545 headings overall (compared to the National Shelflist Count's 354 headings),[6] and how they modified the SUNY tables to create the final product.

Although researchers quibble over some attributes of the Collection Analysis CD (Richard Wood, for example, lists eight "limitations and disadvantages"),[7] Wood himself and other researchers such as Albert Joy,[8] Marcia Findley,[9] Jeanne Harrell,[10] and Michael G. Webster[11] have generally extolled the product for its ability to compare subject strengths and to perform the other tasks for which they have used it. There can be little doubt that for most purposes the Collection Analysis CD compares subject collecting effectively and certainly almost effortlessly compared to any alternative. Wood cites the most common complaint–that the product covers only eleven imprint years–and that is certainly a limitation for comparisons of subject coverage among major research libraries. Findley defends the limited date span with the argument that "it is generally those books published within the last five or ten years that provide the dynamic collection most used by patrons."[12] Findley's argument has merit, but it is also true that the restriction to eleven imprint years makes comparisons much more valid than they otherwise would be. Libraries are very inconsistent in which older materials of theirs are represented on OCLC; a comparison among a library with ten years of cataloging on OCLC, one with twenty years but no retrospective holdings, and one with twenty years plus all retrospective holdings would be meaningless. For total collection counts, we are still dependent on the National Shelflist Count (now titled *The North American Title Count*), despite its shortcomings.

STUDIES OF OVERLAP

If the pre-electronic study of subject strengths in collections was difficult, at least librarians had recourse to the measurement of shelf-list cards. The study of overlap for librarians of the pre-electronic era had to be far more formidable. Overlap, to simplify the concept, might be thought of as the duplication of titles between or among libraries. But the concept of overlap goes beyond duplication: In a group of, say, thirteen libraries, it makes a major difference in our understanding of their efficiency if a title is simply duplicated between two libraries or whether it is held by all thirteen. Overlap studies can make that distinction. Buckland, Hindle, and Walker describe a Lancaster overlap study of 1971 in which sample cards were extracted from catalogs and photocopied or transcribed. "The entire sample (some 23,000 items), was then alphabetised, mounted on sheets of paper and numbered."[13] They go on to describe the reproduction and distribution of the lists but leave to the imagination the excruciating process which older librarians know only too well of looking up 23,000 items in traditional library catalogs.

The SUNY Overlap Study

Glyn Evans of SUNY, with the assistance of OCLC, created the first sophisticated electronic engine for determining overlap. Unfortunately, the brilliance of his design was eclipsed by the faultiness of its application. In a study of the collections of SUNY libraries, Evans and his associates determined that a stunning 86.7% of the titles were unique to one collection only. They reached this fallacious figure by examining a twelve-week period of cataloging only and failing to accommodate the fact that the same books can be purchased and cataloged at different times. Evans conceded this flaw in his study, but he never allowed for how extreme the resulting distortion was. His work was cited repeatedly at conferences in the 1970s and 1980s as proof of the small amount of duplication occurring among university libraries.[14]

The Study of Overlap in the University of Wisconsin System

In a study conducted from 1977 to 1979, Moore, Miller, and Tolliver conducted an overlap analysis of the libraries in the University of Wisconsin system that was, according to their own description, similar to the SUNY study. Instead of utilizing only twelve weeks of cataloging, they used a full two years. Similarly to SUNY, they found that 81.84% of the titles at Wisconsin libraries were unique when they did not restrict imprint date. When they restricted their study to titles published between 1976 and 1979, their uniqueness rate fell to 68.01%.[15]

The authors chose to emphasize the lack of overlap in the Wisconsin system. They began the article by citing studies that found much greater duplication of titles in New England and California, and they concluded that their results were more similar to those at SUNY. Surely it is desirable for overlap to be relatively low among collections, and for that reason it is unfortunate that the Wisconsin study is almost as fallacious as the SUNY study was. Consider, first, the broad issue of comparing books of any date that happened to be cataloged between July 1977 and June 1979. An objective observer might suppose that the primary problem would be in a library's adding, say, a 1965 or a 1975 imprint already held by other libraries that would nonetheless be the only copy of the title cataloged in the system during those two years and therefore erroneously considered unique. The authors' concern instead is for the rare book that might be cataloged, and they conjecture that the true rate of uniqueness should fall between the 68% of the current imprints and the 82% uniqueness rate of all imprints.[16]

In fact, I would conjecture that the rate of uniqueness in the Wisconsin system is substantially exaggerated even by the 68% figure. A narrow analysis of their methodology tells why. They considered any book with an imprint date from 1976 to 1979. This means that any straggling library being the last to catalog a 1976 book in late 1977 would, according to their methodology, have a "unique" copy, even if many other libraries had cataloged it earlier. Similarly, on the other end, the first library to catalog 1979 titles toward the end of the study would be awarded with "unique" titles if no other library cataloged it before the end of the study. For a reader skeptical about the impact of these distortions, I suggest a look at my next section, "Studies of National Collecting," where I revisit the computations of a researcher who employed a better methodology, exercised a longer delay before her computations, and treated a subject less sensitive to distortion than overlap. This researcher still came to highly erroneous conclusions by not giving time for all books of an imprint period to be cataloged. No one will ever pay to revisit the University of Wisconsin study, but my conjecture based on my own experience and on other studies is that the true rate of uniqueness in the Wisconsin system from 1976 to 1979 is not just lower than their figure of 68% to 82%. I suspect that it is significantly lower than 50% and that the majority of the unique books from that time reside at the Madison campus.

The Study of Overlap at the University of California

In the mid-1970s Cooper, Thompson, and Weeks conducted a study of duplication in the University of California library system.[17] Their study entails a minimal use of computerization, and the validity and sensitivity of its results show what is sometimes lost in an undiscerning acceptance of computer output. The California survey distinguishes between an "exact match" and "approximate matches." An exact match includes exact reprints and books identical except for place of printing. An approximate match applies to textually similar books in different editions or books slightly changed in other ways.[18] Readers familiar with modern cataloging will know that none of the approximate matches would be regarded as overlap by a computerized study, and of the exact matches, reprints would not be regarded as overlap. According to the study, at that time Berkeley approximately owned 80% of the San Francisco titles, 74% of the Santa Cruz titles, and 66% of the Davis titles. For exact matches, Berkeley owned 67% of San Francisco's, 56% of Santa Cruz's, and 50% of Davis's titles. The difference between approximate and exact matches amounted to about a 15% difference in overlap. In a head-to-head comparison between Berkeley and UCLA, however, the distinction made less difference. UCLA had an exact match for 46% of Berkeley's titles and an approximate match for 50%. Berkeley had an exact match for 58% of UCLA's titles and an approximate one for 52%.[19] The authors do not tell us what percentage of titles examined are reprints, but perhaps it would be wise to add something like 10% to computerized accounts of overlap to account for extremely similar material that the computer treats as utterly different.

Overlap Studies: Analysis and Recommendations

If non-computerized studies of overlap can be more sensitive, is there any use for computerized studies such as those offered by the OCLC/AMIGOS Collection Analysis CD? There is a use for computerized studies of overlap, and the OCLC/AMIGOS CD offers both convenience and an excellent framework for overlap studies. We have already seen how the restriction of a comparison of subject strengths to eleven imprint years employed by the Collection Analysis CD allows for a much more accurate electronic comparison than is possible without an imprint restriction. The restriction of imprint dates is even more important in overlap studies because different libraries have such different cataloging histories on OCLC. When one library has total retrospective holdings on OCLC and another has only their cataloging of the last twenty years, the count of their holdings of books in common on OCLC profoundly distorts the truth about their holdings in common. The Collection Analysis CD deftly avoids this problem with its focus on eleven years of imprint dates. With its provision of instant overlap statistics and a title-by-title analysis to back up the statistics, it offers an excellent combination of convenience and reliability.

There are three weaknesses in the Collection Analysis CD's ability to do overlap studies, and they are mostly inevitable in an electronic product that scans the collections of multiple libraries. The first is the tendency for there to be at times two different entries on OCLC for one book. From extensive experience with title-by-title lists, I estimate this tendency to introduce about a five percent distortion. Secondly, there is the problem of exact matches versus approximate matches. In examining a list of books provided by the Collection Analysis CD's overlap analysis that SMU seemingly had failed to purchase in ancient history, I discovered that a very high percentage of the most desirable titles on the list were at SMU in earlier editions or in the original edition on which the reprint was based. Thirdly, there is the ironic problem that the Collection Analysis CD is timelier than it should be for accurate overlap analyses. As we shall see in the next section of this study, libraries do not uniformly add and catalog new books at the same speed, and the portion of the overlap study that is based on the most recent year's imprints is certain to be severely distorted.

The merits of the Collection Analysis CD's overlap studies greatly outweigh the demerits, and the product offers a flexibility that can serve almost any user. A user desiring a quick study of overlap between a library and a group of libraries of her choosing can painlessly receive instantaneous statistics from the CD. Because of the tendency that I just described of an electronic product to understate overlap and overstate uniqueness, I would recommend adding 15 to 20 percent to overlap figures and subtracting 15 to 20 percent from uniqueness figures. For most purposes, the results will be accurate enough to determine which subjects in a library are overlapping collections in other libraries the most and how much in general a library's collections overlap those at other libraries.

If a greater degree of precision is needed, a user can go to the title-by-title analysis provided by the CD and achieve as much accuracy as he wants by running it against his and other libraries' holdings. Using the title-by-title analysis in this way can overcome the problem of two entries for one book, the problem of approximate matches, and the problem of the cataloging of the same book at different times by different libraries. In a word, the Collection Analysis CD provides the opportunity for whatever degree of precision a researcher desires. Because it is so convenient and easy-to-use, it is ideal for a quick study of overlap. Because it offers a solid starting point and a title-by-title list to provide the base for as much further analysis as a researcher could desire, it is also an excellent product to use as the beginning point for even a minutely detailed study of overlap. It is hard to imagine anyone studying overlap among any libraries whose recent holdings are in OCLC not wanting to begin the study with this tool.

STUDIES OF NATIONAL COLLECTING

Anna Perrault and Charles Schwartz have recently published articles using the OCLC/AMIGOS Collection Analysis CD to study national collecting patterns. Schwartz has performed a series of studies in anthropology,[20] Judaica,[21] political science,[22] and psychology,[23] and Perrault has studied the entire span of subjects collected by ARL (Association for Research Libraries) institutions.[24] As their titles indicate, both authors are pessimistic about trends in academic collecting. Perrault finds an alarming and precipitous decline in the number of monographs that the greatest academic libraries in North America are collecting. Schwartz believes that these libraries are collecting a decreasing percentage of the works in their areas. Perrault's study, which is the most ambitious and most influential work of its kind, will be the primary subject of this section.

Following the concern voiced by the Mellon Foundation that research libraries will increasingly collect the same basic materials and narrow the range of esoteric materials that they collect,[25] Anna Perrault published her influential and award-winning article based on her own award-winning dissertation. The conclusion that she reaches in her dissertation and her article is that the concern of the Mellon Foundation is well placed: From 1985 to 1989 the collection of monographic non-serial titles by the 72 ARL libraries with bibliographic records in the OCLC/AMIGOS Collection Analysis CD declined 27.76%.[26] Perrault does not qualify or hedge her figures; in another article based on her study, she states, "The study establishes that the rate of acquisitions for new imprints in the collective resources base declined 27.76 percent from 1985 to 1989."[27]

In almost every way, Perrault's study is a good piece of research. The justifiability of her basic idea of comparing these ARL libraries' collecting of monographic titles in 1985 and 1989 in order to study the difference in the range of titles collected by research libraries is arguable, but it certainly has a validity well beyond the impressionistic estimates upon which we must otherwise rely. Her conclusions that she reaches based on the statistical results of her research are generally measured and perceptive, except for the categorical nature of some of her pronouncements on her results that she cites to the second decimal place, when the experience of these libraries is at best an approximation of what is happening in all research libraries. On the whole, it is understandable that the research won awards. Unfortunately, the chief problem with her research is not that it subtly misleads; it is that a tiny flaw in its design makes its statistics utterly wrong and its conclusions false.

The seemingly small flaw in Perrault's design is that she compared the purchasing of ARL libraries in 1985 and 1989 too soon. By using the Collection Analysis CD of 1991, she did not allow time for as many 1989 imprints to be cataloged as 1985. The comparisons below reflect an update of the world history part of her study, using the Collection Analysis CD of 1995 instead of that of 1991. Figures reflect the number of titles owned by ARL libraries with bibliographic records in the OCLC/AMIGOS Collection Analysis CD. In 1991 there were 72 libraries; in 1995 there were 80.

Geographical Region	1985 Imprints	1989 Imprints	Change	Rate of Change
Britain (1991 CD)	569	477	− 92	− 16%
Britain (1995 CD)	592	652	+60	+10%
Austro-Hungary (1991)	388	212	− 176	− 45%
Austro-Hungary (1995)	447	434	− 13	− 3%
France (1991)	737	659	− 78	− 11%
France (1995)	802	1,159	+357	+45%
Germany (1991)	784	672	− 112	− 14%
Germany (1995)	899	904	+5	+1%
Greece (1991)	225	121	− 104	− 46%
Greece (1995)	246	206	− 40	− 16%
Italy (1991)	650	340	− 310	− 48%
Italy (1995)	707	546	− 161	− 23%
Russia (1991)	1,207	925	− 282	− 23%
Russia (1995)	1,292	1,476	+184	+14%
Spain, Port. (1991)	476	319	− 157	− 33%
Spain, Port. (1995)	510	529	+19	+4%
Asia (1991)	4,743	3,704	− 1,039	− 29%
Asia (1995)	5,512	5,861	+349	+6%
Africa (1991)	1,023	728	− 295	− 29%
Africa (1995)	1,143	1,175	+32	+3%[28]

The four years of cataloging intervening between 1991 and 1995 clearly had a drastic effect on the ratio of books collected with 1985 imprints and those collected with 1989 imprints. In the sampling above, which is not especially atypical, the least improvement that

1989 imprints made in a subject area over the additional four years is in German history, where 1989 imprints improved 15 percentage points compared to 1985 imprints. The greatest difference is in French history, where the improvement was 56 percentage points. Overall, between 1991 and 1995 the total number of books collected with 1985 imprints increased just 13% while the number of books with 1989 imprints increased 57%. Contrary to Perrault's finding in 1991 of a decrease of 27.76% in the collection of 1989 imprints compared to 1985 imprints in ARL libraries, by 1995 there was actually an increase of .56% in the collection of 1989 imprints over those of 1985.

CONCLUSION

Perrault's study has been influential, and this study's most important conclusion for the academic world relates to it. There was not a decline in the acquisition of 1989 imprints from those acquired in 1985 of almost 28%. The collection of different imprint titles collected by ARL libraries and registered on the OCLC/AMIGOS Collection Analysis CD did not significantly vary between those years, increasing, in fact, as of 1995 by a little less than one percent. Researchers should beware of using her figures for the basis of their thinking about national collecting patterns during the years of her study.

We have seen from studies of the SUNY and University of Wisconsin library systems and a study of the collecting of ARL libraries that small errors can easily invalidate statistics when researchers use electronic products to compare and analyze collections. Especially in the case of Perrault's study of ARL collecting, the error seems minor indeed, yet it has led to grossly misleading conclusions regarding the nation's collecting over the time period studied. The possibility of error should not, however, keep us from using excellent new products such as the OCLC/AMIGOS Collection Analysis CD. Older means of data collection are extremely cumbersome compared to using the Collection Analysis CD, and the more complex analyses that the CD enables researchers to do would be pragmatically impossible without it.

If researchers are very careful to acknowledge the problems with imprint dates and approximate matches inherent in any electronic product and make allowances for them, the Collection Analysis CD can perform a wide range of useful analyses, including the analysis conceived by Perrault of comparing collecting in ARL libraries over time. The analyses that the Collection Analysis CD performs will be sufficiently accurate for most purposes, and when they are not, the title-by-title lists offered in the Bibliographic Lists section offer the most exacting researcher a basis for the highest degree of precision in her research.

NOTES

1. *Titles Classified by the Library of Congress Classification: Seventeen University Libraries*, preliminary edition (Berkeley, General Library, University of California, 1973).

2. *Titles Classified by the Library of Congress Classification: National Shelflist Count* (Berkeley, General Library, University of California, 1975).

3. LeRoy D. Ortopan, "National Shelflist Count: A Historical Introduction," *Library Resources & Technical Services* 29 (October/December 1985), 328-332.

4. Ibid., 332.

5. Thomas E. Nisonger, "Editing the RLG Conspectus to Analyze the OCLC Archival Tapes of Seventeen Texas Libraries," *Library Resources & Technical Services* 29 (October/December 1985), 311-312.

6. Ibid., 322.

7. Richard J. Wood, "Building a Better Library Collection: The CACD Way," *Library Software Review* 15 (1996), 22-23.

8. Albert H. Joy, "The OCLC/AMIGOS Collection Analysis CD: A Unique Tool for Collection Evaluation and Development," *Resource Sharing and Information Networks* 8/1 (1992), 23-45.

9. Marcia Findley, "Using the OCLC/AMIGOS Collection Analysis Compact Disk to Evaluate Art and Art History Collections," *Technical Services Quarterly* 10/3 (1993), 1-15.

10. Jeanne Harrell, "Using the OCLC/AMIGOS CD to Determine Comparative Collection Strength in English and American Literature: A Case Study," *Technical Services Quarterly* 9/3 (1992), 1-14.

11. Michael G. Webster, "Using the AMIGOS/OCLC Collection Analysis CD and Student Credit Hour Statistics to Evaluate Collection Growth Patterns and Potential Demand," *Library Acquisitions: Practice and Theory* 19/2 (1995), 197-210.

12. Findley, p. 1.

13. William K. Buckland, Anthony Hindle, and Gregory P.M. Walker, "Methodological Problems in Assessing the Overlap Between Bibliographic Files and Library Holdings," *Information Processing and Management* 11 (August 1975), 101.

14. Glyn T. Evans, Roger Gifford, and Donald R. Franz, *Collection Development Analysis Using OCLC Archival Tapes: Final Report* (Albany, NY: SUNY Office of Library Services, 1977). ERIC document no. ED152 299.

15. Barbara Moore, Tamara J. Miller, and Don L. Tolliver, "Title Overlap: A Study of Duplication in the University of Wisconsin System Libraries," *College & Research Libraries* 43/1 (January 1982), 14-21.

16. Ibid., 17.

17. William S. Cooper, Donald D. Thompson, and Kenneth R. Weeks, "The Duplication of Monograph Holdings in the University of California Library System," *Library Quarterly* 45/3 (July 1975), 253-274.

18. Ibid., 261.

19. Ibid., 262-263.

20. Charles A. Schwartz, "Literature Loss in Anthropology," *Current Anthropology 33 (1992), 315-317.*

21. Charles A. Schwartz, "Empirical Analysis of Literature Loss," *LRTS* 38/2 (April 1994), 133-138.

22. Charles A. Schwartz, "Literature Loss in International Relations," *PS: Political Science and Policy* 25 (1992), 720-723.

23. Charles A. Schwartz, "Gap Analysis of Book Publication Output and Aggregate Research Collections in Psychology," *American Psychologist* 48 (1993), 1151-1152.

24. Anna H. Perrault, "The Shrinking National Collection: A Study of the Effect of the Diversion of Funds from Monographs to Serials on the Monograph Collections of Research Libraries," *Library Acquisitions: Practice & Theory* 18/1 (1994), 3-22.

25. Anthony M. Cummings et al., *University Libraries and Scholarly Communication: A Study Prepared for the Andrew W. Mellon Foundation* (Washington, DC, Published by the Association of Research Libraries for the Andrew W. Mellon Foundation, 1993 [1989]), p. 3.

26. Perrault (1994), p. 19.

27. Anna H. Perrault, "The Changing Print Resource Base of Academic Libraries in the United States," *Journal of Education for Library and Information Science* 36/4 (Fall 1995), 295.

28. The figures for 1991 in this table come from Perrault (1994), p. 17.

Chapter Five:
Distributed Education and Libraries

Robert Skinner

"Any time/any place" education continues to grow unimpeded on college campuses. Even though it may not always be clear if this is because institutions are anxiously responding to the demand of students to become more customer-centered or just exploiting the opportunity to collect extra tuition dollars without a corresponding commitment to infrastructure, libraries face the challenge of providing the same quality of library services to all students and faculty whether on- or off-campus.

The traditional view of "any time/any place" involves either faculty and student convening physically together in a single off-campus location or students viewing and perhaps responding to the talking head of an instructor transmitted over phone lines (or recorded on cassette for viewing by individual students). In either case, this "one to many" distance education model is often only a remote version of traditional instruction.

But this is not the only model. Teaching and learning unencumbered by time or location increasingly involves some type of "electronic conferencing," an umbrella term that covers everything from email to virtual reality. It is even more likely to occur on- than off-campus which is why distributed education or learning may be the

Robert Skinner is Director, Central University Libraries Technology Development, Fondren Library, Southern Methodist University, Dallas, TX 75275.

[Haworth co-indexing entry note]: "Chapter Five: Distributed Education and Libraries." Skinner, Robert. Co-published simultaneously in *Collection Management* (The Haworth Press, Inc.) Vol. 22, No. 1/2, 1997, pp. 71-80; and: *Collection Development: Access in the Virtual Library* (ed: Maureen Pastine) The Haworth Press, Inc., 1997, pp. 71-80. Single or multiple copies of this article are available for a fee from The Haworth Document Delivery Service [1-800-342-9678, 9:00 a.m. - 5:00 p.m. (EST). E-mail address: getinfo@haworth.com].

more appropriate term than distance education or learning.[1] Many librarians (not to mention faculty!) are unfamiliar with all of the aspects of distributed education and electronic conferencing. This article will explore how faculty and students are using these technologies and then give examples of how libraries are or could be taking advantage of electronic conferencing, particularly as regards collections and collections-related services.

A basic characteristic of electronic conferencing is whether communication between participants (faculty-student or student-student) occurs synchronously or asynchronously. Synchronous communication takes place in "real time" whether with participants speaking face-to-face or via electronic conferencing over a distance. Asynchronous communication (sometimes called "store and forward") can occur at the convenience of the participants, "on demand" as it were.

Because asynchronous communication adds a layer of disintermediation by removing physical contact, you may be surprised to learn how many faculty and students feel that electronic conferencing can promote the rapid establishment of a sense of community among the members of the class and between them and instructor. It serves as a timely reminder that when we are networking computers we are really networking computers.

Faculty using asynchronous technologies often find more frequent and more substantive interactions with a larger number of individual students than ever before. Some types of electronic conferencing act as "groupware," promoting team projects that require "problem analysis, discussion, spreadsheet analysis or report-preparation."[2] Once students are working in teams, faculty enjoy the ability to intervene with suggestions, encouragement, praise, questions in the deliberations of student groups working on projects, as well as in the spirited general discussions. Rather than inhibiting communication, asynchronous communication encourages both students and instructor to share spontaneously ideas, insights, and information that are not otherwise part of the course. We have all experienced classes where a few students dominate the conversation and others never speak. For classes with over 40 students, communication becomes even more restricted. Electronic conferencing helps correct this. It also increases the willingness on the part of some students to write–whether privately or publicly–about topics, sometimes controversial, which they are uncomfortable discussing in class. In short, electronic conferencing aids the transformation of the class from a punctual time-place event to an open-ended, asynchronous experience, which can include communication and exchange seven days a week, at many different times of night and day."[3]

There is an emphasis today on encouraging faculty moving from "instructor as lecturer" who imparts wisdom to a passive audience to "instructor as tutor-facilitator" (or, as someone has quipped, going "from stage to sage"). In the tutor-facilitator model, electronic conferencing promotes "(a) faculty replying to queries and requests from students, (b) faculty providing advice and guidance, (c) helping students to solve problems with regard to the subject matter, (d) serving as a transmission medium for homework and test papers, (e) discussing projects and work with the tutor, (f) bringing students together in accordance with their interests and their needs, and (g) encouraging team projects and setting up self-help groups."[4]

No one method of electronic conferencing is best for all of these. The following is an overview of some of the principal technologies being used today in the classroom. For each technology, I will list some general advantages and disadvantages and then look at how libraries are using or might use these technologies to support distributed learning or as a vehicle to provide library services.

Email is the most ubiquitous and the most familiar to all of us. *Advantages:* Many students already know how to use email and those that do not can easily learn. At most institutions, email is accessible from dorm, classroom, computer lab or off-campus. Instructors can even create alias or nickname files that will send a message to everyone in the class at one time. *Disadvantages:* It is difficult for messages to contain anything besides unformatted ASCII text. Attaching files from other programs, such as MS Word documents, is not easy for most students (or faculty!). Email for a class becomes intermixed with email from everywhere else. If not saved, deleted email is gone forever. The alias/nickname capability puts the onus on instructors to maintain an up-to-date list of recipients.

Mailing Lists (a.k.a. listservs, electronic discussion groups, electronic conferences). *Advantages:* Easy to learn, especially if the participants already know how to use email. Students can take care of adding themselves to class mailing lists so there is no need for alias/nickname file maintenance. The instructor can restrict traffic on the mailing list to only those in the class and even approve messages if desired. *Disadvantages:* Same as with email (minus the nickname maintenance) plus the annoyance of messages accidentally sent to the list rather than the mailing list administrator or administrative software.

Usenet new reader software or capability (e.g., TRN on UNIX machines, the news module in Web browses such as Netscape Navigator, or client software that runs on microcomputers). *Advantages:* "Thread" function of Usenet brings all messages with the same subject together making it easy to follow discussions with many replies; messages (called "articles" in Usenet parlance) can be archived on the news server for an entire semester. Usenet has more advanced options for replying to messages than email. Access on campus can be password protected. *Disadvantages:* Usenet is more difficult to master than email. Most people find it difficult to decode messages containing anything besides ASCII text.

Chat (a.k.a. IRC) allows real time communication between multiple people: the computer equivalent to CB radio. Some faculty have found that this is a useful way of encouraging student groups to meet outside class or to facilitate breaking into small groups in a large class to work on a project. *Advantages:* Most students enjoy chats. Chats generally are very easy to use. A log of the chat can usually be saved and given to the instructor. *Disadvantages:* Most Internet network administrators do not like chats and some even ban them. It can be difficult for students to keep the discussion focused on the item at hand. Chat puts slow typists at a disadvantage.

World Wide Web.[5] Requires Web browser such as Netscape Navigator or Microsoft Explorer. *Advantages:* Many students appreciate the ability to use the Web to access syllabi, readings, or assignments, or do research via the Internet. The Web supports multimedia better than older Internet technologies. Student projects or assignments can be made accessible to others. It is possible to restrict access to a class site or portions of the site to a campus or even make it password protected. At the other extreme, class assignments can be accessible to anyone anywhere in the world with Web access. Some faculty are recruiting professionals outside of an institution to review student's work posted on class Web pages as a way to improve student writing or argumentation. *Disadvantages:* Web conferencing feature is not built-in and must be programmed for each class or use a commercial product to provide this functionality. In spite of the existence of WYSIWYG Web editors, creating homepages does require training, especially if graphics or other multimedia are imbedded. The wide range of enhancements to Web browsers (such as helper applications, plug-ins, Javascript and Java capability) can hamper students without these ad-ons or the capability to install them. Use of Web browsers from home or off-campus (except for the few non-graphical browsers such as Lynx) require SLIP, PPP or other software to make the computer, modem, and phoneline act like a TCP/IP connection over a network such as Ethernet.

All of the technologies discussed so far are part of the TCP/IP application suite and thus are usually "free" on campus to faculty and students. There exist commercial conferencing products that offer functions or ease of use not otherwise available in the free products. Two examples in use on college campuses are FirstClass and Lotus Notes.[6] (We are ignoring commercial email programs, such as Microsoft Mail, which add ease of use but not significant differences in functionality.)

FirstClass is a product of SoftArc of Canada. It is a multiplatform communications system that integrates email with workgroup communication services, and support for Internet standards. FirstClass offers the exact same ease of use, functionality and performance over network or remote connections. It integrates electronic mail, workgroup conferencing for electronic discussions, file sharing and collaboration, access to institutional databases, and file transfer and directory protocols. *Advantages:* FirstClass sports a graphical, user-friendly interface which looks the same on Macs and Windows. It is comparatively easy to attach or transfer files, such as MS Word documents, making it easy to distribute course material, such as Syllabi or reading lists. FirstClass can display some types of images. Messages can contain different fonts, font sizes, styles, and colors. Files can be archived until the semester is over. FirstClass supports a chat function allowing students to hold online discussions in real time, either during class or outside it. *Disadvantages:* Because FirstClass is commercial, institutions must purchase server software and licenses (the client software is free), and install the clients on individual machines throughout the system. FirstClass is not automatically integrated with the Internet, meaning yet a second place to read email.

Lotus, the leader in networked groupware, has developed Lotus LearningSpace to address the need for Learning Team Centered education that is facilitated by a content expert and delivered anytime, anywhere. It integrates the collaborative, workgroup technologies of Lotus Notes and the World Wide Web. Lotus Notes is a "groupware" tool that permits students to interact asynchronously via a technique known as "replication," which permits users to get on a network, send comments and messages, and simultaneously receive comments and messages that were sent since the last time they logged onto the network. Drexel currently uses Notes within Engineering classes, as well as for independent study opportunities. Outside the classroom, students on co-op gain flexibility in meeting course prerequisites by being able to sign up for Notes-based distance learning courses. Drexel is currently using Notes to roll out an entirely on-line, Internet-based curriculum degree program, which will enable students to earn Drexel degrees from anywhere in the world by using Notes generated Internet courses.[7]

Online Services, such as American Online and CompuServe, represent another use of commercial services to deliver distributed information. For example, The Center for Media and Independent Learning (CMIL), a statewide division of University of California Extension, offers 25 courses online via America Online, and, in collaboration with UC Berkeley Extension and with help from the Alfred P. Sloan Foundation, plans to put 175 courses online over the next three years. UC Berkeley has planned cooperative events and online events with AOL, including contests, surveys, chats and exhibits. *Advantages:* Online services offer ease of use that may allay participants' fears about technology as many students and faculty may already be users of the service. Clients are usually available for all major computer platforms. These services are available internationally thus being more "any place" than any other technology discussed. In addition to the core services, there is some gatewayed access to the Internet. Institutions do not have to authenticate login ids and passwords making online services an attractive vehicle for non-credit or extension courses. *Disadvantages:* As AOL has demonstrated, major online services can be so popular that participants may have difficulty getting into the system. Access to some Internet resources required for class may be restricted. (For example, AOL does not support tn3270 connections required to access many NOTIS online public access catalogs.) Online services were not designed for academic use and may not have all of the customization features desired. Access in remote areas may involve toll calls to nearest large city.

Now that we have looked at the main forms of electronic communications, what happens if we attempt to categorize some library services into synchronous and asynchronous? An example of "synchronous" could include an instructor being able to request delivery during class–regardless of location or time–of collection materials. The need for the materials may have developed serendipitously or could have been anticipated in advance. The most obvious example of "in-advance" is audio-video delivery systems over coax cable or other video distribution networks. Most institutions still rely on human staff to load and unload media into playback units, but advances in storage technology and developments in related areas, such as delivery of video to hotels by companies such as SpectraVision, may eventually automate these functions.[8]

"Just in time" delivery during class has different requirements. This requires access to catalogs of information resources and real-time delivery of materials, which, realistically, means materials already in digital format. Many instructors are incorporating materials on Web sites, local and non-local, that can be accessed during class, and are then available for study by students after class.[9] By making any part of its collections available in digital form, libraries are supporting the possibility of "just in time" delivery to the class. Numerous libraries are experimenting or providing reserve materials online or linking to faculty sites serving these materials. For example, San Diego State University operates the Electronic Reserve Book Room which uses the latest in image scanning technology to provide electronic document delivery. "The E-RBR allows multiple access of documents put on Reserve for course use. This service is particularly helpful for large classes, when the Reserve Book Room copy of a document may be frequently checked out. The E-RBR contains selected sample exams, homework solutions, and readings submitted by the faculty. No books are on the system."[10]

The University of Buffalo Libraries maintains a "Course Materials for Distance Learning" page. Their system provides links to "course related materials including homework, handouts, course notes, etc., for classes offered through distance learning programs at UB. In addition, these Web pages provide access to electronic library resources and services, including database access, electronic journals, electronic reference and interlibrary loan."[11] These resources range from the UB Libraries Catalog to the Encyclopedia Britannica and OVID Biomedical Databases. This approach suggests that a wide variety of existing online library services, such as CD-ROM networks and fulltext databanks, might prove useful resources to instructors using electronic conferencing. Obviously, any of these materials would also be available at other times, thus supporting asynchronous teaching and learning.

What about specific electronic conferencing technologies? The ubiquity of email makes it a viable means for students and faculty to communicate with librarians and vice-versa. In the SPEC Kit on distance education mentioned above, 36 of the responding libraries used email to provide reference services to distance education students. Some libraries are accepting suggestions for acquisitions electronically, usually through their online catalogs, and alerting the requester when the materials are available. Online catalogs increasingly are able to send lists of hits from searches via email.

The main use of electronic mailing lists has been for librarians to exchange information among themselves. But another possibility would be for libraries to establish "listservs" to distribute lists of new acquisitions by subject field or to disseminate information to faculty on issues such as serial costs. The same suggestions for mailing lists could be applied to Usenet groups with the added advantage that subscribers would have easy access to past lists as long as these were still archived. (Usenet messages, called articles, are usually purged automatically by the system after a certain amount of time to provide space for incoming articles.)

The principal use of the Web today by libraries is to disseminate information. Some libraries are using the Web to communicate collection-related issues. For example, Morris Library of Southern Illinois University at Carbondale has included collections-related announcements on their Web pages, such as "Proposed Journal Cuts."[12] The Scripps Institute of Oceanography at the University of California at San Diego has an extensive page of journal price increases, including sections on "What are the most expensive journals" and other tables.[13] Michigan State University has its annual report online which includes sections on collections and collection management.[14] Dartmouth College has monthly acquisitions lists online broken down by subject.[15] A great starting place for more examples and ideas is Barbara Stewarts' *Top 200 Technical Services Benefits of Homepage Development* (http://tpot.ucsd. edu/Cataloging/Misc/top200.html).

Few libraries are using commercial products such as Lotus Notes and FirstClass outside of their own internal Intranets. An exception is Babson College which has used Notes extensively in top level collegiate reengineering efforts. Current plans involve making Notes universal across campus. Existing Notes applications involve classroom integration projects, such as student based international collaborations, MBA IS classes, and class section coordination projects. Library projects involve the reference desk, LEXIS/NEXIS, and financial data apps.[16]

As electronic communication becomes familiar to faculty and students in the classroom, they become viable vehicles for academic libraries to use in reaching patrons. Libraries also need to stay abreast of distributed education on their campus and work to support these courses through offering both synchronous and asynchronous resources and services.

NOTES

1. Definitions for these teaching approaches are fluid. A recent Association of Research Libraries *SPEC Kit* (Role of Libraries in Distance Education, SPEC Kit 216, July 1996, Association of Research Libraries, p. 4) defines distance education "as the delivery of education where the student and the instructor are

geographically separated. Distance Learning is defined as the use of interactive video which allows students and faculty in two or more locations to communicate with each other." This latter definition might properly be expanded to include two way audio only, one way video and two way audio, and mixtures of electronic communication concurrent with audio and video, either using telephone or Internet technologies. The Institute for Academic Technology at the University of North Carolina defines distributed learning as integrating "the interactive capabilities of networking, computing and multimedia with learner-centered teaching approaches such as collaboration, discovery learning and active learning." (http://www.iatunc/dle/dle.html). The Lotus Education Web site defines distributed learning as "a type of distance learning that we define as technology-enabled, learning-team focused education, facilitated by a content expert, and delivered anytime and anywhere (HTTP://WWW.LOTUS.COM/laec/2442.htm).

2. Asynchronous Learning Networks: Alfred P. Sloan Foundation's Program in Learning Outside the Classroom (http://w3.scale.uiuc.edu/education/ALN.new.html).

3. William Beauchamp communication to author, November 1996.

4. F. Henri ("Distance education and computer-assisted communication," in Prospects 18(1): 85-90).

5. An excellent starting point for Web-based conferencing is a site maintained by David R. Woolley (http://www.iat.unc.edu/guides/irg-36.html).

6. A good list of electronic conferencing products and some other useful links has been compiled by Carolyn Kotlas (http://www.iat.unc.edu/guides/irg-36.html).

7. "Asynchronous Learning Networks: Drexel's Experience," *Dr. Stephen J. Andriole, Richard H. Lytle and Charlton A. Monsanto, T.H.E.* Journal, October 1995 (http://thejournal.com/past/oct/510andriole.html).

8. For some additional examples of companies and an introduction to the technology, see http://www.iat.unc.edu/publications/technotes/teknote2.txt

9. An excellent site for seeing how faculty are using the Web in teaching is the World Lecture Hall (http://www.utexas.edu:80/world/lecture/).

10. http://libweb.sdsu.edu/blr/bokmks/rbr.html

11. http://ublib.buffalo.edu/libraries/course/course.html

12. http://www.lib.siu.edu/

13. http://scilib.ucsd.edu/sio/guide/five-yr.html

14. http://www.lib.msu.edu/about/

15. http://www.dartmouth.edu/acad-support/library/NewBookPage.html

16. For a list of schools with innovative uses of Lotus Notes see HTTP://WWW.LOTUS.COM/school/212e.htm

Chapter Six:
The Politics of the Virtual Collection

James J. Kopp

The notion of the virtual collection, the virtual library, and other flavors of "virtuality" that have become standard fare in the library literature at times tend to give the impression that these wall-less or boundary-less entities are achieved through some technological wizardry out of thin air. There is a certain type of Oz-ness about the concept, but those who stand behind the curtain know that there is much more involved in achieving these bibliographic horses of a different color. There are plenty of lions, tigers, and bears (not to mention flying monkeys) that must be avoided, overcome, or tamed to achieve this objective.

The nature of most of these obstacles is well known to librarians. They are terms that generally are qualified by the word "limited," such as in limited budgets, limited staff, limited time, and so on. Yet even when the opportunity arises to move beyond these limitations, an even more ominous force comes into play. One of the largest obstacles on the road to "virtuality" (yellow brick or otherwise) centers on the political struggles that must be undertaken to move into this realm. As implied in the pseudo-definition of virtual

James J. Kopp, PhD, is currently serving as Interim Executive Director of PORTALS, the Portland Area Library System, a consortium of 16 libraries in the greater Portland, Oregon area. He is on leave from the University of Portland where he has served as Library Director since 1994.

[Haworth co-indexing entry note]: "Chapter Six: The Politics of the Virtual Collection." Kopp, James J. Co-published simultaneously in *Collection Management* (The Haworth Press, Inc.) Vol. 22, No. 1/2, 1997, pp. 81-100; and: *Collection Development: Access in the Virtual Library* (ed: Maureen Pastine) The Haworth Press, Inc., 1997, pp. 81-100. Single or multiple copies of this article are available for a fee from The Haworth Document Delivery Service [1-800-342-9678, 9:00 a.m. - 5:00 p.m. (EST). E-mail address: getinfo@haworth.com].

collections or virtual library above (and a less "pseudo" definition appears below), these concepts suggest a transgression of virtual "boundaries" and virtual "walls." Anytime you are dealing with boundaries or walls, virtual or real, politics is going to be involved. In fact, the politics of establishing the virtual collection is perhaps one of the most difficult tasks confronting libraries in this day, and, most likely, in days to come. For creating the virtual collection compounds the already multi-layered political environment of libraryland.

LIBRARYLAND POLITICS

To say that libraries and librarianship are enmeshed in politics is perhaps to state the obvious. Nearly two decades ago Richard DeGennaro, in writing about the political environment in which libraries operate, noted that "nearly all the really important decisions that are made at the highest level have an overriding political component."[1] But it is not only those "really important decisions that are made at the highest level" that are political in nature. More and more, it seems, just about any decision in libraries appears to take on a political dimension, from broad-based political aspects of censorship and universal service to every day back room decisions such as relocating a cubicle or an OCLC workstation or even whether to brew regular or decaffeinated coffee. (The currently popular comic strip "Dilbert" even focuses on the political ramifications of the size and locations of boxes in an organizational chart.)

Thus we can start with the premise that libraries are steeped in politics. Even the librarian is by nature (at least according to some) a political creature. Frederick and Joann Frankena have posited that librarians as "experts" are essentially by definition political entities. They note that "Expertise has come to serve as a political resource, a tool" and librarians as "experts" in their roles as information professionals wield certain power and influence because of that. As the Frankenas state:

Technical expertise is a crucial political resource in controversies because access to knowledge and the resulting ability to question the data and information used to legitimate decision is an essential base for power and influence.²

So not only are libraries immersed in a political environment but librarians themselves are by nature political animals.

The literature is rife with examination of the role of politics in libraries, from "lessons we can learn from politics" to the "politics of the library of the future."³ We can learn of the politics of building a library to the politics of preservation.⁴ There are numerous places to read about the politics of budgeting, funding, and allocations.⁵ And even such aspects of librarianship as reference reorganization as well as broader topics like the curriculum in American higher education have been examined through the lens of politics.⁶

Just about any element of librarianship seems ripe for examination of its political implications. And the virtual collection is no exception. In fact, an examination of the politics of the virtual collection would encompass most, if not all, of these other areas. Such an examination would fill a virtual volume and the intent here is not to cover all the elements of the politics of the virtual collection. Rather two specific areas that serve as the basis for the development of the virtual collection will be explored here: technology, the vehicle by which these collections are made "virtual," and collection development, or more specifically, cooperative collection development, which shapes, molds, and frames the virtual collection (or should).

DEFINITIONS

It is time to provide some boundaries or walls around the boundary-less and wall-less concept that is being explored here. The term "virtual collection" is being used in this paper rather than the more commonly used "virtual library" because the former term is more "precise," if you will, in describing the nature of most efforts being undertaken to establish a virtual presence in cyberspace. "Library" has so many different connotations and represents so many different things that to discuss its "virtualness" is a much larger task and well beyond the intent of this paper.

The virtual collection, as being used in this paper, consists of two basic elements, one technological, the other "intellectual." The technological component refers to the existence of a cooperative or shared online system that reflects the holdings of two or more institutions in a "common" database or through a "common" service that allows users at any of the participating institutions (or others, for that matter) to view the shared holdings of the participating institution. Such a definition might apply to a multitude of online systems from OCLC to a shared local system. Thus we must introduce the second element of the definition of a virtual collection, the intellectual component. This component centers on the notion that there has been some cooperative or collaborative effort among institutions to bring together information on their respective collections in a manner that will provide enhanced service to their respective users, may provide for some efficiencies in resource sharing, and potentially can serve as the catalyst for establishment of some cooperative collection development initiatives among the participating institutions (in either a direct or formal manner, or in some indirect or informal manner). By adding this component to the definition of virtual collection a more specific type of entity is being presented. The essential elements of a technological shared bibliographic database, such as OCLC, would not thus be included in this definition of a virtual collection. Nor would the broader concept of "virtuality" that is represented by broadcast type searching capable through systems with Z39.50 capabilities, unless those systems that were being queried by such methods had participated in the second level of this definition, an intellectual decision to develop this collection. As parenthetically noted above, the collaborative or cooperative agenda to build this "collection" together does not necessarily have to be with the direct intent of the participating institutions getting into a formal cooperative collection development plan. The informal or indirect nature of building this virtual collection may stem from the basic fact that "like" institutions with similar programs have come together through some technological plan to establish this database. It is only after the fact that participating institutions may decide to use the shared database to assist them in their own collection development activities or possibly even to the cooperative or consortial level.

Thus the virtual collection used as the basis for discussion in this paper is based on two elements:

- a technologically based structure of a shared online system
- an intellectually based decision to bring collections together in such a system.

This definition is limiting and it is intended to be so for the sake of the discussion below. Many of the points related to politics presented here could be relevant in various other scenarios. Some, however, are most noticeable when the above criteria are in place.

What then of "politics"? The reader probably has already constructed some working definitions of what politics means in the context of this paper and essentially those are all accurate. For "politics" can and does work on several levels, from the organized political undertakings of government, be it at the national, state, or local level, to the institutional politics associated with one's organization (e.g., a campus), to very specific politics of one's own immediate workplace (e.g., office politics or, as defined in one dictionary, "factional scheming for power and status within a group").[7] As will be discussed below, all these levels (and others) can come into play in dealing with the politics of the virtual collection.

TECHNOLOGY AND POLITICS

One would think that technology would be the great leveler (maybe in some Orwellian fashion) and because of this, politics would not be encountered in dealing with the technological aspects of the virtual collection. Think again. As just about any perusal of the archive of any listserv on the Internet dealing with a technologically related issue will demonstrate, technology and politics go hand-in-hand. In fact, technology itself (i.e., the use of the Internet as a broadband broadside) can be viewed as keeping the human element away from the political-less world depicted by Orwell and other dystopians. But it is not the role of technology as the tool of politics that is the focus here. Instead it is the politics within the discussion of technology that is significant in the discussion of the virtual collection.

These politics work again on various levels. They can be as base in technological terms as the issue of what operating system or hardware platform is preferred. In the past twenty years or so, this has led to significant political chasm as those centered on the main-frame faction versus the distributed computing faction, from the MVS users to the VMS users, from the PC aficionados to the Mac antagonists, and so on. Toss in some software debates and sprinkle with issues of security, access, and costs, and there is a political concoction for just about every taste bud. There are those who will say that these are technological issues alone, but each of these issues has some type of boundaries around them and when those boundaries are crossed, this raises the level of discussion to a political level.

Within the library landscape there are numerous ways in which the politics of technology come into play. Consider, for example, when technology was largely the domain of the technical services staff and the politics surrounding this situation. Once online catalogs, CD-ROMs, and other means of technology were not only introduced in the public areas but became the norm, the political pendulum swung in the opposite direction. When the issue of a virtual collection is added to the equation, the issues become more complex, interrelated, and, quite often, inflammatory. Included among the various ways in which technology and politics have come together in libraries over the years and that play a role in the development of the virtual collection are:

- vendor systems
- building vs. buying
- control of system.

Each of these topics will be explored briefly below, but these are only the proverbial tip of the iceberg and there are many subplots and variances to each issue. The intent here is to provide a flavor of the nature of the technological politics at the core of the virtual collection.

Vendor Politics

The emotions, energies, and exultations (or, in other cases, expletives) that are evident in libraries regarding vendors of integrated library systems characterize the political setting of these technological solutions. Although such systems presumably are selected on the basis of functionality, technological integrity, and budgetary considerations, once a system has been selected, installed, and implemented, the environment quickly shifts to one of a political nature. Boundaries have been drawn and the attitude of "My system can beat your system" comes to the forefront. Librarians become politicized in their allegiance to their vendor systems. The widespread development of national and international user groups for such systems takes on a national political party flavor and, speaking of parties, the vendor galas are not unlike the political gatherings of Democrats or Republicans around a favorite watering hole. The idea of switching vendors, even if there are functional, technical, and fiscal justifications for this, often times can be as traumatic as the notion of switching political allegiances within an administration.

In the virtual collection arena, the politics of vendors systems can quickly become a major obstacle in achieving an environment in which institutions can work together without the fear of a vendor takeover or an acceptance of a mutual understanding among the players from diverse vendor backgrounds. Even if there is a love-hate relationship between one institution and the vendor of their online system, the thought of encroachment by an outside entity (i.e., another institution with a disparate vendor system) leads to throwing down the political gauntlet. In most cases, the issues become less technical and more political (a situation in which vendors generally try to stand clear).

Build versus Buy

This issue, which was predominant in the 1980s, has become less evident in recent years but there are still strong feelings regarding this issue that fuel the political flames within some institutions. Like several issues discussed here, the politics associated with this issue often focus on the intra-institutional environment, particularly that of the relationship of the library and the computer center. In this situation, one entity wants to build a system with internal resources while the other seeks to find an off-the-shelf solution. As with other issues in the political landscape, the focal points are boundaries which further break down into territories, control, and ownership.

On the scale of the virtual collection, these issues translate more to the potential for disagreement and dispute among the collective "agency," be it a consortium, a statewide system, or even a for-profit service. However, the basis for the political confrontations remain the same–territory, control, and ownership. Although the build vs. buy concept has been reduced on the local (i.e., institutional) level, such technological developments as Z39.50 and the World Wide Web have restructured this issue. Potentially with such a protocol as Z39.50 or by use of the Web, the notion of "build" takes on different connotations and, of course, is at the center of the evolving concept of the virtual collection. For potentially anyone can "build" a virtual collection, but, as implied in the definitions set out for this paper, is this truly a virtual collection? The answer to that question, as one might expect, itself is overflowing with political overtones.

Another way in which the build vs. buy issue has been revamped in the late 1990s is that commercial entities, previously not directly in the realm as "competitors" for libraries, have entered this market. Their existence itself sets off some political warning lights but it also leads to the issue of whether libraries will once more buy the services and products of such vendors or seek to develop them on their own. Once more, the issues of territory, control, and ownership come to the fore.

Control of System

As noted above, an issue that comes into play in both the dueling vendors model and the build vs. buy scenario is that of control. Specifically in this situation is the matter of who has the responsibility for the care and feeding of the online system. Institutions have been torn asunder by such issues. Not only do they occur at the institutional level (e.g., library vs. computer center) but they also take place within institutional entities (e.g., between administrative and academic computing in a computing center, or between technical services and a separate systems office in the library). There are again very sound arguments on all sides for technical reasons for control and ownership of the hardware, the maintenance of the software, and various other aspects of the system, but the political implications of such arrangements are the most long lasting and difficult issues to address (and overcome). Many of these issues have been dealt with or side-stepped as changes in technology have taken place. For instance, from a hardware perspective, smaller computers requiring less in terms of power and environmental controls have lessened some of the issues related to larger and more complex machinery of earlier systems. The adoption of client/ server technology by library systems also has changed the landscape. However, even as some of these issues became minimized, other issues tended to fill the void. The introduction of the World Wide Web and its multiplicity of options for an institution has created a new political battlefield at many institutions in terms of who "controls" the looks, feel, and even hardware associated with this powerful resource. To the previous combatants of the library and computer center, new players such as the public relations office, the alumni office, and even the athletics department enter the struggle for control of the Web.

Switch the focus to the virtual collection lens in which multiple institutions may be involved with a variety of subplots being played out at the local level and the political permutations are mind boggling.

In addition to the technological politics associated with territory, control, and ownership, there are a number of issues that work at a different level to underscore the politics of technology at the institutional level as well as for the virtual collection. Included among these issues are:

- pressure to move toward new technologies
- technological change
- technological uncertainty.

Again, the attempt here is to provide a sampling of the issues involved and each of these will be discussed briefly below. Undoubtedly institutions have come across many other issues that have played a part in the politics of working toward a virtual collection.

Newer Technologies

Most, if not all, institutions have had to address the question of where they want to be on the technological curve. Is it in the institution's best interest to be on the leading edge, or even on the bleeding edge? Is being a follower an adequate role to play? Even if those questions have been asked and answered, the follow-up question too often has been overlooked or underestimated–What is it going to take to maintain our status as a leader, bleeder, or a follower? These questions and the discussions and decisions that come out of them can be some of the most divisive political issues with an organization.

For an academic institution which is seeking to posture itself better in terms of recruiting and retaining students, faculty, and staff, the response and action to these questions can be mission-critical. However, the necessary action and direction easily can present serious confrontations related to priorities (as well as territory, control, and ownership). Libraries generally have found themselves in the middle of such debates for most libraries must deal with some aspects of traditional resources and services but also must be able to respond to the demands of those who are front-runners in the technological marathon.

The multi-layered politics of dealing with the issues of keeping up with technology at the institutional level is only a hint of the complexities of such issues within the virtual collection environment. In such a situation, the variances in technological sophistication, directions, and expectations of the many players can create a political Tower of Babel in which even the very language of the politics may not be understandable by all the players.

Technological Change

Compounding the issues of keeping up with the technology, of course, is the matter that the technology changes. Although this is a foregone conclusion, the manner in which an institution chooses to deal with such changes depends on their position, as noted above, on where they want to be riding on the technological wave. From the virtual collection perspective, this issue is even more real for participants than that of the philosophical decision of where the collective "whole" wishes to be, for once the technology changes there has to be a response in some fashion as to where to go as a virtual "organization," and this in turn impacts each institution locally. Once more, boundaries, territory, ownership, and control are tossed into the question of the virtual collection.

Technological Uncertainty

Perhaps even more threatening to the political stability of an institution or for a virtual collection is the question of the certainty of a particular technological path that is chosen. Although the use of technology is a given as is the fact that it will change, the uncertainty of the viability and duration of any one technology fuels the fires of political discussion and debate from the local level up through various channels of discourse and decision, depending on what type of governance and fiscal structure on which an institution or virtual collection is founded.

This rather sweeping overview of the technological politics associated with the virtual collection has been provided to show that there are many levels of potential political pitfalls that can impede progress toward the virtual collection. As noted earlier, most of the issues really do not deal with technology itself but focus on the "human factor" of dealing with technology. It is the human factor of politics that often makes decisions, plans, and actions for technological achievement of the virtual collection so difficult. But, as complex and taxing as these issues are, it is the politics of the second aspect of the virtual collection that perhaps presents the largest challenge for libraries. That challenge is addressing the politics of cooperative collection development.

COOPERATIVE COLLECTION DEVELOPMENT AND POLITICS

In his examination of "Cooperative Collection Development" in *Collection Management: A New Treatise*, Joseph J. Branin lays it out plain and simple. He states that "Cooperative collection development is at its most basic level a political, not a technical, issue."[8] Anyone who has been involved with any aspect of a cooperative collection development activity, or who has observed it from the sidelines, would come to the same conclusion. As Branin points out, "Regardless of the type of cooperative collection development activity . . . it always involves two or more libraries in the governance of programs that extend beyond local, autonomous boundaries."[9] There is perhaps no better recipe for concocting a political brew (or brouhaha) than involving two or more libraries in the governance of programs that extend beyond local, autonomous boundaries. But there is more in the cooperative collection activity besides the governance issue that makes this a potent ferment for potential political parlaying. In fact, the collection development process itself can be viewed as being steeped in issues of a highly political nature, a situation that necessitates, as Peggy Johnson has noted, that the collection development officer have the "political skills of Disraeli."[10]

Politics of Collection Development

There is a wealth of literature on the politics of the collection development process, from approval plans to weeding. Only a portion of the literature will be examined here, but throughout the discussion in the literature several recurring themes are evident and should not be much of a surprise. These include:

- limited resources
- environmental factors
- "ownership."

As with the politics of technology discussed earlier, each of these areas shares something in common, boundaries. It is defining those boundaries, monitoring those boundaries, and, in the ultimate instance of lighting the political fuse, crossing those boundaries that makes the collection development process so political. A few specific examples of how this is so in various areas of the collection development process will highlight the significance of boundaries and the resulting political impact.

To look at some elements at the "beginning" of the collection development process (although one can argue if there indeed is a "beginning" in the process since it is more circular in nature), consider approval plans. Robert Nardini in examining the "politics and performance" of such plans notes that "Approval plans remain controversial because by nature they are inherently political." They are so, Nardini notes, because "They raise questions about how library decisions are made and who has authority to make them." And then Nardini gets to the heart of the matter:

> Approval plans trespass upon library boundaries: boundaries between teaching faculty and library, between acquisition and collection development, between one subject selector and another, and between library and book vendor.[11]

Just with approval plans alone, Nardini has identified several boundaries that establish the basis for political conflict. And it is important to note that these are not just within the library or the library and its broader institution but also extend beyond the institution to for-profit players in the equation.

At the other "end" of the collection development cycle, Robert Stueart has examined the politics and policies associated with weeding. Stueart notes the importance placed on weeding in the literature but then asks the provocative question "Why then is the process so highly recommended in theory and so rigorously ignored or avoided in practice?" He also provides the answer–"The reasons are many, and include politics, priorities, and other perceived problems associated with the process."[12] The word "weeding" alone is a political hot potato and many institutions have tried to cool that off by adopting alternative words or phrases for the process of "weeding," as Stueart notes, with terms such as retirement, pruning, reverse selection, negative selection, deselection, and relegation. The politics of removing materials from library collections, in fact, may be trickier than the politics of adding materials. In addition to the issues of "ownership" of materials by segments of the user population, there is the larger issue, at least in the case of federal, state, or local agencies of public ownership of those materials. And increasingly, there is also an environmental concern about how and where items are disposed, touching off political powder kegs of a different sort.

Between approval plans and weeding in the collection process (and, one might add, in the collection development "alphabet"), lie many other aspects of collection development that present widespread opportunities for engaging the political process. None, perhaps, is so characteristic in touching so many areas of an institution and thus crossing so many boundaries as the budgetary process, from the requesting of funds to the allocation of those funds.

In examining the "Politics, pressure, and power in the budgetary process," Barbara G. Leonard notes the all-important obvious point that ". . . there are forces outside the library pulling and vying for scarce resources" and that this sets up the complex situation of conflicting political pressures.[13] These complexities stem from the fact that there are internal and external factors involved, and that within both sets of factors there are further complicating situations. Regarding internal factors in an academic environment, Leonard notes

> it is important to differentiate those that are institutional and/or programmatic and those that are individual, i.e., the faculty, the students, and the librarians.
>
> The institutional/programmatic factors include stagnant budgets, curriculum changes, the relative importance of the schools, colleges, departments, or programs within the university's hierarchy, and the changing mission of the university.[14]

Among the individual factors Leonard notes are the conflicts of research needs of individual faculty members, the issue of support of the curriculum versus the promotion and tenure needs of faculty, student pressure for just-in-time information, and even the subject bias of the selector.[15]

Among the external pressures examined by Leonard are publishing output, state and federal budgets and level of support, private funding initiatives and sources, and such items as included earlier in the technological politics discussion–technological change and uncertainty, and pressure to adopt newer technologies.[16]

Anthony W. Ferguson, although coming to the issue from a perspective broader than the budgetary process, arrives at a very similar list of issues that make up the "decision-making environment" of the collection development officer in an academic institution. In the "immediate environment" (i.e., internal), Ferguson includes:

- personnel costs
- needs for research materials
- multiple copy needs

- stressed selectors
- poor environmental conditions
- acidic papers
- faculty demands
- OTP [other than personnel] costs.[17]

In the sphere beyond the library and the university environment (i.e., external factors), Ferguson includes:

- currency fluctuations
- competing paradigms
- stagnant world economy
- benefits crisis
- student needs
- philanthropy laws
- consortial partnerships
- print publishing
- electronic publishing
- for-profit publishers.

Most, if not all, of the factors in Leonard's and Ferguson's examples present opportunities for boundaries, territories, control, and ownership and thus are ripe for political posturing. (Ferguson's "environments" are even graphically represented to identify certain boundaries.) These then are many of the basic elements of collection development politics.

The Matrix of Virtual Collection Politics

When extrapolating the political issues of collection development from the institutional to the cooperative (or virtual) setting of an inter-institutional arrangement, each of the issues identified at the institutional level is still present as an underlying factor. Compounding the situation is the fact that each institution is grappling with these matters within its own environment. The introduction of cooperatively developing a virtual collection raises the political significance of each factor to a new rung on the political ladder. Consider the institutional/programmatic factors identified by Leonard that include curriculum changes, relative importance of the schools, college, and departments. The political aspects of addressing these factors in a multi-institutional environment can be immense.

Although it was stated earlier that Branin lays out the fact that cooperative collection development is a political issue plain and simple, the issue itself is far from plain or simple. To understand the political environment of cooperative collection development (and the virtual collection) requires something in the order of a three-dimensional matrix with the factors related to potentially political issues running along the "y" axis with the impact of these issues upon the local (or institutional) environment on the "x" axis on the top level of the matrix, while the inter-institutional (cooperative or virtual) environment on the "x" axis at another level or plane. Many of the issues are going to be factors at both the local and inter-institutional level but the issues may be more complex the "deeper" one proceeds down the matrix.

Compounding the matter further is another set of issues that arises when another organizational entity comes into play, whether it is a library consortium, an inter-governmental agency, or some other multi-institutional endeavor which has a role in cooperative activities, including cooperative collection development. For such an entity, even if it is the most simplistic in nature, poses many of the same political issues as those discussed above. Not only are there the matters of institutions (and individuals) getting along together and working cooperatively but there is now the relationship of the institutions with the collective institution and a new set of issues of territory, ownership, and control that comes into play. Included among these are such issues as:

- governance
- types of Institutions
- suspicions between agencies.

A brief examination of these topics will suggest even more levels of complexity in the matrix of virtual collection politics.

Governance

As noted above, the relationships of institutions with one another and the relationships of each institution with the collective entity, in whatever form it takes, is a critical issue in the politics of the virtual collection. Centered in the middle of these types of relationships is the issue of governance of the collective "whole." Is the governance tied in with the institutions themselves or is it a separate organization administered by individuals outside any of the participating institutions? The models of organization of such entities cover the spectrum of possibilities but the common element in all is that in whatever shape, form, size, or location the governance "body" exists, it is bound to be a focal point of inter-institutional politics.

Types of Institutions

Efforts to establish a virtual collection among multi-type libraries (e.g., academic, public, special) present additional challenges and a different level of politics that must be addressed. The boundaries of institution type are often shaped differently, have different border crossing laws, and, in many cases, have an increased patrol of border police to monitor those boundaries. The politics associated with these situations also work at a different level and need to be understood better, perhaps, than with "like" institution arrangements.

Suspicions Between Agencies

This last point, perhaps, does not need to be elaborated upon for when there are politics involved, there are going to be suspicions of the intent of each player in the political arena. In a multi-institutional setting, however, the potential for this perhaps increases proportionally to the number of institutions involved. The suspicions are in most cases not ill-natured (although they certainly can be) but they stem from a number of underlying concerns that come into play including competition between institutions (whether it is for enrollment, grant funds, even athletic prominence) and image and prestige issues (for libraries the size and nature of collections might come into play). Then there are the suspicions of one multi-institutional organization toward another. Joel Rutstein identified such a situation in his examination of issues in cooperative collection development.[18] Such suspicions can often be some of the most harmful aspects of the politics of cooperative collection development and of the virtual collection.

CONCLUSION

It is upon this backdrop of politics that the virtual collection must be built. So is the virtual collection too much like Oz, an over-the-rainbow, utopian dream whose realization is unlikely to be fulfilled? Maybe, but there are strong indications that important strides have been made toward this bibliographic vision.

Cooperative activities have been around in libraries for decades and serve as the foundation for many strong and successful organizations and activities. Collection development also has been around for a long time but it only has been raised to a new level of focus in the past two decades, coinciding with the rise in the use of technologies in libraries. Technology itself has evolved significantly in the past ten years providing new levels of opportunity and realization of many dreams earlier thought to be unattainable. It is, as defined earlier in this paper, the combination of technology and the cooperative collection development efforts that sets the stage for the realization of the virtual collection. Libraries continue to be moving steadily toward the concept of the virtual collection and there is no reason to believe that they will not continue on that path.

As the technology and cooperative collection development foundations take shape, it is time to focus on the intangible but critically important aspect of the politics of the virtual collection. As Mara Niels pointed out several years ago in discussing the "Politics of the library of the future":

> We sometimes view politics as a dirty business that is nevertheless necessary in order to accomplish major initiatives like implementing new technology in the library.[19]

Libraries and librarians are at the stage of evolution when they must focus not just on the technical aspects of the work that they undertake, but they should also be seeking to understand better the nature and extent of the political situation and process that surrounds this work, in all its manifestations. As Niels points out, "Working the political process is also essential and is often ignored by libraries."[20]

Seeking to understand the politics of the virtual collection and to learn how to work with the political process at all levels will aid considerably in the realization of the virtual collection. Without that effort and accomplishment, the virtual collection is very likely to remain a utopian vision.

NOTES

1. Richard DeGennaro, "Library Administration and New Management Systems," *Library Journal* 103 (December 1978), 2480.

2. Frederick Frankena and Joann Koellin Frankena, "The politics of expertise and role of the librarian," *Behavioral & Social Sciences Librarian* 6 (1986) 39.

3. Sheila S. Intner, "Lesson we can learn from politics," *Technicalities* 16 (1996), 1; Mara Niels, "Politics of the library of the future," *The Electronic Library* 8 (1990), 408-11.

4. See, for example, Patricia Swanson, "The politics of library buildings: a case study of the John Crerar Library," *IATUL Quarterly* 4 (1990), 115-21, and Karl G. Schmude, "The politics and management of preservation planning," *IFLA Journal*, 16 (1990), 332-5.

5. See, for example, Judith F. Niles, "The politics of budget allocation," *Library Acquisitions* 13 (1989), 51-5; Diane R. O'Brien, "The politics of funding," *New Jersey Libraries* 28 (1995), 3-24; and Donna Packer, "Acquisitions allocations: equity, politics, and formulas," *The Journal of Academic Librarianship* 14 (1988), 276-86.

6. Karyle S. Butcher and Michael P. Kinch, "Who calls the shots? The politics of reference reorganization," *The Journal of Academic Librarianship* 16 (1990), 280-4; Irving J. Spitzberg, Jr., "It's academic: the politics of the curriculum in American higher education," in *Libraries and the search for academic excellence* (Scarecrow, 1988).

7. *Webster's New World Dictionary*, 2nd College edition (New York: World Publishing Co., 1970), s.v. "politics."

8. Joseph J. Branin, "Cooperative Collection Development," in Charles B. Osburn and Ross Atkinson, eds., *Collection Management: A New Treatise*. Foundations in Library and Information Science, Volume 26 (Part A). (Greenwich and London: JAI Press, Inc., 1991), 104.

9. Branin, 104-105.

10. Johnson also adds the successful collection development officer also needs "the financial acumen of Trump, the wisdom of Solomon, Churchill's way with words (written and spoken), and a bit of Houdini's ability to get out of tight spots!" Peggy Johnson, "Collection Development Officers, A Reality Check: A Personal View," *Library Resources & Technical Services* 33 (1989), 153.

11. Robert F. Nardini, "Approval plans: politics and performance," *College & Research Libraries* 54 (1993), 418.

12. Robert D. Stueart, "Weeding of library materials–politics and policies," *Collection Management* 7 (1985), 47.

13. Barbara G. Leonard, "Politics, pressure, and power in the budgetary process," in *Conference on Acquisitions, Budgets, and Collection* (Genaway & Assocs., 1990), p. 243.

14. Leonard, 243.

15. Leonard, 245-46.

16. Leonard, 246.

17. Anthony W. Ferguson, "Collection Development Politics: The Art of the Possible," in Peggy Johnson and Bonnie MacEwan, eds., *Collection Management and Development: Issues in an Electronic Era*. Proceedings of the Advanced Collection Management and Development Institute. Chicago, Illinois, March 26-28, 1993. (Chicago: American Library Association, 1994), p. 31.

18. Joel Rutstein, "National and Local Resource Sharing: Issues in Cooperative Collection Development," *Collection Management* 7 (Summer 1985), p. 13-14.

19. Mara Niels, "Politics of the library of the future," *The Electronic Library* 8 (Dec. 1990), p. 408.

20. Niels, p. 408.

Chapter Seven:
Library Acquisitions 1986-1995:
A Select Bibliography

Jim Vickery

Dr. Jim Vickery is Head of Acquisitions, The British Library, Boston Spa, Wetherby, L S23 7BQ England.

[Haworth co-indexing entry note]: "Chapter Seven: Library Acquisitions 1986-1995: A Select Bibliography." Vickery, Jim. Co-published simultaneously in *Collection Management* (The Haworth Press, Inc.) Vol. 22, No. 1/2, 1997, pp. 101-186; and: *Collection Development: Access in the Virtual Library* (ed: Maureen Pastine) The Haworth Press, Inc., 1997, pp. 101-186. Single or multiple copies of this article are available for a fee from The Haworth Document Delivery Service [1-800-342-9678, 9:00 a.m. - 5:00 p.m. (EST). E-mail address: getinfo@haworth.com].

INTRODUCTION

This work was compiled as part of the programme to celebrate the first decade of the National Acquisitions Group, which was founded in 1986.

The bibliography comprises the entries from all the Acquisitions Updates which appeared in *NAG Newsletter* and *Taking Stock*, covering material published in the years 1986-1995. It has not been supplemented with publications from other sources, except that articles and books which appeared under NAG's own imprint are included. Works on serials, retail bookselling and general trade publishing are excluded, as are annuals, directories and market surveys. All the publications are in English.

I hope that this subject listing will serve as a useful source of material for readers interested in library acquisitions, library collections and the book trade.

Jim Vickery
The British Library
May 1996

ACQUISITIONS

Acquisitions–General

1. Buying good pennyworths: a review of the literature of acquisitions in the eighties, by K.A. Schmidt. *Library Resources and Technical Services 30* (4) October/December 1986 333-340.
2. *Library acquisitions: constraints and opportunities. Proceedings of the inaugural conference of the National Acquisitions Group, Oxford, April 1986*, edited by G.A. Gilbert. Loughborough, National Acquisitions Group, 1986. ISBN 1870269004
3. *Selecting and ordering British books and journals: a guide.* London, British Council, 1987.
4. A select bibliography of library acquisitions, by J.T. Deffenbaugh and H.H. Yelich. *RTSD Newsletter 13* (4) 1988 33-36.
5. The acquisitions librarian as informed consumer, by T.W. Leonhardt. *Library Acquisitions Practice and Theory 12* (2) 1988 149-154.
6. *The eternal triangle? Proceedings of the second annual conference of the National Acquisitions Group, York, September 1987*, edited by Vivienne Menkes. Loughborough, National Acquisitions Group, 1988. ISBN 1870269020

7. Librarians and booksellers: working together in the Year of the Young Reader, by E.A. Hass. *School Library Journal 35* (5) January 1989 24-27.

8. *Acquisitions management and collection development in libraries*, by Rose Mary Magrill and John Corbin; 2nd. ed. Chicago, American Library Association, 1989. ISBN 0838905137.

9. Acquisitions and collection development in Italy, by P. Biancofiore and L. Vespucci. *Library Acquisitions Practice and Theory 13* (3) 1989 303-313.

10. *Statistics for managing library acquisitions*, by Eileen D. Hardy. Chicago, American Library Association, 1989. ISBN 0838933742 (Acquisitions guidelines, 6)

11. On the nature of acquisitions, by J. A. Hewitt. *Library Resources and Technical Services 33* (2) April 1989 105-122.

12. The business of acquisitions, by P. Johnson. *Technicalities 9* (6) June 1989 5-7.

13. Education for acquisitions: a history, by K.A. Schmidt. *Library Resources and Technical Services 34* (2) April 1990 159-169.

14. Acquisitions, budgets and collections: Acquisitions '90. [Conference report by B. Alley]. *Technicalities 10* (6) June 1990 10-11.

15. The year's work in acquisitions and collection development, 1988, by W. Schenk. *Library Resources and Technical Services 34* (3) July 1990 326-337.

16. What do librarians do? They buy books, by H. S. White. *Library Journal 115* (5) 15 September 1990 57-58.

17. *Acquisitions 90: conference on acquisitions, budgets and collections, St. Louis, Missouri, May 1990.* Proceedings, edited by David C. Genaway. Canfield, Ohio, Genaway & Associates Inc, 1990. ISBN 943970067.

18. *Understanding the business of library acquisitions*, edited by Karen A. Schmidt. Chicago, American Library Association, 1990. ISBN 0838905366.

19. *Charleston Conference 1990* [papers on various acquisitions topics]. New York, Pergamon, 1991 (*Library Acquisitions Practice and Theory 15* (3) 1991 257-421).

20. The education of the acquisitions librarian: a survey of ARL acquisitions librarians, by K.A. Schmidt. *Library Resources and Technical Services 35* (1) January 1991 7-22.
21. *Dealing with the unexpected–policy and procedures involved in document acquisition at the Institute of Development Studies,* by J.A. Downey. Brighton, University of Sussex Institute of Development Studies Resource Unit, 1991 (Documentation and Library Advisory Report, 16).
22. *Acquisitions 91: Conference on acquisitions, budgets and collections, Minneapolis, April 1991.* Proceedings, edited by David C. Genaway. Canfield, Ohio, David C. Genaway & Associates. 1991. ISBN 0943970075.
23. Education for acquisitions: an informal survey, by W. Fisher. *Library Acquisitions Practice and Theory 15* (1) 1991 29-31.
24. Please sir, I want some more: a review of the literature of acquisitions, 1990, by K.A. Schmidt. *Library Resources and Technical Services 35* (3) July 1991 245-254.
25. Divided by a common language, united by common problems: buying foreign books for UK academic libraries, by L. Chapman. *Library Acquisitions Practice and Theory 15* (4) 1991 447-452.
26. Acquisitions in the library school curriculum, by D.B. Marcum. *Library Acquisitions Practice and Theory 15* (4) 1991 471-473.
27. Why we need acquisitions in the library science curriculum, by J.L. Ogburn. *Library Acquisitions Practice and Theory 15* (4) 1991 475-479.
28. The acquisitions librarian as change agent in the transition to the electronic library, by R. Atkinson. *Library Resources and Technical Services 36* (1) January 1992 7-20.
29. *Australian studies: acquisition and collection development for libraries,* edited by G.E. Gorman. Mansell, 1992. ISBN 0720121345.
30. The professional education of acquisitions librarians: a survey, by Jim Vickery. *Taking Stock 1* (1) May 1992 33-53.
31. Supply from Europe: East and West Germany, by Knut Dorn. *Taking Stock 1* (2) November 1992 11-16.

32. Supply from Europe: Italy, by Mario Casalini. *Taking Stock 1* (2) November 1992 21-24.
33. Supply from Europe: The Netherlands, by A. Houtschild. *Taking Stock 1* (2) November 1992 25-28.
34. Supply from Europe: The Commonwealth of Independent States, by Gregory Walker. *Taking Stock 1* (2) November 1992 29-31.
35. Acquisitions personnel management: a librarian's perspective, by R. Brumley. *Library Acquisitions Practice and Theory 16* (2) 1992 119-126.
36. *Popular culture and acquisitions*, edited by Allen Ellis. New York, The Haworth Press, Inc., 1992. ISBN 156024299X (*The Acquisitions Librarian*, no. 8).
37. *Managing acquisitions and vendor relations*, by Heather S. Miller. New York, Neal-Schuman, 1992. ISBN 1555701116 (How-to-do-it manual for librarians, 23).
38. A closer world: a review of acquisitions literature, 1992, by Lisa German. *Library Resources and Technical Services 37* (3) July 1993 255-260.
39. Acquisitions from Yugoslavia's successor states, by Michael Biggins. *Library Resources and Technical Services 38* (1) January 1994 47-55.
40. Western European political science: an acquisitions study, by Barbara Walden, Charles Fineman, William S. Monroe and Mary Jane Parrine. *College and Research Libraries 55* (4) July 1994 286-296.
41. Building and managing an acquisitions program, by Carol Pitts Hawks. *Library Acquisitions Practice & Theory 18* (3) Fall 1994 297-308.
42. Acquisitions–long distance, by Murray S. Martin. *Collection Management 20* (1/2) 1995 3-13.
43. The vision thing: developing a vision for acquisitions, by Karen A. Schmidt. *Library Acquisitions Practice and Theory 19* (1) Spring 1995 5-7.
44. E-mail discussion lists: an acquisitions perspective, by Catherine Nicholson. *Taking Stock 4* (1) May 1995 33-34.

45. Acquisitions management information: do administrators really care?, by Cynthia Gozzi. *Library Administration and Management 9* (2) Spring 1995 85-87.
46. Closing the loop: how did we get here and where are we going? [on the future of acquisitions], by Marion T. Reid. *Library Resources and Technical Services 39* (3) July 1995 267-273.
47. The value-added acquisitions librarian: defining our role in a time of change, by Alex Bloss. *Library Acquisitions Practice and Theory 19* (3) Fall 1995 321-330.

Procurement Methods
(See also 176, 796)

48. Selling direct to the consumer, by D. Tuller. *Publishers Weekly 31* October 1986 39-40.
49. The dangers of discounting, by J. Davis. *Book Research Quarterly 3* (2) Summer 1987 79-80.
50. The case for direct purchasing, by I.A. Phillips. *Public Library Journal 2* (6) December 1987 103-104.
51. Third party buying vs buying direct, by A. Melkin. *Library Acquisitions Practice and Theory 12* (2) 1988 225-228.
52. *Public tendering: books and other library materials–model documents.* Hertfordshire Library Service, 1988. ISBN 0901354465.
53. Public interest versus private profit, by M. Turner. *Bookseller* (4346) 7 April 1989 1241-1248.
54. *Public library procurement specifications and contract arrangements,* by Capital Planning Information Ltd. British Library, Boston Spa, 1989. ISBN 0712332014 (British National Bibliography Research Fund report, 42).
55. *Buying books: a how-to-do-it manual for librarians,* by Audrey Eaglen. New York, Neal-Schuman, 1989. ISBN 1555700136.
56. Buying direct: the vendor perspective, by K. Farrell. *Library Acquisitions Practice and Theory 14* (3) 1990 285-287.
57. Bidness as usual: the responsible procurement of library materials, by S.D. Clark and S.A. Winters. *Library Acquisitions Practice and Theory 14* (3) 1990 265-274.

58. How not to buy books for libraries: contracts, bids and recent developments in New York State, by H. S. Miller. *Library Acquisitions Practice and Theory 14* (3) 1990 275-281.

59. *Managing the purchasing process: a how-to-do-it manual*, by Arnold Hirshon and Barbara A. Winters. New York, Neal-Schuman, 1991. ISBN 1555700810.

60. African acquisitions: strategies to locate and acquire current and retrospective Africana, by P. Malanchuk. *Library Acquisitions Practice and Theory 15* (4) 1991 453-462.

61. Collection development through exchanges: the experience of the Third World, by J. Otike. *New Library World 93* (1100) 1992 14-18.

62. *Tendering for bibliographic services in a competitive market; report to Norfolk Library and Information Service*, by Capital Planning Information Ltd. Stamford, Capital Planning Information, 1993. ISBN 0906011892.

63. The role of the international exchange of publications in the National Library in Prague: yesterday and tomorrow, by Vojtech Balik and Adolf Knoll. *Resource Sharing and Information Networks 8* (2) 1993 57-64.

64. Direct schools supply: how booksellers can hit back, by Jayne de Courcy. *Bookseller* (4564) 11 June 1993 18-27.

65. Contract acquisitions: change, technology and the new technologies in acquisitions, by Gary M. Shirk. *Library Acquisitions Practice and Theory 17* (2) Summer 1993 145-53.

66. Information access with the former East Germany: book procurement and other information access issues before and after reunification, by Thomas Kilton. *Library Resources and Technical Services 37* (4) October 1993 415-422.

67. Don't get anxious, get active! Bromley's approach to competitive tendering, by Ruth Alston. *New Library World 94* (1108) 1993 4-11.

68. Contracting out, by Ann Lawes. *New Library World 95* (1114) 1994 8-12.

69. Outsourcing: what does it mean for technical services? by Sheila S. Intner. *Technicalities 14* (3) March 1994 3-5.

70. Outsourced library technical services: the bookseller's perspective, by Gary M. Shirk. *Library Acquisitions Practice and Theory 18* (4) Winter 1994 383-395.

71. Toward a new world order: a survey of outsourcing capabilities of vendors for acquisitions, cataloguing and collection development services, by Carmel C. Bush, Margo Sasse and Patricia Smith. *Library Acquisitions Practice and Theory 18* (4) Winter 1994 397-416.

72. The tendering process: a supplier's view, by M.T. Taylor. *Taking Stock 3* (2) November 1994 1-5.

73. Compulsory competitive tendering: a worthwhile experience, by Catherine Machin. *Taking Stock 3* (2) November 1994 15-17.

74. Win, lose or draw? The pros and cons of the principal supplier agreement in the light of the NAG Code of Conduct, by Michael Maxwell. *Taking Stock 3* (2) November 1994 7-10.

75. Principal supplier arrangements: the supplier's view, by Peter Jones. *Taking Stock 3* (2) November 1994 11-14.

76. The more things change, the more they stay the same: East-West exchanges, 1960-1993, by Margaret S. Olsen. *Library Resources and Technical Services 39* (1) January 1995 5-21.

77. *Tendering for library supply: a practical guide.* Leeds, National Acquisitions Group, 1995. ISBN 1870269128.

78. The RFP [Request for Proposals] process: rational, educational, necessary or there ain't no such thing as a free lunch, by Frances C. Wilkinson and Connie Capers Thorson. *Library Acquisitions Practice and Theory 19* (2) Summer 1995 251-268.

79. *Library materials acquisition: the tender process*, by Brenda White. Leeds, National Acquisitions Group, 1995. ISBN 1870269152.

80. The tender trap, by Brenda White. *Taking Stock 4* (2) November 1995 4-7.

81. Facilities management: a real opportunity, by Diana Edmonds. *Taking Stock 4* (2) November 1995 13-17.

82. Books for Britain, by Mike Casale. *Library Manager* (12) November 1995 18-19.

Net Book Agreement

83. The Net Book Agreement: a personal view from the trade, by R. Knowles. *Assistant Librarian 80* (8) August 1987 117-118.
84. *Library bookselling under the Net Book Agreement.* London, Booksellers Association Library Booksellers Group, 1987. ISBN 0907972055.
85. The library case for the Net Book Agreement, by R. Pybus. *Bookseller* (4288) 26 February 1988 744-750.
86. With and without rpm [resale price maintenance]: the French experience, by V. Menkes. *Bookseller* (4301) 27 May 1988 2067-2071.
87. Without rpm [resale price maintenance]–the Belgian experience, by M. Mertens. *Bookseller* (4308) 15 July 1988 216-218.
88. The NBA debate–a view from Australia, by M. Zifcak. *Bookseller* (4305) 24 June 1988 2459-2460.
89. The economic implications of the Net Book Agreement, by Frank Fishwick. London, Publishers Association, 1989.
90. The Net Book Agreement and health service libraries, by A. Strange and E. Hochland. *Health Libraries Review 6* (1) 1989 3-19.
91. A short and bloody history of the free market in books, by M. Grindley. *Bookseller* (4296) 22 April 1988 1610-1615.
92. *The Net Book Agreement: to break or not to break, that is the question*, edited by Derek Jones. Library Association, 1989. ISBN 085365669X.
93. Net book pricing, by C.V. Marsh and E. Lockman. *Library Acquisitions Practice and Theory 12* (2) 1988 169-176.
94. Net Book Agreement: the case for abrogation, by T. Maher. *Bookseller* (4339) 17 February 1989 499-502.
95. *Non-net books: some possible consequences*, by F. Fishwick. London, Booksellers Association, 1990.

96. What future without the Net Book Agreement? A library supplier's point of view, by D. Turner. *Public Library Journal 5* (1) January/February 1990 14-15.
97. *The Net Book Agreement: an economic assessment*, by E. Davies and S. Flanders. London Business School, 1991.
98. Abolishing resale price maintenance: lessons from Sweden, by Per I. Gedin. *Logos 4* (2) 1993 84-87.
99. Licence to kill? [on the Library Licence], by Frank Edwards. *Bookseller* (4613) 20 May 1994 22-25.
100. A toothcomb to the NBA, by Frank Fishwick. *Bookseller* (4632) 30 September 1994 26-29.
101. Going, going, gone: the NBA and the Library Licence; a librarian's view, by Ruth Alston. *Taking Stock 3* (2) November 1994 27-30.

Out-of-Print Books

102. Here today, gone tomorrow: the growing out-of-print crisis, by C. Marsh. Library *Acquisitions Practice and Theory 12* (3/4) 1988 439-443.
103. The grass was greener in the good old days: the "crisis" of out-of-print books, by J.P. Seth. *Book Research Quarterly 5* (4) Winter 1989/90 75-78.
104. Organising out-of-print and replacement acquisitions for effectiveness, efficiency and the future, by J.W. Barker, R.A. Rottman and M. Ng. *Library Acquisitions Practice and Theory 14* (2) 1990 137-163.
105. An overview of the out-of-print trade from the book dealer's perspective, by V.L. Gordon. *Library Acquisitions Practice and Theory 15* (1) 1991 53-62.
106. It's out of print? What libraries need to know, by W.W. Williams. *Library Journal 116* (3) February 1991 155-160.
107. Out-of-print but not out of mind, by H. S. Miller. *The Bottom Line 5* (4) Winter 1991-1992 11-17.
108. Comparison of out-of-print searching methods, by Mary Eldredge and William Ludington. *Library Acquisitions Practice and Theory 17* (4) 1993 427-432.
109. Antiquarian books and bookselling, by Ben Weinreb. *Logos 5* (1) 1994 31-36.

110. A study of OP [out of print] and OSI [out of stock indefinitely] cancellations in an academic library, by Min-Huei Lu. *Library Acquisitions Practice and Theory 18* (3) Fall 1994 277-287.
111. The use of CD-ROM to investigate the in-print/out-of-print subject patterns of books, by Thomas E. Nisonger. *Library Resources and Technical Services 39* (2) April 1995 117-132.

Approval Plans

112. Capturing the mainstream: publisher-based and subject-based approval plans in academic libraries, by K.A. Schmidt. *College and Research Libraries 47* (4) July 1986 365-369.
113. Use of approval plans with automated acquisitions, by M. Kreyche et al. *Library Acquisitions Practice and Theory 11* (3) 1987 207-219.
114. Science and technology book reviews as supplements to an approval program, by B. Magnuson. *Science and Technology Libraries 8* (2) Winter 1987/88 75-94.
115. An evaluation of a blanket order plan for French publications, by R. Austin. *Collection Management 10* (4) 1988 137-148.
116. A quantitative methodology for evaluating approval plan performance, by C.E. Pasterczyk. *Collection Management 10* (1/2) 1988 25-38.
117. An approval plan vendors review: the organisation and process, by K. Womack et al. *Library Acquisitions Practice and Theory 12* (3/4) 1988 363-378.
118. British approval plan books: American or British vendor? by A.W. Ferguson. *Collection Building 8* (4) Spring 1988 23-26.
119. Using approval plans and blanket ordering, by I. Sternberg and J. Grantier. *American Studies Library Newsletter* (27) August 1988 2-9.
120. Collection assessment and development using Blackwell North America approval plan referral slips, by B. Childress and N. Gibbs. *Collection Management 11* (1/2) 1989 137-143.
121. Approval plan versus conventional selection: determining the overlap, by P.B. Kaatrude. *Collection Management 11* (1/2) 1989 145-150.

122. Engineering books on approval: a selector's viewpoint, by H. Franklin. *Technicalities 9* (3) March 1989 12-15.

123. Vendor studies redux: evaluating the approval plan option from within, by J.W. Barker. *Library Acquisitions Practice and Theory 13* (2) 1989 133-142.

124. Science and technology approval plans, by G. St. Clair and J. Treadwell. *Library Resources and Technical Services 33* (4) October 1989 382-392.

125. Modeling an academic approval program, by J.C. Calhoun, J.K. Bracken, K.L. Firestein and P.A. Eskoz. *Library Resources and Technical Services 24* (3) July 1990 367-379.

126. Analysis of selection activities to supplement approval plans, by J.L. Loup and M.L. Snoke. *Library Resources and Technical Services 35* (2) April 1991 202-216.

127. Approval plans for religious and theological libraries, by W.J. Hook. *Library Acquisitions Practice and Theory 11* (2) 1991 215-227.

128. Approval plan processing: integrating acquisitions and cataloguing, by Vicki Grahame. *Technical Services Quarterly 10* (1) 1992 31-41.

129. Approval slips and faculty participation in book selection at a small university library, by Amy E. Arnold. *Collection Management 18* (1/2) 1993 89-102.

130. Approval plans: politics and performance, by Robert F. Nardini. *College and Research Libraries 54* (5) September 1993 417-425.

131. United Kingdom approval plans and United States academic libraries: are they necessary and cost-effective? by Mary Eldredge. *Library Acquisitions Practice and Theory 18* (2) Summer 1994 165-178.

132. The approval plan profiling session, by Robert F. Nardini. *Library Acquisitions Practice and Theory 18* (3) Fall 1994 289-295.

133. The origin of the library approval plan, by Richard Abel. *Publishing Research Quarterly 11* (1) Spring 1995 46-56.

134. Sci/tech book approval plans can be effective, by Hugh L. Franklin. *Collection Management 19* (1-2) 1994 135-145.

135. The evolution of approval services, by Martin Warzala. *Library Trends 43* (3) Winter 1994 514-523.

Donations

136. Donations: the unacceptable face of acquisitions, by L. Chapman. *Library Association Record 88* (10) October 1986 503-504.
137. How to look a gift horse in the mouth: saying no to donations, by K.R. Huston. *The Bottom Line 3* (1) 1989 14-17.
138. Options for the disposal of unwanted donations, by E.R. Cooper. *Bulletin-Medical Library Association 78* (4) October 1990 388-394.
139. Killing us with kindness, or what to do with those gifts, by E. Buis. *Collection Building 11* (2) 1991 10-12.
140. Gifts to libraries: coping effectively, by M.J. Bostic. *Collection Management 14* (3/4) 1991 175-184.
141. When to look a gift horse in the mouth, by Peggy Johnson. *Technicalities 13* (6) June 1993 10-13.
142. Grace under pressure: relations with library donors, by Peggy Johnson. *Technicalities 13* (8) August 1993 4-9.
143. Aid for libraries: should one look the proverbial gift horse in the mouth? by Carol Mills. *Australian Academic and Research Libraries 25* (4) December 1994 240-246.
144. Extracting the gold from book surpluses, by Sara Harrity. *Logos 5* (3) 1994 153-157.
145. How to look a gift horse in the mouth, or how to tell people you can't use their old junk in your library, by Benita Strnad. *Collection Building 14* (2) 1995 29-31.

Book Suppliers
(See also 70, 75, 82, 244, 250, 281, 293)

146. Library supply and electronic mail, by W. J. Connolly. *Bookseller* (4211) 5 September 1986 984-985.
147. Alternative bookselling, by C. Tunstill. *Information and Library Manager 7* (5) 1988 110-112.
148. The Nashville connection: a vendor profile [of Ingram Library Services], by B. Alley, F. Philipp and L. Price. *Technicalities 8* (5) May 1988 1-4.

149. Baker and Taylor targets the trade, by J. Mutter. *Publishers Weekly 234* (4) 22 July 1988 34-36.

150. Heffers: a company profile, by J. Richardson. *British Book News* January 1989 8-11.

151. Children's booksellers and teachers: partners in literacy, by S. Wilensley-Lanford. *Publishers Weekly 235* (3) January 20 1989 101-103.

152. Library vendors: how do they use us? by K. Hendrickson. *Library Acquisitions Practice and Theory 13* (2) 1989 121-124.

153. Do vendors cost too much for the service they provide? by F.E. Link. *Library Acquisitions Practice and Theory 13* (2) 1989 125-128.

154. T.C. Farries: friendly and flexible book suppliers, by J. Richardson. *British Book News* November 1989 768-770.

155. Information ferret, by D. Duchin. *Journal of Library Administration 12* (3) 1990 99-107.

156. The bookseller and the community: a British experience, by I. Nonie. *Logos 1* (2) 1990 38-43.

157. Berger and Tims: supplying libraries worldwide, by C.J. Fallows. *European Bookseller 1* (9) January/February 1991 68-70.

158. Which supplier? Book supply agreements: a case study, by B. Gambles. *Public Library Journal 6* (6) November/December 1991 153-156.

159. *Vendors and library acquisitions*, edited by Bill Katz. New York, The Haworth Press, Inc., 1991. ISBN 1560241217 (*Acquisitions Librarian*, no. 5).

160. Western European vendors: a critical survey of their use by American academic libraries, by T.D. Kilton and R.G. Sewell. *Collection Management 16* (1) 1992 1-54.

161. Library supply: adapting for survival, by M. Pewtress. *Bookseller* (4505) 24 April 1992 1195-1198.

162. The library as a library supplier, by Brian Lantz. *Taking Stock 2* (1) June 1993 1-7.

163. The business of library supply, by Jonathan Waring. *Taking Stock 2* (1) June 1993 24-31.

164. International library supply: the view from Florence, by Barabara Casalini. *Logos 6* (4) 1995 188-194.
165. What cost service? by Suzy Brain. *Bookseller* (4692) 24 November 1995 24-25.

Evaluation of Suppliers

166. Measuring book supply efficiency, by A.J. Oulton. *Bookseller* (4206) 2 August 1986 493-495.
167. Random vendor assignment in vendor performance evaluation, by J.W. Barker. *Library Acquisitions Practice and Theory 10* (4) 1986 265-280.
168. *Guide to performance evaluation of library materials vendors*, by the American Library Association Collection Management and Development Committee. Chicago, ALA, 1988. ISBN 0838933696 (Acquisition guidelines, 5).
169. Vendor evaluation: a selected annotated bibliography, 1955-1987, by Z. M. Shafa et al. *Library Acquisitions Practice and Theory 12* (1) 1988 17-28.
170. Measuring the performance of library suppliers, by Lawrence Rawsthorne. *National Acquisitions Group Newsletter* (9) July 1990 19-26.
171. Vendor performance evaluation: numeric formula, by T. Koln. *Library Acquisitions Practice and Theory 14* (3) 1990 307-312.
172. Acquisitions survey: the vendors respond, by L.A. Zoyner. *Library Acquisitions Practice and Theory 14* (3) 1990 313-316.
173. *Vendor evaluation and acquisition budgets*, edited by Sul H. Lee. New York, The Haworth Press, Inc., 1992. ISBN 1560242531 (*Journal of Library Administration*, vol. 16 no. 3).
174. Supplier performance evaluation at Surrey County Library, by Ted Mawby. *Taking Stock 1* (1) May 1992 17-25.
175. Regional study of vendor performance for in-print monographs, by the Vendor Study Group. *Library Acquisitions Practice and Theory 16* (1) 1992 21-29.
176. Evaluating suppliers for South Australian public libraries: the PLB principal supplier agreement, by Lindsay Harris.

Library Acquisitions Practice and Theory 16 (4) 1992 451-457.

177. A firm order vendor evaluation using a stratified sample, by Steven M. Rouzer. *Library Acquisitions Practice and Theory 17* (3) Fall 1993 269-278.

178. The quest for quality: evaluating supplier performance. Papers from Australian seminar [by various authors], edited by Jerelynn E. Brown. *Library Acquisitions Practice and Theory 18* (1) Spring 1994 43-92.

179. Measuring performance: from initiation to supply, by Geoffrey Ford. *Taking Stock 3* (1) May 1994 7-15.

Organisation of Work
(See also 236, 487)

180. *ISBNs in book ordering and control: Proceedings of the MARC Users Group seminar, 23 January 1986.* MARC Users Group, 1986. ISBN 0905463056.

181. Evaluation of technical service functions, by B. Lantz. *Journal of Librarianship 18* (4) October 1986 257-279.

182. Verification: is it pre-order or pre-cataloguing? by D. Phelps. *Cataloguing and Classification Quarterly 9* (1) 1988 5-9.

183. A case for pre-order searching in the catalog department, by J.H. Lambrecht. *Cataloguing and Classification Quarterly 9* (1) 1988 27-36.

184. Robbing Peter . . . balancing collection development and reference responsibilities, by D.G. Null. *College and Research Libraries 49* (5) September 1988 448-452.

185. *Cost-effective technical services: how to track, manage and justify internal operations*, by Bary M. Pitkin. New York, Neal-Schuman, 1989.

186. The ISBN: a good tool sorely misused, by A. Eaglen. *Collection Building 10* (2) 1990 74-76.

187. The creative use of acquisitions mechanisms in the college library, by C.S. Likness. *Collection Management 12* 1990 3-10.

188. *Operational costs in acquisitions*, edited by James R. Coffey. New York, The Haworth Press, Inc., 1990. ISBN 1560240083 (*Acquisitions Librarian*, 4).

189. Organizational models, by B.A. Winters et al. [8 articles on the reorganization of acquisitions departments]. *Library Acquisitions Practice & Theory 16* (4) 1992 345-389.
190. Technical services in the 1990's: a process of convergent evolution, by G.M. McCombs. *Library Resources and Technical Services 36* (2) April 1992 135-148.
191. Analysis of technical services throughput on a sample of monographic orders, by Susan A. Cady. *Technical Services Quarterly 10* (2) 1992 17-27.
192. Evaluating the success of acquisitions departments: a literature review, by A.L. O'Neill. *Library Acquisitions Practice and Theory 16* (3) Fall 1992 209-219.
193. A time analysis of a technical services workflow in a representative library: year one implementation of an integrated system, by Jeanne Harrell, Suzanne D. Gyeszly and Joni Gomez. *Technical Services Quarterly 9* (4) 1992 49-61.
194. The dis-integrating library system: effects of new technologies in acquisitions, by Ron L. Ray. *Library Acquisitions Practice and Theory 17* (2) Summer 1993 127-36.
195. *Interfaces: relationships between library technical and public services*, by Sheila S. Intner. Engelwood, Colorado, Libraries Unlimited, 1993. ISBN 1563080591.
196. A skeptic's view of the future for combined acquisitions and document delivery, by Ron L. Ray. *Library Acquisitions Practice and Theory 17* (3) Fall 1993 347-351.
197. The reading lists project at Aston University, by N.R. Smith. *British Journal of Academic Librarianship 8* (2) 1993 89-97.
198. The impact of computerization on library support staff; a study of support staff in academic libraries in Wisconsin, by Cathleen C. Palmini. *Library Resources and Technical Services 55* (2) March 1994 119-127.
199. *Management And Organization Of The Acquisitions Department*, Edited By Twyla Racz and Rosina Tammany. New York, The Haworth Press, Inc., 1994. ISBN 1560245832 (*Acquisitions Librarian*, 12).
200. Local government review: the implications for central support services, by Linda Hopkins. *Taking Stock 3* (2) November 1994 20-26.

201. Modelling technical services in libraries: a microanalysis employing domain analysis and Ishikawa ("fishbone") diagrams, by Lynne C. Howarth. *Technical Services Quarterly 12* (3) 1995 1-16.
202. Can you cut costs without cutting service? by Susan Mendelsohn. *Library Manager* (9) July-August 1995 12-14.

Automated Acquisitions Systems
(See also 111, 113, 193, 194, 198, 589, 607, 652, 661, 689)

203. *Automating acquisitions*, by Richard W. Boss, Susan Harrison and Hal Espo. Chicago, American Library Association, 1986. (Library Technology Reports vol. 22 no. 5)
204. The microcomputer in the library, 4: cataloguing and acquisitions software, by P. Leggate and H. Dyer. *Electronic Library 4* (3) June 1986 152-165.
205. The Geac acquisition system as a source of management information, by C. P. Hawks. *Library Acquisitions Practice and Theory 10* (4) 1986 245-253.
206. Standards for automated acquisitions systems, by S.R. Bullard. *Library Acquisitions Practice and Theory 11* (4) 1987 357-358.
207. Cost analysis of the LIBRIS II automated acquisitions system at the University of Texas at Dallas Library, by T.E. Nisonger. *Library Acquisitions Practice and Theory 11* (3) 1987 229-238.
208. A versatile dBase acquisitions program at Worcester Polytechnic Institute, by H.M. Shuster. *Library Acquisitions Practice and Theory 11* (3) 1987 241-253.
209. Vendor's view of library automation standards, by A. Miller. *Library Acquisitions Practice and Theory 11* (4) 1987 359-361.
210. DOBIS/LIBIS acquisitions subsystem in operation at King Fahd University, by Z. Khurshid. *Library Acquisitions Practice and Theory 11* (4) 1987 325-334.
211. Automated invoice processing at the National Library of Medicine, by D.E. McCutcheon and M.R. Fishel. *Information Technology and Libraries 6* (3) September 1987 205-211.

212. The LIBERTAS acquisitions system, by A. Britton. *Vine* (69) December 1987 4-12.
213. Library-wide use of a dBase acquisitions system, by M. Wineburgh-Freed, A.W. Karasick and D.R. Morse. *Bulletin-Medical Library Association 76* (11) January 1988 73-74.
214. Midwest Automated Technical Services System, by N. Desmarais. *Library Software Review 7* (2) March/April 1988 116-127.
215. Development of an automated acquisitions system at the University of Lancaster Library, by K. Harrison and D. Summers. *Program 22* (2) April 1988 143-162.
216. Tracking vendor discounts on a micro, by L.T. Snyderwine. *The Bottom Line 2* (2) 1988 36-37.
217. *Acquisitions systems for libraries*, by Norman Desmarais. Westport, Conn, Meckler, 1988. ISBN 0887361854 (The essential guide to the library IBM PC series, vol 11).
218. Implementing the automated acquisitions system: staffing considerations, by P. Schroeder. *Library Acquisitions Practice and Theory 12* (3/4) 1988 423-429.
219. Implementing the automated acquisitions system: perspectives of a personnel administrator, by D.C. Rooks. *Library Acquisitions Practice and Theory 12* (3/4) 1988 431-436.
220. Maintaining business as usual with vendors while implementing the Innovacq automated acquisitions system, by C.F. Hyslop. *Library Acquisitions Practice and Theory 12* (11) 1988 105-108.
221. BookBase: a tailor-made ordering alternative, by M.J. O'Brien. *Publishers Weekly 235* (2) January 1989 52-53.
222. Library acquisitions system: a micro application, by C.C. Lee. *Library Software Review 8* (1) January/February 1989 2-7.
223. Automated acquisitions in small academic libraries, by B.K. Nelson. *Library Acquisitions Practice and Theory 13* (4) 1989 335-341.
224. Automated acquisitions, by A. Eaglen. *Collection Building 9* (2) 1989 43-48.

225. BIP on CD-ROM, OCLC, and dBaseIII+ combine to improve acquisitions workflow, by M. J. Thayer. *Library Acquisitions Practice and Theory 13* (4) 1989 371-379.

226. Book budgets, community college libraries and Lotus 1-2-3, by D. Hillman. *Computers in Libraries 9* (4) April 1989 17-21.

227. Expanding horizons in collection development with expert systems, by S.L. Sowell. *Special Librarian 80* (1) Winter 1989 45-50.

228. *Automated acquisitions: issues for the present and future*, edited by Amy Dykeman. New York, The Haworth Press, Inc., 1989. (*Acquisitions Librarian*, 1) ISBN 0866569138.

229. The turnkey systems marketplace: ten years on [by K. Bloxham]. *Vine* (76) November 1989 3-8.

230. Automation in the Department of Printed Books at the National Library of Wales, part 1: system configuration and acquisitions, by D. Jeremiah. *Program 24* (3) July 1990 233-252.

231. Full acquisitions systems, by M. McLaren. *Library Acquisitions Practice and Theory 14* (3) 1990 247-250.

232. Internal control, auditing and the automated acquisitions system, by C.P. Hawks. *Journal of Academic Librarianship 16* (5) November 1990 296-301.

233. Detroit Area Library Network: bringing up acquisitions, by B. Heath. *Resource Sharing and Information Networks 7* (1) 1991 91-97.

234. Creating bibliographic records in the GEAC acquisitions module efficiently, by G. Rollins. *Library Acquisitions Practice and Theory 15* (4) 1991 427-432.

235. Automated acquisitions and OCLC: a brief history, present concerns, future options, by R.H. Stankowski. *Technical Services Quarterly 8* (3) 1991 59-63.

236. Automation and non-professional staff: the neglected majority, by P. Sykes. *Serials 4* (3) November 1991 33-43.

237. Automated acquisitions: the future of collection development, by M. Sasse and R.A. Smith. *Library Acquisitions Practice and Theory 16* (2) 1992 135-143.

238. A knowledge-based expert systems application in library acquisitions: monographs, by P. Zager and O. Smadi. *Library Acquisitions Practice and Theory 16* (2) 1992 145-154.
239. *Bar coding for books–a guide for publishers.* London, Book Industry Communication, 1992. ISBN 1873671008.
240. Management information from library systems, by Anthony J. Wood. *Taking Stock 2* (1) June 1993 16-18.
241. The MSUS/PALS acquisitions subsystem vendor file, by Gary A. Hudson. *Acquisitions Librarian* (11) 1994 161-186.
242. Expert systems in technical services and collection management, by Carol Pitts Hawks. *Information Technology and Libraries 13* (3) September 1994 203-212.
243. The potential of the Internet and networks for library acquisitions, by Gordon Dunsire. *Taking Stock 3* (2) November 1994 44-49.
244. Library supply and the technology triangle, by Suzy Brain. *Bookseller* (4665) 19 May 1995 26-29.
245. Acquisitions operational requirements for a new or replacement computer system, by Colin Galloway. *Taking Stock 4* (2) November 1995 47-50.
246. *New automation technology for acquisitions and collection development*, edited by Rosann Bazirjian. New York, The Haworth Press, Inc., 1995. (*Acquisitions Librarian*, 13/14) ISBN 1560247320.

Electronic Data Interchange

247. International teleordering: worldwide electronic access to British books. *British Book News* July 1987 477.
248. The promise of PUBNET, by J. Mutter. *Publishers Weekly 233* (11) 18 March 1988 44-46.
249. Teleordering–an international service in the making. *Bookseller* (4319) 30 September 1988 1304-1307.
250. ACQUIRE: electronic book ordering [from Baker and Taylor], by C. Larew and B. Alley. *Technicalities 8* (9) September 1988 3-4.
251. PC-Order: electronic book ordering, by J. Sanders. *Technicalities 8* (12) December 1988 3-5.

252. Books and electronic data transmission: the role of BTECC, by D. Greenwood. *British Book News* January 1989 16-17.
253. Library-to-vendor electronic transmission today, by J.W. Barker. *Library Acquisitions Practice and Theory 13* (3) 1989 275-279.
254. Teleordering and EDI in the book trade, by R. Dove. *Bookseller* (4397) 30 March 1990 1074-1078.
255. *Electronic data interchange: purchase orders*, by Elaine W. Woods. Bethesda, MD, National Information Standards Organization, 1990.
256. Parlez-vous X12? Do you speak EDI? by J. Mutter. *Publishers Weekly 237* (41) 9 November 1990 27-30.
257. *Report of the working parties of the UK Book Trade Electronic Data Interchange Standards Committee (BEDIS).* London, J. Whitaker & Sons Ltd., 1990. ISBN 0850212211.
258. Teleordering. *British Book News* February 1991 90-91.
259. B & B: BEDIS and BLCMP, by K. Smith. *Vine* (84) October 1991 15-17.
260. Interactive online acquisitions using BEDIS: three perspectives, by G. McCrae, J. Hardinge and D. Scrimgeour. *New Library World 93* (1099) 1992 15-21.
261. Killing the paper tiger: electronic communications in the book trade, by B. Green. *British Book News* January 1992 18-19.
262. *EDI the future of library supply: the strategic importance of EDI in the library world.* Leeds, National Acquisitions Group, 1993. ISBN 187026908X.
263. *EDIBIB: harmonising standards for bibliographic data interchange,* by Juliet Leeves. London, The British Library, 1993. ISBN 0712332812 (British National Bibliography Research Fund, report 62).
264. EDILIBE: an experiment based on the technological relationship between booksellers and libraries, by Berndt Dugall. *Taking Stock 2* (1) June 1993 19-23.
265. *Bringing EDI to book: the impact of EDI in the book industry,* by Coopers & Lybrand. London, BNB Research Fund, 1993.

266. *Standard book subject categories for EDI*, by Russell Sweeney. London, British National Bibliography Research Fund, 1994. ISBN 0712332901 (BNB Research Fund report, 67).

267. Implementing electronic data interchange in the library acquisitions environment, by Wilbert Harri. *Library Acquisitions Practice and Theory 18* (1) Spring 1994 115-117.

268. EDI standards for acquisitions, by Betty Landesman. *Library Acquisitions Practice and Theory 18* (1) Spring 1994 119-121.

269. In at the deep end: sandwiched between publishers and the libraries [on EDI], by Stephen Scott. *Taking Stock 3* (1) May 1994 1-4.

270. At the end of the line [on EDI], by Brenda Ponton. *Taking Stock 3* (1) May 1994 5-6.

271. EDI: a systems supplier's view, by Tony Hall. *Taking Stock 3* (1) May 1994 7-10.

272. EDI: a publisher's view, by Karl Lawrence. *Taking Stock 3* (1) May 1994 12-14.

273. First Edition: preface and first chapter, by Mark Hodder-Williams. *Taking Stock 3* (1) May 1994 16-20.

274. *The impact of electronic data interchange on library operations: implementation issues*, by Craig Fairley. The Hague, IFLA, 1995. (IFLA professional report 42).

275. Implications of implementing EDI, by Janet Broome. *Taking Stock 4* (2) November 1995 8-12.

276. *Data elements for an EDI 'book product information' message*, by David Martin. London, Book Industry Communication, 1995. (British National Bibliography Research Fund report 75) ISBN 0873671075.

277. Towards international standards for book sector EDI, by Brian Green. *International Cataloguing and Bibliographic Control 24* (4) October/December 1995 59-60.

Bibliographic Data
(See also 128)

278. *MARC in the market place: harmonising book trade and library systems.* Proceedings of the MARC Users Group

annual seminar, Lancaster, September 24 1986. London, MARC Users Group, 1987.

279. The book trade and library bibliographic control, by D. Whitaker. *Catalogue & Index* (86) Autumn 1987 1-6.

280. Technology and the British National Bibliographic Service, by A. Stephens. *Journal of Librarianship 20* (3) July 1988 194-204.

281. *Guidelines for the layout and contents of booksellers' catalogues.* London, Art Libraries Society, 1988. ISBN 0950106356.

282. *Publishers' bibliographic databases: standards and design,* by John Allison. Boston Spa, British Library, 1988. ISBN 0712331654 (British National Bibliography Research Fund report no 35).

283. Standards for book and serial publishers, by S.K. Paul. *Book Research Quarterly 4* (3) Fall 1988 61-65.

284. Satisfying bibliographic needs in the future: from publisher to user, by M.B. Line. *Catalogue and Index* (90/91) Autumn/ Winter 1988 10-14.

285. BISAC: an industry update, by B.L. Blatz. *Technicalities 8* (11) November 1988 9.

286. *Downloading 88: Online supply of bibliographic records,* edited by Pat Manson. MARC Users Group, 1989. ISBN 0905463072.

287. The use and usefulness of publishers' catalogues to medical and nursing librarians, by P. Moorbath. *Aslib Proceedings 41* (2) February 1989 65-73.

288. *Currency with coverage: a survey report* by Lorcan Dempsey. ISBN 0905463080 London, MARC Users Group, 1989.

289. Creating publishers' catalog database in a curriculum materials center, by R. Stavis. *Education Libraries 14* (2) Spring 1989 68-70.

290. *Effective bibliographic management in the publishing house,* by Mary Anne Bankes. London, Publishers Association, 1989. ISBN 0853861870.

291. Bowker's Ingram Books In Print Plus: a case study, by M. Brooks. *Laserdisk Professional 2* (4) July 1989 46-52.

292. How much help are publishers' catalogues and why do publishers send out their bumph? by Paul Moorbath. *National Acquisitions Group Newsletter* (8) January 1990 31-33.
293. Library suppliers as a source of bibliographic information, by J.P. Bunce. *Aslib Proceedings 42* (2) February 1990 51-60.
294. Users' requirements of bibliographic records: publishers, booksellers, librarians, by L. Dempsey. *Aslib Proceedings 42* (2) February 1990 61-69.
295. An approach to cataloguing using trade data, by J. Seddon. *Marc Users Group Newsletter 89* (2)/*90* (1) March 1990 10-19.
296. A worldwide bibliographic database of books: why it is needed and how it could be achieved, by M.B. Line. *Logos 2* (3) 1991 145-149.
297. Publishers and libraries: an all-through system for bibliographic data? by L. Dempsey. *International Cataloguing and Bibliographic Control 20* (3) July/September 1991 37-41.
298. Authority control in the order process [5 papers], by various authors. *Library Acquisitions Practice and Theory 16* (1) 1992 61-83.
299. New acquisitions lists, by Sheila S. Intner. *Technicalities 12* (9) September 1992 4-8.

Finance, Expenditure and Budgeting
(See also 226, 232, 400, 403, 542, 543, 546, 549, 552, 561, 563, 564, 565, 571, 657, 725, 732, 754)

300. *The effectiveness of library expenditure*, by Peter Brophy et al. Bristol Polytechnic Library, 1985. ISBN 09049516504.
301. Issues in books and serials acquisitions: all you ever wanted to know about finances, by S.W. Somers. *Technical Services Quarterly 4* (1) 1986 69-73.
302. *Library book and periodical spending in universities, polytechnics and colleges, 1981-1984*. London, National Book League, 1986.
303. Public libraries and book funds, by P.H. Mann. *Bookseller* (4210) 30 August 1986 863-865.
304. University library book budgets, 1860, 1910 and 1960, by J.P. Danton. *Library Quarterly 57* (3) July 1987 284-302.

305. Reduction budgeting hits home: the Dallas story, by P. O'Brian. *The Bottom Line 1* (2) 1987 4-7.
306. Changing enrolment patterns: the implications for university library funding, by J.R. Brockman. *British Journal of Academic Librarianship 2* (1) Spring 1987 1-11.
307. Public libraries and bookfunds by P.H. Mann. *Bookseller* (4260) 14 August 1987 630.
308. The development of an objective budget allocation procedure for academic library acquisitions, by G.G. Allen and C.T. Lee. *Libri 37* (3) September 1987 211-221.
309. Deposit accounts for monograph acquisitions: a budget-stretching technique, by S. Hayes. *The Bottom Line 1* (4) 1987 28-29.
310. Library materials budget crisis, by F.C. Lynden. *Book Research Quarterly 3* (4) Winter 1987/88 58-61.
311. Book budget formula allocations: a review essay by M. Sellen. *Collection Management 9* (4) Winter 1987 13-24.
312. Effects of polytechnic library funding, by P. Lund. *COPOL Newsletter* (45) January 1988 30-33.
313. The great leveler: the library budget by J.S. Lopez. *Library Acquisitions Practice and Theory 12* (2) 1988 229-234.
314. Bitter book news, by P.H. Mann. *Bookseller* (4295) 15 April 1988 1530-1531.
315. *Acquisitions, budgets and material costs: issues and approaches*; edited by Sul H. Lee. New York, The Haworth Press, Inc., 1988. ISBN 0866566902 (*Journal of Library Administration* Monographic Supplement no 2).
316. STM: in search of new library funding, by P. Oakeshott. *Bookseller* (4306) 1 July 1988 19.
317. Public libraries and bookfunds, by P.H. Mann. *Bookseller* (4309) 22 July 1988 292-293.
318. University libraries–the straw gets shorter, by P.H. Mann. *Bookseller* (4315) 16 September 1988 901-902.
319. Deposit accounts and their economic impact in medium-sized academic libraries, by W. Hardin. *Collection Management 11* (1/2) 1989 97-107.
320. Budgeting for collection development, by R. Ring. *Collection Building 9* (3) 1989 25-28.

321. A rose is a rose is a rose [on acquisitions budgets], by P. Johnson. *Technicalities 9* (7) July 1989 7-8, 12.
322. *University and polytechnic libraries: book and journal spending: 1978/79-1986/87, a report* by the University, College and Professional Publishers Council. Publishers Association/Book Trust, 1989. ISBN 0853861684.
323. Public libraries and book funds, by P. H. Mann. *Bookseller* (4361) 21 July 1989 217-218.
324. University libraries: books make a come back, by P.H. Mann. *Bookseller* (4367) 15 September 1989.
325. *Public libraries and their book funds*, by the National Book Committee. London, Book Trust, 1989. ISBN 0853861846.
326. Stagnant budgets: their effects on academic libraries, by M.S. Martin. *The Bottom Line 3* (3) 1989 10-16.
327. When we buy books, we know what we pay for—or do we? by C.M. Boissannas. *Library Acquisitions Practice and Theory 13* (2) 1989 87-102.
328. Library funding and economics: a framework for research, by Y.M. Braunstein. *IFLA Journal 15* (4) 1989 289-298.
329. *The acquisitions budget* edited by Bill Katz. New York, The Haworth Press, Inc., 1989. (*Acquisitions Librarian*, 2) ISBN 0866569308.
330. Library materials budget justifications, by F.C. Lynden. *Book Research Quarterly 5* (4) Winter 1989/90 68-74.
331. The serial/monograph ratio in research libraries: budgeting in light of situation studies, by R.B. Devin and M. Kellogg. *College and Research Libraries 51* (1) January 1990 46-54.
332. Spending in polytechnic libraries, by P.H. Mann. *Bookseller* (4387) 19 January 1990 176.
333. Cost analysis of monographs and serials, by C.A. Hamaker and S. Grimall. *Journal of Library Administration 12* (3) 1990 41-49.
334. Real money [on budgeting for library materials], by P. Johnson. *Technicalities 10* (2) February 1990 10-13.
335. Universities in Great Britain: some comparisons of costs, 1983/84-1987/88, by P.H. Mann. *Newsletter–University College and Research Section of the Library Association* (30) Spring 1990 2-3.

336. Allocating the academic library's book budget: historical perspectives and current reflections, by R.H. Werking. *Journal of Academic Librarianship 14* (3) 1990 140-144.

337. More library materials budget justifications, by A. Henderson. *Book Research Quarterly 6* (3) Fall 1990 81-88.

338. Public libraries and book funds, by P.H. Mann. *Bookseller* (4422) 21 Sept 1990 824-825.

339. Budgeting: the major task of the financial manager, by D. Bausch and N. Bausch. *Bottom Line 4* (4) 1990 27-30.

340. Modeling library materials expenditure: initial experiments at Arizona State University, by C.W. Brownson. *Library Resources and Technical Services 35* (1) January 1991 87-103.

341. University Libraries: the lull before the storm? by A. Mac-Dougall. *The Bookseller* (4437) 4 January 1991 20-22.

342. *Budgets for acquisitions: strategies for serials, monographs and electronic formats*, edited by Sul H Lee. New York, The Haworth Press, Inc., 1991. ISBN 560241586 (*Journal of Library Administration*, volume 14 no. 3).

343. Equity, efficiency and reality: budgeting as battle with a hydra, by P. Johnson. *Technicalities 11* (2) February 1991 5-8.

344. *Guide to budget allocation for information resources*, edited by Edward Shreeves. Chicago. American Library Association, 1991. ISBN 0838933971 (Collection management and development guide, 4).

345. Zero-based budgeting: a tool for cutting back, by Carol Hodlofski. *Bottom Line 5* (2) Summer 1991 13-19.

346. Depreciation of library collections: terminology of the debate, by E. Christanson and S. Hayes. *The Bottom Line 5* (3) Fall 1991 35-37.

347. Libraries in crisis, by G. Cunningham. *Bookseller* (4494) 7 February 1992 356-358.

348. Budgeting in libraries [4 papers], by various authors. *Serials 5* (1) March 1992 35-61.

349. Resource allocation in university libraries, by D. Baker. *Journal of Documentation 48* (1) March 1992 1-19.

350. *Public library materials fund and budget surveys, 1991-1993*. Loughborough, Library and Information Statistics Unit, 1992. ISBN 0948848448.

351. The invasion of the library materials budget by technology serials and databases: buying more with less? by M.S. Martin. *Serials Review 18* (3) 1992 7-17.

352. More books, higher prices, declining budgets: where do we go from here? by Maurice Line. *Taking Stock 1* (1) May 1992 6-11.

353. The politics of budgeting, by Carla J. Stoffle. *The Bottom Line 6* (2) Summer/Fall 1992 9-16.

354. *Keeping the books: public and financial practices*, edited by Jane R. Robbins and Douglas L. Zweizig. Fort Atkinson, Wisconsin, Highsmith Press, 1992. ISBN 0917846117.

355. Collection assessment and acquisitions budgets: highlights of a conference, by Carol Pitts Hawks. *Library Acquisitions Practice and Theory 16* (4) 1992 431-438.

356. Library funding in the 90s; report of the state of the nation's libraries as documented by the American Library Association. *Technicalities* 6 (3/4) Winter 1992/Spring 1993 18-21.

357. Academic library book spend: the decline continues, by John Sumsion. *Bookseller* (4548) 19 February 1993 44-54.

358. Louisiana's gift horse: funding library acquisitions with bond money, by Stanley Wilder. *Journal of Academic Librarianship 19* (2) 1993 78-80.

359. Sponsorship in libraries, by Rex Bird. *Taking Stock 2* (1) June 1993 12-15.

360. *Academic library budgets*, edited by Murray S. Martin. JAI Press inc, 1993. ISBN 1559385979 (Foundations in library and information science series, 28).

361. Assessing the adequacy of academic library budgets, 1960-1990, by Michael R. Gabriel. *Technicalities 13* (10) October 1993 2-5, 11.

362. Accruals accounting and library materials acquisitions, by Nancy M. Stanley. *The Bottom Line 7* (2) Fall 1993 15-17.

363. No bucks, no books, by Beverly J. Bagan. *Bottom Line 7* (3/4) Spring 1994 12-16.

364. Library book funds back in the melting pot, by Cathy Aitchison. *Bookseller (4613)* 20 May 1994 26-27.

365. *Declining acquisitions budgets: allocation, collection development and impact communication*, edited by Sul H. Lee.

New York, The Haworth Press, Inc., 1994. (*Journal of Library Administration*, vo. 19 no. 2) ISBN 1560246138.

366. The audit trail and automated acquisitions: searching for road signs, by Carol Pitts Hawks. *Library Acquisitions Practice and Theory 18* (3) Fall 1994 333-339.

367. Financial record-keeping in acquisitions departments: University of Iforin Library case study, by Richard Olorunsola. *Acquisitions Librarian* (11) 1994 187-195.

368. *University libraries.-a report on book and journal spending, 1978/79-1992/93.* London, Council of Academic and Professional Publishers, 1994.

369. Recent trends in academic library materials expenditures, by Chandra Prabha and John E. Ogden. *Library Trends 42* (3) Winter 1994 499-513.

370. Preparing materials budget requests, by Peggy Johnson. *Technicalities 15* (4) April 1995 1,8-10.

371. A method for establishing a depreciated monetary value for print collections, by Edward Marman. *Library Administration and Management 9* (2) Spring 1995 94-97.

372. Public library funding: preparing for gloom, by John Sumsion. *Bookseller* (4660) 14 April 1995 22-24.

373. The value of library materials, by Sheila S. Intner. *Technicalities 15* (8) August 1995 9-11.

374. How we spent $2.7 million–with the help of centralized selection, by Catherine Gibson. *Library Journal 120* (14) 1 September 1995 128-130.

375. *Collection development and finance: a guide to strategic library materials budgeting*, by Murray S. Martin. Chicago, American Library Association, 1995. (Frontiers of access to library materials, 2) ISBN 0838906486.

376. German university library budgets: model and reality, by Rolf Griebel. *Library Management 16* (7) 1995 3-8.

377. Reduced budgeting: an exercise in prioritisation; an academic viewpoint, by Geoffrey Gilbert. *Taking Stock 4* (2) November 1995 18-24.

378. Book selection and bookfund management at Imperial College Libraries, by Janice Yeadon and Ruth Cooper. *New Review of Academic Librarianship 1* 1995 33-40.

Prices and Pricing

379. Academic book price index, by D. Biblarz. *Book Research Quarterly 2* (2) Summer 1986 83-87.
380. *Towards a public library book price index*, by Peter H. Mann. Loughborough, Centre for Library and Information Management, 1986. ISBN 0948848 05 (CLAIM Report no. 57).
381. Foreign book prices, by F.C. Lynden. *Book Research Quarterly 2* (3) Fall 1986 89-91.
382. Reporting book prices: managing the rising costs in materials, by F.C. Lynden. *Book Research Quarterly 3* (1) Spring 1987 82-84.
383. Inflation indexes for academic library purchases, by J. Fletcher. *Library Association Record 89* (8) August 1987 400-401.
384. *Pricing and costs of monographs and serials: national and international issues*, edited by Sul H. Lee. New York, The Haworth Press, Inc., 1987. ISBN 0866566201 (*Journal of Library Administration*, vol 8: Monographic supplement no. 1).
385. Reporting book prices [in Germany], by R. Griebel. *Book Research Quarterly 3* (4) Winter 1987/88 67-76.
386. Take a look at the RTSD RS Library Materials Price Index Committee, by R. Lenzini. *RTSD Newsletter 13* (2) 1988 17-19.
387. Pricing and discounts, by F.C. Lynden. *Library Acquisitions Practice and Theory 12* (2) 1988 255-258.
388. Price versus coverage: calculating the impact on collection development, by E.K. Welsch. *Library Resources and Technical Services 32* (2) April 1988 159-163.
389. Prices of foreign library materials, by F.C. Lynden. *College and Research Libraries 49* (3) May 1988 217-231.
390. Getting the price right, by N. Ross. *Bookseller* (4319) 16 September 1988 1096-1098.
391. Differential pricing in the international book market, by U. Montag. *IFLA Journal 15* (1) 1989 37-43.
392. Book prices and costs for a small hospital library: a subject analysis, by C.A. Johnson. *Bulletin–Medical Library Association 77* (1) January 1989 38-41.

393. The apparently automatic self-inflating price of books, by D. Duchin. *Library Acquisitions Practice and Theory 13* (2) 1989 115-118.

394. Markets and prices, by D. Whitaker. *Bookseller* (4351) 12 May 1989 1620-1626.

395. What price indexes? by P.H. Mann. *Bookseller* (4372) 6 October 1989 1146-1147.

396. Publishers' pricing: the public librarian's dilemma, by R. Stoakley. *Bookseller* (4366) 25 August 1989 580-583.

397. *Book prices in the United Kingdom: a study by Peat Marwick McLintock*, by Vicky Pryce and Michael Littlechild. Boston Spa, British Library, 1989 ISBN 0712331972 (British National Bibliography Research Fund report, 41).

398. *The Impact of rising costs of serials and monographs on library services and programs*, edited by Sul H. Lee. New York, The Haworth Press, Inc., 1989. ISBN 0866568859 (*Journal of Library Administration*, volume 10, part 1).

399. The price of books, by R. Stanley. *Public Library Journal 5* (1) January/February 1990 9-13.

400. Getting into this mess wasn't easy; it took a lot of effort on our part [on rising prices], by H.S. White. *Technical Services Quarterly 8* (2) 1990 1-16.

401. Cost analysis of monographs and serials, by F.C. Lynden. *Journal of Library Administration 12* (3) 1990 19-40.

402. Trends in American book and periodical price indexes, by F.C. Lynden. *LIBER Bulletin* (36) 1990 120-132.

403. Price and cost indexes as instruments of budgetary planning, by R. Griebel. *LIBER Bulletin* (36) 1990 133-149.

404. *Information and documentation–determination of price indexes for books and serials purchased by libraries* [standard]. Milton Keynes, British Standards Institution. 1991. ISBN 0580202607.

405. Problems in documenting international prices, by F.C. Lynden. *Collection Management 15* (3/4) 1992 527-532.

406. AAP-BISG book industry data, by R.F. Winter. *Publishing Research Quarterly 8* (3) Fall 1992 5-11.

407. Book industry statistics from the R.R. Bowker Company, by J. Peters. *Publishing Research Quarterly 8* (3) Fall 1992 12-23.
408. *Will the chain break? Differential pricing as part of a new pricing strategy for research literature and its consequences for the future of scholarly communication*, edited by Ulrich Montag. Munchen, Saur, 1992. ISBN 3598217897 (IFLA publications, no. 61).
409. The growing gap in book industry statistics, by John P. Dessauer. *Publishing Research Quarterly 9* (2) Summer 1993 68-71.
410. The page price of popular fiction and nonfiction books: an exploratory study, by William C. Robinson. *Library Resources and Technical Services 37* (4) October 1993 351-366.
411. Data on prices for publications purchased by libraries: progress report, by Frederick C. Lynden. *IFLA Journal 19* (4) November 1993 410-416.
412. Indexing price trends of French academic books in the humanities and social sciences, by Ronald E. Austin. *College and Research Libraries 55* (1) January 1994 37-40.
413. VAT on books: a publisher's perspective, by Simon Master. *Taking Stock 3* (2) November 1994 31-34.
414. Perception of economics in a digital publishing environment; a report of a field study, by Elisabeth Davenport. *Interlending and Document Supply 22* (4) 1994 8-16.
415. *Library material costs and access to information*, edited by Sul H Lee. New York, The Haworth Press, Inc., 1994. ISBN 1560241462 (*Journal of Library Administration*, volume 12 no. 3).
416. On the cost differences between publishing a book in paper and in the electronic medium, by Tom Clark. *Library Resources and Technical Services 39* (1) January 1995 23-28.
417. Price of materials and collection development in larger public libraries, by William C. Robinson. *Library Acquisitions Practice and Theory 19* (3) Fall 1995 299-312.
418. Acquisitions and inflation, by Amy Hartman. *Collection Building 14* (4) 1995 5-11.

The Book Trade

419. *Liaison in the book world*, by Priscilla Oakeshott. British National Bibliography Research Fund, 1986 (BNB Research Fund report, 24).
420. *The market for books in the Republic of Ireland*, by Francis Fishwick. Irish Books Marketing Group, 1987. ISBN 0951246100.
421. *The book trade in Wales*, prepared by the Welsh Studies Department of the College of Librarianship Wales. Aberystwyth, Market Research Working Party, 1988. ISBN OB6383437X.
422. Whitaker and Sons, by V. Menkes. *British Book News* October 1988 724-728.
423. The BNB Research Fund: cutting across boundaries, by D. Greenwood. *Journal of Librarianship 21* (4) October 1989 246-259.
424. The book trade, by the Scottish Arts Council. *Scottish Libraries* (18) November 1989 5-6.
425. *Education and training for the book and information world*, by Maurice B Line. British Library, 1990 (British National Bibliography Research Fund report, 45).
426. The book is dead–long live the book, by T. Rix. *Assistant Librarian 84* (1) January 1991 7-10.
427. The library doomsday machine, by A. Okerson and K. Stubbs. *Publishers Weekly 238* (8) 8 February 1991 36-37.
428. *Information UK 2000: publishing, new products, distribution and marketing; bookselling and library supply*, by P.L. Holmes et al. Boston Spa, The British Library, 1991 (BLR&D Department report 6019).
429. Training for the book trade and acquisition: is there a common core? by John Feather. *Taking Stock 1* (1) May 1992 26-32.
430. *The economic aspects of the information system*, by DJB Associates. London, The British Library, 1993 (British Library R&D Report no. 6121).
431. The best book trade organization in the world? [Borsenverein des Deutschen Buchhandels], by Klaus Saur. *Logos 4* (3) 1993 120-123.

432. Building bridges with books: the British Council's sixty-year record, by Brigid O'Connor and Stephan Roman. *Logos 5* (3) 1994 133-138.
433. The library, the bookshop and the literature centre, by Robert Walters. *New Library World 96* (1116) 1995 21-27.
434. *Title output in the UK: figures, causes and implications*, by Philip Bryant. London, British Library, 1995 (British National Bibliography Research Fund, report 77).
435. Intellectual convergence in a mass communication course for librarians and publishers, by Stuart Hannabuss, Jane Barford and Fiona Campbell. *Journal of Librarianship and Information Science 27* (2) June 1995 67-76.
436. How publishers, librarians and booksellers could collaborate to achieve the virtual library, by Charles Oppenheim. *Logos 6* (3) 1995 153-157.

The Library Market
(See also 287)

437. Monographs in decline, by A. Hellemans. *Publishers Weekly* 31 October 1986 39-40.
438. Scholarly publishers and research libraries: cooperation in the information age, by K. Hunter. *Research Libraries in OCLC* (22) Spring 1987 1-5.
439. The relationship between publisher and librarian, by F. O'Donovan. *American Studies Library Newsletter* (26) December 1987 11-17.
440. The future library market for scholarly books, by B.P. Lynch. *Scholarly Publishing 19* (2) January 1988 86-90.
441. Libraries and the "other" booktrade, by S. Masson. *Assistant Librarian 81* (5) May 1988 66-70.
442. Replacing the myths about marketing to libraries, by M. Sexton. *Publishers Weekly 236* (9) 10 March 1989 56-57.
443. Book publishers focus on librarian focus groups, by R. Burroughs. *Library Journal 114* (5) 15 March 1989 48-49.
444. Libraries: an important end-market for book publishers, by D. Selsky. *Library Journal 114* (8) 1 May 1989 28.
445. Why do publishers send out their catalogues? by P. Moorbath. *Aslib Proceedings 41* (6) June 1989 213-216.

446. Dispelling more myths about marketing to libraries, by M. Sexton. *Publishers Weekly 236* (25) 22 December 1989 38.
447. Marketing to libraries in the 1990s. [Conference report by M. Sexton]. *Publishers Weekly 237* (35) 31 August 1990 45.
448. Publishers, librarians and readers, by G. Graham. *Publishers Weekly 238* (3) 18 January 1991 84.
449. Publishers are looking at you [on the library market], by B. Hoffert. *Library Journal 116* (3) February 1991 146-154.
450. Strengthening the partnership [between publishers and librarians], by H.M. Epstein. *Publishers Weekly 238* (24) 31 May 1991 33-34.
451. Reaching the library market with Christian books, by Graham Hedges. *Christian Librarian* (17) 1993 45-53.
452. *Are books different? Marketing in the book trade*, by Alison Baverstock. London, Kogan Page, 1993. ISBN 0749409002.
453. Publishing and the library market, by Liz Chapman. *Taking Stock 2* (1) June 1993 8-11.
454. Modeling scholarly book literature, by Charles A. Schwartz. *Publishing Research Quarterly 10* (2) Summer 1994 29-35.
455. Librarians and publishers: an uneasy dance, by Patricia Glass Schuman. *Wilson Library Bulletin 69* (4) December 1994 40-43.
456. A publisher and a librarian talk, or: everything you've always thought but were too afraid to say out loud–a tongue-in-cheek look at ourselves, by Barbara Meyers and Charles Germain. *Library Acquisitions Practice and Theory 19* (2) Summer 1995 219-224.
457. Why Russian libraries are vital to the book trade, by Evgeny Kuzmin. *European Bookseller* (11) August 1995 53-55.
458. Debunking ten myths publishers have about libraries, by Nancy Pearl. *Library Journal 120* (14) 1 September 1995 132-134.
459. How much or how little: the state of the market, by Leslie Henry. *Taking Stock 4* (2) November 1995 29-37.

Publishing
(See also 290, 428, 735, 815, 868)

460. *The world book industry,* by Peter Curwen. London, Euromonitor, 1986. ISBN 086338093X.
461. Thor tax ruling after 5 years: its effect on libraries and publishing, by M.H. Loe. *Library Acquisitions Practice and Theory 10* (3) 1986 203-213.
462. The growing partnership between small presses and independent booksellers, by J. Kremer. *Book Research Quarterly 3* (1) Spring 1987 75-77.
463. University presses and libraries. *Library Journal 112* (13) August 1987 55-68.
464. Publishing: the future, by Peter Owen. London, Peter Owen, 1988. ISBN 0720607205.
465. Planning and budgeting in publishing: the link with marketing, by M.E. Curtis. *Book Research Quarterly 4* (2) Summer 1988 3-9.
466. The future pattern of publishing, by N. Morley. *Catalogue and Index* (90/91) Autumn/Winter 1988 14-16.
467. The impact of new technology on the distribution of books and journals, by S.K. Paul. *Book Research Quarterly 4* (4) Winter 1988-89 87-90.
468. Technology and convergence in publishing, by N. Morley. *Outlook on Research Libraries 11* (3) March 1989 1-3.
469. University presses: highs and lows, by W. Nixon. *Publishers Weekly 236* (12) 22 September 1989 18-24.
470. *Getting in print, staying in print,* edited by William A. Forster. Hatfield, HERTIS, 1990 ISBN 0852672845.
471. Book culture and book business: the UK vs the US, by M.H. Lee. *Journal of Academic Librarianship 16* (1) March 1990 4-10.
472. Scholarly publishing in the 90s, by R. Campbell. *Bookseller* (4415) 3 August 1990 320-322.
473. Between academic and commercial publishers: an ill-defined demilitarized zone, by D.S. Lamm. *Logos 1* (3) 1990 55-59.
474. Barriers to the flow of books, by the Working Group of Europeans Librarians and Publishers. *Book Research Quarterly 6* (3) Fall 1990 76-81.

475. Publish *and* perish, by A.L. Henon. *Serials Librarian 17* (3/4) 1990 35-41.
476. Book production and library purchases: looking beyond the Thor ruling, by A.L. O'Neill. *Publishing Research Quarterly 7* (2) Summer 1991 39-51.
477. Children's book publishing on the ascent. by J. Donovan. *Publishing Research Quarterly 7* (3) Fall 1991 7-14.
478. *Competition and choice in the publishing industry*, by Walter Allan and Peter Curwen. London, Institute of Economic Affairs, 1991. ISBN 0255362455.
479. The trend towards self-publishing, by P. Hayward. *Canadian Library Journal 49* (4) August 1992 287-293.
480. Publishing under constraint, by Andy McKillop. *Taking Stock 1* (2) November 1992 6-10.
481. Self-publishing: an honourable history, a new dynamism and a bright future, by Ann Kritzinger. *Logos 4* (1) 1993 21-25.
482. Publishing for a future: publishers' options in an electronic world, by Richard Siegersma. *Australian Academic and Research Libraries 24* (1) March 1993 26-29.
483. *As I was saying: essays on the international book business*, by Gordon Graham. London, Hans Zell, 1993. ISBN 1873836015 (Studies on publishing, 2).
484. Vicious circles: trade publishing in the US today, by Donald Lamm. *Logos 4* (4) 1993 198-203.
485. How the US book industry developed a new field of study: itself, by Sandra K. Paul. *Logos 5* (4) 1994 195-199.
486. European academic publishing: the British academic librarian's view, by Ian R.M. Mowat. *Learned Publishing 8* (1) January 1995 11-17.
487. *Policies of publishers: a handbook for order librarians*; 1995 edition, by David U. Kim and Craig A. Wilson. Scarecrow Press, 1995. ISBN 0810830175.
488. Bestsellers and the British book industry, by John Feather and Martin Reid. *Publishing Research Quarterly 11* (1) Spring 1995 57-72.
489. *International book publishing–an encyclopedia*, edited by Philip G. Altbach and Edith S. Hoshino. New York, Garland Press, 1995. ISBN 0815307861.

490. *Book publishing in Britain.* London, Bookseller/MTI, 1995 [inc. CD-ROM of the text].
491. The flow of publishing, by Murray S. Martin. *Technicalities 15* (11) November 1995 1, 7-8.

COLLECTIONS

Collection Development
(See also 8, 9, 15, 17, 22, 29, 237, 737, 785, 814, 824)

492. The dichotomous collection, by D.L. Vidor and E. Futas. *Library Resources and Technical Services 31* (3) July/September 1987 207-213.
493. Epistemological dead-end and ergonomic disaster? The North American Collections Inventory Project, by D. Henige. *Journal of Academic Librarianship 13* (4) September 1987 209-213.
494. *Collection development: options for effective management,* edited by Sheila Corrall. Taylor Graham, 1988. ISBN 0947568255.
495. Why books are bought and borrowed, by D.W. Lewis. *The Bottom Line 2* (4) 1988 21-24.
496. Collection development in action, by B. Linklater. *Australian Academic and Research Libraries 19* (1) March 1988 32-38.
497. Collection development: an overview of the research, by D.F. Kohl. *Collection Management 10* (3) 1988 1-14.
498. *Collections: their development, management, preservation and sharing.* Washington, DC, Association of Research Libraries, 1989.
499. The North American Collections Inventory Project, by D. Farrell and J. Reed-Scott. *Library Resources and Technical Services 33* (1) January 1989 15-28.
500. Stock selection guidelines, by the Association of Assistant Librarians. *Assistant Librarian 82* (2) February 1989 27-28.
501. Library acquisitions policy by consultation out of Conspectus, by M. Henty. *Australian Academic and Research Libraries 20* (1) March 1989 47-50.

502. Book selection, collection development and bounded rationality, by C.A. Schwartz. *College and Research Libraries 50* (3) May 1989 329-343.

503. *Collection development for libraries*, by G.E. Gorman and B.R. Howes. Bowker-Saur, 1989. ISBN 0408301007.

504. The roles of collections and the scope of collection development, by M.K. Buckland. *Journal of Documentation 45* (3) September 1989 213-226.

505. Old forms, new forms: the challenge of collection development, by R. Atkinson. *College and Research Libraries 50* (5) September 1989 507-520.

506. Collection development in Canadian studies: a practical model, by T.C. Dahlin. *Collection Management 13* (1/2) 1990 97-102.

507. Conspectus as a tool for art libraries in Australia, by M. Shaw. *Australian Academic and Research Libraries 21* (1) March 1990 33-38.

508. Case studies in collection development: setting an agenda for future research, by D. Gonzalez Kirby. *Collection Building 11* (2) 1991 2-9.

509. Issues in developing a religious studies collection, by M.S. Alt. *Library Acquisitions Practice and Theory 15* (2) 1991 207-214.

510. Books aren't us? The year's work in collection development, 1990, by D.S. Sullivan. *Library Resources and Technical Services 35* (3) July 1991 283-293.

511. An interview with Ann Okerson (Office of Scholarly and Academic Publishing), by P. Johnson. *Technicalities. 11* (10) October 1991 2-6.

512. Collection development today: coping with reality, by P. Johnson. *Technicalities 12* (6) June 1992 5-8.

513. The future of collection development in an era of financial stringency: a symposium, by J.G. Schad et al. *Journal of Academic Librarianship 18* (1) March 1992 4-15.

514. *Collection assessment: a look at the RLG Conspectus*, edited by Richard J. Wood and Katina Strauch. New York, The Haworth Press, Inc., 1992. ISBN 1560242582 (*Acquisitions Librarian*, No 7).

515. The end of collection development as we know it? by P. Johnson. *Technicalities 12* (8) August 1992 5-8.
516. Canon formation, library collections and the dilemma of collection development, by Mark Cyzyk. *College and Research Libraries 54* (1) January 1993 58-65.
517. The year's work in collection development, 1992, by Stephen Lehmann and James H. Spohrer. *Library Resources and Technical Services 37* (3) July 1993 299-313.
518. Collection development education: an Australian perspective, by G.E. Gorman. *Library Acquisitions Practice and Theory 17* (3) Fall 1993 333-344.
519. Collection development as performance measurement, by Gundu Shibanda. *Library Review 43* (8) 1994 44-48.
520. The Conspectus approach to collection evaluation: panacea or false prophet? by Virgil L.P. Blake and Renee Tjoumas. *Collection Management 18* (3/4) 1994 1-31.
521. *Recruiting, educating and training librarians for collection development*, edited by Peggy Johnson and Sheila S. Intner. Westport, Conn., Greenwood Press, 1994. ISBN 0313285616 (New directions in information management, no. 33).
522. Collection development issues of academic and public libraries: converging or diverging? by Kirsti Nilsen. *Collection Building 13* (4) 1994 9-17.
523. The library collection crisis: what is to be done? by Richard Abel. *Publishing Research Quarterly 10* (2) Summer 1994 40-44.
524. *Collection management and development issues in an electronic era*, edited by Peggy Johnson and Bonnie MacEwan. Chicago, American Library Association, 1994. ISBN 0938934471 (ALCTS papers on library technical services and collections, no. 5).
525. A study of the collection inventory assessments for psychology in the Canadian Conspectus database and an analysis of the Conspectus methodology, by Daniel G. Dorner. *Library and Information Science Research 16* (4) Fall 1994 279-297.
526. Some implications of the canon debate for collection development, by Brian Quinn. *Collection Building 14* (1) 1994 1-10.

527. *Collection management and development: issues in an electronic era*, edited by Peggy Johnson and Bonnie MacEwan. Chicago, American Library Association, 1994. ISBN 0838934471.
528. The bottleneck in research communications [the decline in library collections], by Albert Henderson. *Publishing Research Quarterly 10* (4) Winter 1994/95 5-21.
529. Toward a theory of collection development, by Dennis P. Carrigan. *Library Acquisitions Practice and Theory 19* (1) Spring 1995 97-106.
530. The potential of conjoint analysis for measuring value in collection development, by Hollis T. Landrum. *Collection Management 20* (1/2) 1995 139-147.
531. Collection development in the field of communication studies, by Ann T. Power and Jeanne Pavy. *Collection Building 14* (2) 1995 9-23.
532. *Collection development policies and procedures*, 3rd edition, edited by Elizabeth A. Futas. Phoenix, Oryx Press, 1995. ISBN 0897747976.
533. What will collection developers do? by Michael Buckland. *Information Technology and Libraries 14* (3) September 1995 155-159.
534. Beyond access: new concepts, new tensions for collection development in a digital environment, by Wendy P. Lougee. *Collection Building 14* (3) 1995 19-25.
535. Mastering collection development: a continuum, by Peggy Johnson. *Technicalities 15* (10) October 1995 1, 6-9.
536. *Collection development and collection evaluation: a sourcebook*, by Michael R. Gabriel. Scarecrow Press, 1995. ISBN 0810828774.
537. Collection development strategies for a university center library, by Charlene S. Hurt, Laura O. Rein, Maureen S. Connors, John C. Walsh and Anna C. Wu. *College and Research Libraries 56* (6) November 1995 487-495.
538. *Advances in collection development and resource management, volume 1*, edited by Thomas W. Leonhardt. JAI Press, 1995. ISBN 1559382139.

539. Developing library and information center collections. Third edition, by G. Edward Evans. Littleton, Colorado, Libraries Unlimited, 1995. ISBN 1563081830.
540. *Practical issues in collection development and collection access*, edited by Katina Strauch. New York, The Haworth Press, Inc., 1995. (*Collection Management*, volume 19, no. 3/4) ISBN 1560247339.

Collection Policies
(See also 388, 719)

541. Towards demand-led book acquisitions? by A.N. Peasgood. *Journal of Librarianship 18* (4) October 1986 242-256.
542. Percentage based allocations for acquisitions: the Q formula, by D.C. Genaway. *Library Acquisitions Practice and Theory 10* (4) 1986 287-306.
543. The acquisitions allocation formula at Ohio University, by K. Mulliner. *Library Acquisitions Practice and Theory 10* (4) 1986 318-327.
544. Managing the book selection process: Derbyshire's stock assessment programme, by R. Rippingdale. *Public Library Journal 2* (3) 1987 40-46.
545. A written collection development policy: to have and have not, by M.J. Bostic. *Collection Management 10* (3) 1988 81-88.
546. Acquisitions allocations: equity, politics and formulas, by D. Packer. *Journal of Academic Librarianship 14* (5) November 1988 276-286.
547. *Guide for written collection policy statements*, edited by Bonita M. Bryant. Chicago, American Library Association, 1989. ISBN 0838933718 (Collection management and development guidelines, 3).
548. *Selection for survival: a review of acquisition and retention policies*, by Brian Enright et al. British Library, 1989. ISBN 0712302174.
549. Allocation formulas in practice, by J.M. Budd and K. Adams. *Library Acquisitions Practice and Theory 13* (4) 1989 381-390.

550. Collection development policies in medical rare book collections, by C. Hoolihan. *Collection Management 11* (3/4) 1989 167-179.

551. Acquisition and retention at the British Library, by Richard Christophers and Stephen Green. *National Acquisitions Group Newsletter* (9) July 1990 15-17.

552. Allocation formulas in the literature: a review, by J.M. Budd. *Library Acquisitions Practice and Theory 15* (1) 1991 95-107.

553. Optimality and the best collection: the goals and rules of selectors and collection managers, by R.M. Losee. *Collection Management 14* (3/4) 1991 21-30.

554. Developing special collections in the 90s: a fin-de-siecle perspective, by M.T. Ryan. *Journal of Academic Librarianship 11* (5) November 1991 288-293.

555. Collection development policies of parliamentary libraries, by E. Kohl. *IFLA Journal 17* (4) November 1991 389-394.

556. *Survival of the fittest? Collection management implications of the British Library review of acquisition and retention policies. Papers presented at a NAG seminar, Birmingham, November 1990*, edited by Clare Jenkins and Mary Morley. Loughborough, National Acquisitions Group, 1991. ISBN 1870269047.

557. *Women's studies collection development policies.* Chicago, Association of College and Research Libraries, 1992. ISBN 0838975968.

558. Reconciling pragmatism, equity and need in the formula allocation of book and serial funds. by C.B. Lowry. *College and Research Libraries. 53* (2) March 1992 121-138.

559. Needs analysis and collection development policies for culturally diverse populations, by G.E. Evans. *Collection Building 11* (4) 1992 16-27.

560. A critique of exclusion categories for translations in the acquisitions policies of major research libraries, by A.L. MaKuch. *Collection Management 15* (3/4) 1992 381-387.

561. A quantitative comparison of acquisitions budget allocation formulas using a single institutional setting, by I.R. Young.

> *Library Acquisitions Practice and Theory 16* (3) Fall 1992 229-242.

562. A collection policy for printed Welsh ephemera, by Paul Drew and Michael Dewe. *Library and Information Research News 15* (55) Winter 1992 9-11.

563. Balancing act for library materials budgets: use of a formula allocation, by Mollie Niemeyer et. al. *Technical Services Quarterly 11* (1) 1993 43-60.

564. Formula-based subject allocation: a practical approach, by Laura O. Rein et al. *Collection Management 17* (4) 1993 25-48.

565. The shrinking national collection: a study of the effects of the diversion of funds from monographs to serials on the monograph collections of research libraries, by Anna H. Perrault. *Library Acquisitions Practice and Theory 18* (1) Spring 1994 3-22.

566. Collections development policies: a cunning plan, by Peggy Johnson. *Technicalities 14* (6) June 1994 3-6.

567. Writing collection development policy statements: format, content, style, by Peggy Johnson. *Technicalities 14* (8) August 1994 4-7.

568. Writing collection development policy statements: getting started, by Peggy Johnson. *Technicalities 14* (10) October 1994 2-5.

569. More about core collections, by Sheila S. Intner. *Technicalities 14* (11) November 1994 6-10, 20.

570. Collection development policies in the information age, by Dan C. Hazen. *College and Research Libraries 56* (1) January 1995 29-31.

571. *Allocation formulas in academic libraries*, by Jane H. Tuten and Beverly Jones. Chicago, American Library Association, 1995 (CLIP note, 22).

Selection and Deselection
(See also 114, 129, 138, 227, 292, 374, 378, 799, 839)

572. Can book selection be improved? by M.B. Line. *British Journal of Academic Librarianship 1* (2) Summer 1986 160-166.

573. The process of book selection, by T. Martin. *Bookseller* (4217) 17 October 1986 1590-1595.
574. A decision theoretic model of materials selection for acquisition, by R. M. Losee. *Library Quarterly 57* (3) July 1987 269-283.
575. Deja vu all over again? Book marketing and selection update, by C. Marsh. *Library Acquisitions Practice and Theory 11* (4) 1987 347-355.
576. Improving the textbook selection process, by J. Dole, T. Rogers and J. Osborn. *Book Research Quarterly 3* (3) Fall 1987 18-36.
577. *Selection of library materials in applied and interdisciplinary fields*, edited by Beth J. Shapiro and John Whaley. Chicago, American Library Association, 1987. ISBN 0838904461.
578. Selecting British books: a guide for librarians outside Britain, by D. Spiller. *British Book News* November 1987 732-734.
579. Theoretical adequacy and the scientific study of materials selection, by R.M. Losee. *Collection Management 10* (3) 1988 15-26.
580. Mechanical selection, by C.W. Brownson. *Library Resources and Technical Services 32* (1) January 1988 17-29.
581. The politics of weeding, by H.N. Tillman. *Education Libraries 13* (1) Winter 1988 16-19.
582. Evaluating Third World national bibliographies as selection resources, by G.E. Gorman and J.J. Mills. *Library Acquisitions Practice and Theory 12* (11) 1988 29-42.
583. List-checking in collection development: an imprecise art, by A.H. Lundin. *Collection Management 11* (3/4) 1989 103-112.
584. The impact of weeding on collection development, by B. Kovacs. *Science and Technology Libraries 9* (3) Spring 1989 25-35.
585. *Weeding library collections: library weeding methods*, 3rd edition, by Stanley J. Slote. Engelwood, Co, Libraries Unlimited, 1989. ISBN 0872876660.
586. You can tell a book by its cover: an analysis of blurbs, by A.S. Eaglstein. *Aslib Proceedings 42* (1) January 1990 17-30.

587. *Selection of library materials for area studies, part I: Asia, Iberia, the Caribbean, Latin America, Eastern Europe, the Soviet Union, and the South Pacific*, edited by Cecily Johns. Chicago: American Library Association, 1990. ISBN 0838953285.

588. Beyond the stacks: book disposal and the librarian's torment, by B. Duckett. *Library Association Record 92* (6) June 1990 433-435.

589. Selection adviser: an expert system for collection development, by M. Johnston and J. Weckert. *Information Technology and Libraries 9* (3) September 1990 219-225.

590. Faculty participation in book selection in a large academic library: the case of German studies, by B.L. Walden. *Collection Management 13* (3) 1990 27-42.

591. Weeding without tears, by L. Roy. *Collection Management 12* 1990 83-94.

592. *The decision-making process for library collections: case studies in four types of libraries*, by Beatrice Kovacs. Greenwood Press, 1990. ISBN 0313260427 (Contributions on librarianship and information science, 65).

593. From binmen to bibliophiles: book disposal and the enterprise culture, by B. Duckett. *Library Association Record 92* (9) September 1990 663-667.

594. Needs-led service not acquisitions-led service in the research library, by D.L. Roberts. *Collection Building 11* (1) 1991 23-25.

595. The enemy is us [on relegation of library materials], by L. Barnett. *Collection Building 11* (3) 1991 25-27.

596. *The strange rise of semi-literate England: dissolution of the libraries*, by W.J. West. Duckworth, 1991. ISBN 0715623974.

597. *Book selection: principles and practice*; 5th edition, by David Spiller. London, Bingley, 1991. ISBN 0851574645.

598. Charmed circles not conspiracies? A personal view of academic book reviewing, by B. Morton. *British Book News* March 1991 162-163.

599. Developing selection criteria for special collections, by A. Pacey. *Canadian Library Journal 48* (3) June 1991 187-190.

600. Retention management (or how to decide what to throw out and when), by S. Garland. *Aslib Information 19* (9) September 1991 302-303.

601. The middle road: selecting contemporary German literature for medium-sized academic libraries, by B.F.H. Allen. *Collection Management 16* (1) 1992 117-135.

602. Bibliographic information and book selection: an experimental study of information load on choice behavior in a school library, by Ross J. Todd. *Library and Information Science Research. 14* (4) October-December 1992 447-464.

603. Beyond the mainstream: examining alternative sources for stock selection, by Chris Atton. *Library Review 43* (4) 1994 57-64.

604. A view from across the Pacific: the role of the academic librarian in the selection of monographs, by Barbara G. Leonard. *Australian Academic and Research Libraries 25* (1) March 1994 55-59.

605. A review of qualitative and quantitative measures in collection analysis, by P.E. Ephraim. *Electronic Library 12* (4) August 1994 237-241.

606. *Selection of library materials for area studies, part 2: Australia, Canada and New Zealand*, edited by Cecily Johns. Chicago, American Library Association, 1994. ISBN 0838906311.

607. Hands-off selection, by Cathy Aitchison. *Bookseller* (4665) 19 May 1995 22-24.

608. Favorable and unfavorable book reviews: a quantitative study, by Robert J. Greene and Charles D. Spornick. *Journal of Academic Librarianship 21* (6) November 1995 449-453.

609. *Disposal of printed material from libraries*, by Capital Planning Information. London, British Library, 1995. ISBN 0712333002 (British National Bibliography Research Fund report no.72).

Cooperation and Resource Sharing

610. *Research collections under constraint and the future coordination of academic and national library provision*. Report of

a SCONUL/BL seminar, 28 February-2 March 1986. SCO-
NUL, 1986 (BL Research-and Development report, 5907).

611. Cooperative collection development: a brief overview, by J.
Sohn. *Collection Management 8* (2) Summer 1986 1-9.

612. *Coordinating cooperative collection development: a national
perspective*, edited by Wilson Luquire. New York, The
Haworth Press, Inc., 1986. ISBN 0866565434 (*Resource
Sharing and Information Networks*, volume 2 no. 1/2).

613. Depository libraries: a look at the US scene, by M. Hill.
Information and Library Manager 7 (3) December 1987 74-75.

614. Multilis book exchange process: a 'shuttle' approach to
collection development, by N.A. Fink and R. Boivin. *Library
Hi-tech* (22) 1988 63-70.

615. National repository planning, by M.B. Line. *International
Library Review 20* (3) July 1988 309-319.

616. *Acquisition: principles, coordination, cooperation.* Graz,
LIBER, 1988 (LIBER bulletin 30).

617. Acquisitions and collection development: cooperation in a
changing environment, by T.E. Nisonger. *Library Acquisitions Practice and Theory 12* (11) 1988 73-78.

618. The new mythology: co-operative collection development,
by B. Maass. *Canadian Library Journal 46* (1) February
1989 23-29.

619. Collaborative collection development in an era of financial
limitations, by P.H. Mosher. *Australian Academic and
Research Libraries 20* (1) March 1989 1-15.

620. *Resource sharing: practices and problems*, by K.G.B. Bake-
well. Bradford, MCB University Press, 1990. ISBN
086176501X (Library Management *11* (3)).

621. Little-used duplicates, cooperative collection development,
and storage, by M.K. Buckland. *Collection Management 13*
(4) 1990 39-52.

622. *Advances in library resource sharing, volume 1 1990*, edited
by Jennifer Cargill and Diane J. Cimbala. London, Meckler,
1991. ISBN 088736490X.

623. The distributed national collection, by M. Henty. *Australian
Academic and Research Libraries 22* (4) December 1991
53-59.

624. *Handbook of library cooperation*, edited by Alan F. Mac-Dougall and Ray Prytherch. Aldershot, Gower, 1991. ISBN 0566036274.

625. The evolution of cooperative collection development in Alabama academic libraries, by S.O. Medina. *College and Research Libraries 53* (1) January 1992 7-19.

626. The resource sharing crunch: a brighter future ahead? by D.J. Graves. *Technicalities 12* (4) April 1992 7-10.

627. Cooperative promotion [on the new Scottish Book Centre], by Joanna Mattinson. *Assistant Librarian 85* (10) October 1992 156-158.

628. *The Scandia Plan: a cooperative acquisition scheme for improving access to research publications in four Nordic countries*, by Sigrun Klara Hannesdottir. Metuchen, NJ, Scarecrow, 1992. ISBN 0810825406.

629. A CARL model for cooperative collection development in a regional consortium, by Donnice Cochenour and Joel S. Rutstein. *Collection Building 12* (1-2) 1993 34-53.

630. *Access versus assets: a comprehensive guide to resource sharing for academic libararions*, by Barbra Buckner Higginbotham and Sally Bowdoin. Chicago, American Library Association, 1993. ISBN 0838906079 (Frontiers of access to library materials, no. 1).

631. Cooperative collection development at the Research Triangle University Libraries: a model for the nation, by Patricia Buck Dominguez and Luke Swindler. *College and Research Libraries 54* (6) November 1993 470-496.

632. *Cooperative collection management: the conspectus approach*, edited by Barbara McFadden Allen and Georgine N. Olson. New York, Neal-Schuman, 1994 (Collection Building, vol. 13 no. 2-3).

633. The relationship of acquisitions to resource sharing: an informal analysis, by Sheila S. Intner. *Resource Sharing and Information Networks 9* (2) 1994 61-73.

634. *Resource sharing: new technologies as a must for universal availability of publications*, edited by Ahmed H. Helal and Joachim W. Weiss. Essen, Universitatsbibliothek Essen,

1994. ISBN 3922602185 (Publications–Essen University Library, 17).

635. *Guide to cooperative collection development*, edited by Bart Harloe. Chicago, American Library Association/Association for Library Collections and Technical Services, 1994. ISBN 0838934447 (Collection management and development guides, no. 6).

636. *The Apt review: a review of library and information co-operation in the UK and the Republic of Ireland*, by the Apt Partnership. Sheffield, Library and Information Co-operation Council, 1995. ISBN 1873753063 (British Library R&D report 6212).

637. Stretching the bookfund: resource sharing, by Frances Hendrix. *Taking Stock 4* (1) May 1995 1-7.

638. Resource sharing: the CALIM experience, by Colin Harris. *Taking Stock 4* (1) May 1995 8-11.

639. The consortium as learning organization: twelve steps in collaborative collections projects, by Christy Hightower and George Soete. *Journal of Academic Librarianship 21* (2) May 1995 87-91.

640. Providing collaborative access to German political science and historical resources: a pilot project of the Association of Research Libraries, by Winston Tabb. *European Research Libraries Cooperation 5* (2) 1995 183-191.

641. *The future of resource sharing*, edited by Shirley K. Baker and Mary E. Jackson. New York, The Haworth Press, Inc., 1995. ISBN 1560247738 (*Journal of Library Administration*, vo. 21 nos. 1/2).

Access versus Ownership
(See also 686)

642. When pigs fly: or when access equals ownership, by P. Johnson. *Technicalities 12* (2) February 1992 4-7.

643. Access versus holdings policy with special reference to the University of East Anglia, by David Baker. *Interlending and Document Supply 20* (4) October 1992 131-137.

644. Collection development vs. access in academic science libraries, by Gary Wiggins. *Science and Technology Libraries 13* (1) Fall 1992 57-71.

645. Access and ownership: academic libraries' collecting and service responsibilities and the merging benefits of electronic publishing and document supply, by Michael Wooliscroft. *New Zealand Libraries 47* (9) March 1994 170-180.

646. Acquisition and access in academic libraries: the case for access, today, by Vic Elliott. *New Zealand Libraries 47* (10) June 1994 200-203.

647. Is access a viable alternative to ownership? a review of access performance, by Cheryl B. Truesdell. *Journal of Academic Librarianship 20* (4) September 1994 200-206.

648. Integrating access to formal and informal collections: what is important and what succeeds, by Suzanne S. Bell. *Journal of Academic Librarianship 21* (3) May 1995 181-186.

649. *Access, ownership and resource sharing*, edited by Sul H. Lee. New York, The Haworth Press, Inc., 1995. ISBN 1560247274 (*Journal of Library Administration*, volume 20 no.1).

Collection Management
(See also 205, 524)

650. *Systematic bookstock management*, by John Allred. British Library, 1985 (BL Research and Development Department, report 5889).

651. *Collection management for school library media centres*, edited by Brenda H. White. New York, The Haworth Press, Inc., 1988. ISBN 0866564330 (*Collection Management*, volume 7 no. 3/4).

652. The Unicorn collection management system, by J. Young. *Library Hi Tech 6* (1) 1988 61-66.

653. Librarian accountability for the collection, by M. S. Brown. *Education Libraries 13* (2/3) Spring/Fall 1988 39-40.

654. Preparation for privation: the year's work in collection management, 1987, by R. Atkinson. *Library Resources and Technical Services 32* (3) July 1988 249-262.

655. Automated collection analysis using the OCLC and RLG bibliographic databases, by N.P. Sanders, E.T. O'Neill and S.L. Weibel. *College and Research Libraries 49* (4) July 1988 305-314.

656. Measuring collections use at Virginia Tech, by P. Metz and C.A. Litchfield. *College and Research Libraries 49* (6) November 1988 501-513.

657. The application of life cycle costing in libraries, by A. Stephens. *British Journal of Academic Librarianship 3* (2) 1989 82-88.

658. *Collection management in sci-tech libraries*, edited by Ellis Mount. New York, The Haworth Press, Inc., 1989. ISBN 0866569332 (Science and Technology Libraries, volume 9 no. 3).

659. Collection analysis CD: a new approach to collection assessment, by M. Dillon and C. Mak. *Library Hi-Tech News* (65) November 1989 3-5.

660. *Collection management: background and principles*, by William A. Wortman. Chicago, American Library Association, 1989. ISBN 0838905153.

661. Books in Print Plus as a tool for analyzing US in-print monographs, by T.E. Nisonger. *Library Resources and Technical Services 24* (4) October 1990 477-491.

662. Collection management in British children's libraries: a report of five case studies, by S. Blenkin and H. Lewins. *Collection Management 13* (4) 1990 77-87.

663. Organisation theory and collection management in libraries, by M. Kanazawa. *Collection Management 14* (1/2) 1991 43-57.

664. *Collection management in academic libraries*, edited by Clare Jenkins and Mary Morley. Aldershot, Gower, 1991. ISBN 0566036355.

665. Collection management and development in libraries: some recent books. A review article, by L. Chapman. *Journal of Librarianship and Information Science 23* (4) December 1991 222-224.

666. Academic library bookstock management, by L.O. Nwali. *Library Management 13* (1) 1992 17-21.

667. Remote shelving comes of age: storage collection management at the University of Michigan, by Wendy P. Lougee. *Collection Management 16* (2) 1992 93-107.
668. *Access services in libraries: new solutions for collections management*, edited by Gregg Sapp. New York, The Haworth Press, Inc., 1992 (*Collection Management*, vol.17 No.1-2).
669. Age profile of polytechnic bookstocks, by D. Revill. *COPOL Newsletter* (57) January 1992 44-46.
670. Collection maintenance 101: or, how many librarians can you fit into a VW? by William C. Divens. *Collection Management 17* (3) 1993 7-11.
671. Talking at last: developing the potential of library management information, by Frank Edwards. *British Book News* June 1993 372-373.
672. *Collection management for the 1990s*, edited by Joseph J. Branin. Chicago, American Library Association, 1993 (ALCTS papers on library technical services and collections, no. 3).
673. Empirical analysis of literature loss, by Charles A. Schwartz. *Library Resources and Technical Services 38* (2) April 1994 133-138.
674. Collection management in Australian academic libraries: an American perspective, by Barbara G. Leonard. *Library Acquisitions Practice and Theory 18* (2) Summer 1994 147-156.
675. Education for collection management: results of a survey of educators and practitioners, by John M. Budd and Patricia L. Bril. *Library Resources and Technical Services 38* (4) October 1994 343-353.
676. The management and use of reserve and special collections in public libraries: a study of the East Midlands, by John Feather, Graham Matthews and Carolyn Pritchett. *Journal of Librarianship and Information Science 27* (2) June 1995 89-97.
677. Book deterioration and loss: magnitude and characteristics in Ohio libraries, by Edward T. O'Neill and Wesley L. Boom-

gaarden. *Library Resources and Technical Services 39* (4) October 1995 394-408.

Physical Processing

678. *The shape of things to come? The standardisation of the servicing requirements of public libraries,* by Capital Planning Information. London, British National Bibliography Research Fund. 1990. ISBN 0712332502 (BNBRF Report, 50).
679. *The role of rebinding in modern stock management,* by Alan Watkin. Clwyd County Library, 1992. ISBN 0900121440.
680. *Guide to preservation in acquisition processing,* by Marsha J. Hamilton. Chicago, American Library Association, 1993. ISBN 0838906117 (Acquisition guidelines, no. 8).
681. *The standard for book servicing.* Leeds, National Acquisitions Group, 1993. ISBN 1870269071.
682. *A library manager's guide to the physical processing of nonprint materials,* by Karen C. Driessen and Sheila A. Smyth. Westport, Conn, Greenwood Press, 1995. ISBN 0313279306.

Collection Evaluation
(See also 179, 355, 536, 751)

683. *Collection assessment manual for college and university libraries,* by Blaine H. Hall. Oryx, 1986. ISBN 08977414SX.
684. *New acquisitions, loan strategies, and library use: an assessment using SWALCAP management information,* by Philip Payne. London, City of London Polytechnic, 1986 (Library research digest, 18).
685. Acquisitions and interlibrary loans: a correlation? by B. Burch and A. Davies. *Interlending and Document Supply 15* (3) 1987 84-87.
686. Interlibrary lending and collection development: costs and fees, by G. Kuske. *LIBER Bulletin* (34) 1989 76-77.
687. A use statistic for collection management: the 80-20 rule revisited, by W.A. Britten. *Library Acquisitions Practice and Theory 14* (2) 1990 183-189.
688. Do the books we buy get used? by A.H. Miller. *Collection Management 12* 1990 15-20.

689. Using a turnkey automated system to support collection assessment, by R.K. Baker. *College and Research Libraries 51* (4) July 1990 360-366.
690. Book availability as a performance measure of a library: an analysis of the effectiveness of a health sciences library, by H.F. Rashid. *Journal–American Society for Information Science 41* (7) October 1990 501-507.
691. *Book delivery: a survey: a study carried out with the co-operation of members of the National Acquisitions Group,* by Catherine Cope. Loughborough, LISU, 1990. ISBN 0948848294 (LISU occasional paper, 2).
692. *Evaluating acquisitions and collection management,* edited by Pamela S. Cenzer and Cynthia I. Gozzi. New York, The Haworth Press, Inc., 1991. ISBN 1560241608.
693. Collection evaluation workshops project: consultants' report, by N. Powell and M. Bushing. *New Zealand Libraries 46* (11) September 1991 9-12.
694. The value of evaluation, by Peggy Johnson. *Technicalities 12* (10) October 1992 4-7.
695. Evaluation of the collections of Saudi university libraries based on the ACRL standards, by M. Saleh Ashoor. *International Information and Library Review 24* (1) March 1992 3-14.
696. *Collection evaluation in academic libraries: a literature guide and annotated bibliography,* by Thomas E. Nisonger. Engelwood, Colorado, Libraries Unlimited, 1992. ISBN 0872879259.
697. Comparing characteristics of highly circulated titles for demand-driven collection development, by W.A. Britten and J.D. Webster. *College and Research Libraries 53* (3) May 1992 239-248.
698. A review of some modelling approaches to the loan and duplication of academic texts, by J.P. Warwick. *Journal of Librarianship and Information Science 24* (4) December 1992 187-194.
699. *Availability and value of library management information: a feasibility study.* Book Industry Communication/National

Acquisitions Group, 1992. ISBN 0873671059 (BNB Research Fund report, 61).

700. Meeting modern demands of collection evaluation: a new approach, by Sushella N. Rao. *Collection Building 13* (1) 1993 33-36.

701. *Collection assessment and acquisitions budgets*, edited by Sul H. Lee. New York, The Haworth Press, Inc., 1993. ISBN 1560243902 (*Journal of Library Administration*, Volume 17, no. 2).

702. Obsolescence and stress: a study of the use of books on open shelves at a university library, by Karin de Jager. *Journal of Librarianship and Information Science 26* (2) June 1994 71-82.

703. Comprehensive materials availability studies in academic libraries, by Abdus Sattar Chaudhry and M. Saleh Ashoor. *Journal of Academic Librarianship 20* (5/6) November 1994 300-305.

704. Use of monograph bookstock in the University of Sussex Library for teaching and/or research: an analysis based on loan records 1981-1991, by J.M. Pendlebury, A.N. Peasgood and R.C. Young. *British Journal of Academic Librarianship 9* (1-2) 1994 127-143.

705. *Collection assessment in music libraries*, edited by Jane Gottlieb. Music Library Association, 1994 (MLA technical report 22).

706. Collection evaluation and academic review: a pilot study using the OCLC/AMIGOS Collection Analysis CD, by Anne C. Ciliberti. *Library Acquisitions Practice and Theory 18* (4) Winter 1994 431-445.

707. Time series circulation data for collection development, or: you can't intuit that, by Chuck Hamaker. *Library Acquisitions Practice and Theory 19* (2) Summer 1995 191-195.

708. Measuring book availability in an academic library: a methodological comparison, by N.A. Jacobs and R.C. Young. *Journal of Documentation 51* (3) September 1995 281-290.

709. Towards the active collection: the use of circulation analyses in collection evaluation, by Mike Day and Don Revill. *Jour-*

nal of Librarianship and Information Science 27 (3) September 1995 149-157.

710. *The use of management data in public and academic libraries: four case studies*, by Chambers & Stoll. London, Book Industry Communication, 1995. ISBN 1873671083 (British National Bibliography Research Fund, report 73).

711. The evaluation and improvement of book availability in an academic library, by N.A. Jacobs. *New Review of Academic Librarianship 1* 1995 41-55.

712. *Brief tests of collection strength: a methodology for all types of libraries*, by Howard D. White. Greenwood Press, 1995. ISBN 0313297533 (Contributions in Librarianship and Information Science, 88).

713. Surveying collections: the importance of condition assessment for preservation management, by Graham Matthews. *Journal of Librarianship and Information Science 27* (4) December 1995 227-236.

714. Interlibrary loans and collection failure at La Trobe University Library: report on a research project, by John Horacek and Julie Marshall. *Australian Academic and Research Libraries 26* (4) December 1995 248-259.

AREAS OF SPECIAL INTEREST

Academic Libraries and Scholarly Communication
(See also 306, 309, 312, 318, 322, 324, 326, 332, 335, 336, 341, 349, 357, 368, 486, 528, 537, 594, 601, 610, 664, 813, 821)

715. *Book selection and use in academic libraries*, by Marilyn Hart et al. Loughborough University, Centre for Library and Information Management, 1986. ISBN 0904024718 (CLAIM report no 45).

716. *Book buying in colleges of further education; report of a survey amongst lecturers*, by Bill McClelland. London, Publishers Association, 1986. ISBN 0853861250.

717. Academic libraries in contraction: facts, theories and fancies, by G. MacKenzie. *Aslib Proceedings 38* (9) September 1986 317-325.

718. Collection development in academic libraries: science, art and magic, by P. Metz. *Libraries and Computing Centers* (4) September 1987 3-4 [in *Journal of Academic Librarianship* 13 (4) September 1987].

719. Atkinson revisited? Limiting the growth of West German University libraries, by H. Schnelling. *Outlook on Research Libraries 9* (9) September 1987 6-9.

720. *Research collections under constraint: the effect on researchers*, by Keith Pocklington and Helen Finch of Social and Community Planning Research. British Library, 1987. ISBN 0712331549 (British Library Research Paper no. 36).

721. Trouble at the OK Corrall University Library, by H.S. White. *Library Journal 112* (14) September 1987 154-155.

722. Using the syllabus in collection development, by R.N. Anderson. *Technicalities 8* (1) January 1988 14-15.

723. Effective collection developers: librarians or faculty? by D.L. Vidor and E. Futas. *Library Resources and Technical Services 32* (2) April 1988 127-136.

724. British university libraries 1977-1987: some observations on the challenges of declining resources, by E.M. Rodger. *Journal of Documentation 44* (4) December 1988 346-378.

725. University libraries: a closed book? by P.H. Mann. *Library Association Record 91* (2) February 1989 96.

726. Acquisition of documents in academic libraries, by S.C. Shunmuganathan and J.P.S. Kumaravel. *International Library Review 21* (2) April 1989 241-244.

727. The precarious state of academic science library collections, by P.B. Yocum. *Science and Technology Libraries 9* (3) Spring 1989 37-46.

728. *The ACLS Survey of Scholars: views on publications, computers, libraries*, by Herbert C. Morton and Anne Jamieson Price. American Council of Learned Societies, 1989. ISBN 081917260X.

729. University and polytechnic library expenditure on law materials, 1988/89, by W. Hines. *Law Librarian 21* (1) April 1990 38-39.

730. Changing patterns of scholarly communication: implications for libraries, by M. Glicksman. *Library Acquisitions Practice and Theory 14* (4) 1990 341-346.
731. Changing patterns of scholarly communication and the need to expand the library's role and services, by R.C.W. Brown. *Library Acquisitions Practice and Theory 14* (4) 1990 371-377.
732. Collection growth and expenditures in academic libraries: a preliminary enquiry, by R.H. Werking. *College and Research Libraries 52* (1) January 1991 80-91.
733. Back to academia? The case for American universities to publish their own research, by A. Okerson. *Logos 2* (2) 1991 106-112.
734. *Research libraries in transition*, by Bob Erens. London, The British Library, 1991. ISBN 0712332472 (Library and Information Research Report, 82).
735. Academic libraries and university presses, by J.M. Budd. *Publishing Research Quarterly 7* (2) Summer 1991 27-37.
736. *Collection development in college libraries*, edited by J. S. Hiel, W.E. Hannaford and R.H. Epp. Chicago, American Library Association, 1991. ISBN 0838905595.
737. Changing patterns of faculty participation in collection development, by Margaret R. Dittemore. *Collection Management 16* (4) 1992 79-89.
738. Scholarly publication, academic libraries and the assumption that these processes are really under management control, by Herbert White. *College and Research Libraries 54* (4) July 1993 293-301.
739. *The future of Latin American research collections in the United Kingdom*, edited by Pat Noble and Ann Wade. London, SCONUL, 1993. ISBN 0901145831.
740. Searching for the Holy Grail: a core collection for undergraduate libraries, by Larry Hardesty and Collette Mak. *Journal of Academic Librarianship 19* (6) January 1994 362-371.
741. Academic libraries in continuing decline, by John Sumsion. *Bookseller* (4608) 15 April 1994 18-21.

742. *Survey of resources and users in higher education libraries: UK 1993*, by John Sumsion. Loughborough, LISU, 1994. ISBN 0948848596 (LISU occasional paper, no. 6).

743. A research agenda for libraries, by Frederick C. Lynden. *Publishing Research Quarterly 10* (3) Fall 1994 36-50.

744. Collaboration in a loosely coupled system: librarian-faculty relations in collection development, by Felix T. Chu. *Library and Information Science Research 17* (2) Spring 1995 135-150.

745. Academic partnership: a future for special collections, by Stanley A. Chodorow and Lynda Corey Claasen. *Journal of Library Administration 20* (3/4) 1995 141-148.

746. 'In the beginning was the word . . .': social and economic factors in scholarly electronic communication, by Tom Wilson. *Aslib Proceedings 47* (9) September 1995 195-202.

747. *Filling the pipeline and paying the piper.* Proceedings of the fourth symposium on scholarly publishing on the electronic networks, edited by Ann Okerson. Washington, DC, Association of Research Libraries, 1995. ISBN 0918006251.

748. From books to bytes: the user at the centre of the scientific information centre, by Anthony Pearce. *Learned Publishing 8* (4) October 1995 203-208.

Public Libraries
(See also 7, 151, 307, 317, 325, 338, 350, 380, 396, 417, 676, 762, 771, 792, 823)

749. *Trends in public library selection policies*, by Capital Planning Information. London, BNB Research Fund, 1987. ISBN 0712331166 (BNB Research Fund report, 29).

750. Effects of an English-only law on public library acquisition policies, practices, and librarians' attitudes toward books in Spanish for children and young adults, by G.V. Glass and I. Shon. *Library and Information Science Research 10* (4) 1988 411-424.

751. Bookfunds and book issues in public libraries, by C. Cope and P.H. Mann. *Library Association Record 92* (6) June 1990 436-439.

752. *Developing public library collections, policies and proce-dures*, by Kay Ann Cassel and Elizabeth Futas. New York, Neal-Schuman, 1991. ISBN 1555700608 (How-to-do-it manual for librarians, 12).
753. Collections for the emerging majority, by K. Scarborough. *Library Journal 116* (11) 15 June 1991 44-47.
754. *Public libraries and their bookfunds*, by the National Book Committee. National Book Committee, 1992. ISBN 0853534454.
755. Public libraries: back on the downward path, by John Sumsion. *Bookseller* (4604) March 1994 26-30.
756. *The Seals project: selection, acquisition and loan systems for European language fiction in West Midlands public libraries*, by Geoffrey Warren. Birmingham, West Midlands Regional Library System, 1994. ISBN 0952123916.

School and Special Libraries
(See also 64, 90, 127, 187, 397, 507, 550, 554, 555, 599, 662, 690, 705, 851)

757. *Book buying in commercial and industrial libraries.* Publishers Association, University College and Professional Publishers Council, 1985. ISBN 0853860971.
758. *Class book selection: the teacher's guide*, by Alison Leaks. University of London Institute of Education, 1987. ISBN 0900008253 (Education Libraries Bulletin, Supplement no. 24).
759. Acquisitions problems in school libraries: the Kenyan situation, by J. N. Otike. *International Review of Children's Literature and Librarianship 2* (3) Winter 1987 181-190.
760. Selection tools for school libraries, by J.T. Gillespie. *Catholic Library World 59* (6) May/June 1988 269-270.
761. *Materials selection for the school library of the future*, by Audrey W. Hall. Liverpool Polytechnic School of Information Science and Technology, 1989. ISBN 0901537217 (Occasional paper, 7).
762. *Book acquisition and use by young people: a review of recent research initiatives*, by Margaret Kinnell, Helen Pain-Lewis and Janet Stevenson. Boston Spa, British Library, 1989. ISBN 0712331832 (BNB Research Fund report, 39).

763. Resourcing GCSE: a new approach, by N. Harwood. *Library Association Record 91* (6) June 1989 338-339.
764. In practice: selecting information books in primary school, by K. Barker. *School Librarian 37* (4) November 1989 136.
765. Books special [10 short articles], edited by R. Hyman. *Aslib Information 18* (7/8) July/August 1990 235-252.
766. *Books in schools.* London, Book Trust, 1992. ISBN 0853534446 (British National Bibliography Research Fund report 60; Book Trust report 1).
767. Children's libraries: the expertise squeeze, by Hilary Macaskill. *Bookseller* (4627) 26 August 1994 26-31.
768. The teacher as buyer, by Hilary Macaskill. *Bookseller* (4668) 9 June 1995 30, 35-36.
769. *Survey of acquisitions in special libraries*, by Chambers & Stoll. London, Council of Academic and Professional Publishers, 1995. ISBN 0853862389 (British National Bibliography Research Fund report no. 71).
770. Catch 'em young: marketing and promoting books to children, by Trish Botten. *Taking Stock 4* (2) November 1995 25-28.

Special Materials
(See also 451, 557, 560, 562, 682, 729, 745, 833)

771. *Going soft: some uses of paperbacks in libraries*, by Barry Cropper. St Albans, Library Association Branch and Mobile Libraries Group, 1986. ISBN 0 946461 05 8 (Occasional paper, 12).
772. *Access to ethnic minority materials*, by Pirkko Elliott. Polytechnic of North London, 1986. ISBN 0 946232 27 X (British National Bibliography Research Fund report, 19; Polytechnic of North London School of Librarianship and Information Studies Research Report, 15).
773. Acquisition of French language monographic materials, by W.F. Coscarelli and P.P. Charalon. *Collection Management 8* (11) Spring 1986 45-53.
774. Acquisition of multilingual materials, by M. Zielinska. *Library Acquisitions Practice and Theory 10* (4) 1986 255-260.

775. The life expectancy of paperback books in academic libraries, by R.L. Presley. *Technical Services Quarterly 4* (3) Spring 1987 21-31.

776. Starting a collection of artists books from the USA, by S. Bury. *American Studies Library Newsletter* (25) September 1987 3-6.

777. Hard selling in soft covers, by P. Miller. *Times Literary Supplement* (4433) 18-24 March 1988 313.

778. What the eye doesn't see, the market should grieve over [on large print books], by P. Webb. *Bookseller* (4293) 1 April 1988 1380-1381.

779. Nonprint media selection guidelines, by C. Caywood. *Journal of Youth Services in Libraries 2* (1) Fall 1988 90-94.

780. Dissertations: a need for new approaches to acquisition, by M.D. Lopez. *Journal of Academic Librarianship 14* (5) November 1988 297-301.

781. The national collection of audiovisual materials: some problems and practices, by C.F. Pinion. *IFLA Journal 15* (2) 1989 112-117.

782. "Grau, teurer Freund, ist alle Theorie": the acquisition of exhibition catalogues, by T. Lersch. *Art Libraries Journal 14* (1) 1989 30-37.

783. A local approach to national collecting: a UK feasibility study for the co-operative collection of exhibition catalogues, by B. Houghton and G. Varley. *Art Libraries Journal 14* (1) 1989 38-43.

784. Promoting the paperback, by David Lindley. *National Acquisitions Group Newsletter* (7) July 1989 30-34.

785. Collection development in British legal materials, by A. Noel-Todd. *Law Library Journal 81* (4) Fall 1989 723-731.

786. Collection development, selection and acquisition of agricultural materials, by N.J. Elder, B. Hobrock, D.L. Madsen and W.H. Wiese. *Library Trends 38* (3) Winter 1990 442-473.

787. Universal availability of non-book materials in Australia, by P.T. McNally. *IFLA Journal 18* (3) August 1992 200-211.

788. *Non-standard collection management*, edited by Michael Pearce. Ashgate, 1992. ISBN 1857420209.

789. The collection of printed ephemera in Australia at national, state and local levels, by Michael Dewe and Paul Drew. *International Information and Library Review 25* (2) June 1993 123-140.

790. The evaluation, selection and acquisition of legal looseleaf publications, by Michael J. Petit. *Library Acquisitions Practice and Theory 17* (4) 1993 417-426.

791. *Multicultural acquisitions*, edited by Karen Parrish. New York, The Haworth Press, Inc., 1993. (*Acquisitions Librarian*, vol. 9/10) ISBN 1560244518.

792. Cowboys, horror, romance and crime: genre fiction–the case for the defence, by Susan Moody et al. *Taking Stock 3* (1) May 1994 27-35.

793. *AV in public and school libraries: selection and policy issues*, edited by Margaret J. Hughes. New York, The Haworth Press, Inc., 1994 (*Acquisitions Librarian*, no. 11).

794. Nga taonga tuku iho kei roto i nga whare matauranga o Aotearoa: collection management in the field of traditional Maori knowledge, by Robert Sullivan. *New Zealand Libraries 48* (4) March 1995 5-10.

795. Europe: a novel experience; fiction from France, Germany, Italy and Spain, by Geoff Warren. *Taking Stock 4* (1) May 1995 12-15.

796. Problems in obtaining grey literature, by M.C. Debachere. *IFLA Journal 21* (2) May 1995 94-98.

797. *Video acquisitions and cataloguing: a handbook*, by James C. Scholtz. Greenwood Press, 1995. ISBN 0313293457.

798. GIS [Geographic Information Systems] collection development, staffing and training, by Karl Longstreth. *Journal of Academic Librarianship 21* (4) July 1995 267-274.

799. Selection and audiovisual collections, by Helen P. Harrison. *IFLA Journal 21* (3) August 1995 185-190.

Electronic Publications
(See also 351, 414, 436, 524, 746, 747)

800. Academic librarians and publishers: customers v producers, or partners in the planning of electronic publishing? by K. Hunter. *Journal of Library Administration 9* (4) 1988 35-47.

801. Acquiring software for the academic library: new horizons for acquisitions, by J.L. Ogburn and K.N. Fisher. *Collection Management 13* (3) 1990 69-84.
802. Legal deposit and electronic publishing: results of a survey, by P. McCormick and M. Williamson. *Alexandria 2* (3) December 1990 51-63.
803. Resolving the acquisitions dilemma: into the electronic information environment, by E. Smith. *College and Research Libraries 52* (2) May 1991 231-240.
804. Redefining the textbook: the impact of electronic custom publishing, by J.L. Dionne. *Logos 2* (4) 1991 190-194.
805. Between the visionaries and the Luddites: collection development and electronic resources in the humanities, by Edward Shreeves. *Library Trends 40* (4) Spring 1992 579-595.
806. Electronic book and serial acquisitions: the medium is the message, by Norman Desmarias. *Computers in Libraries 13* (1) January 1993 25-27.
807. Resources for collection development and electronic media, by Peggy Johnson. *Technicalities 13* (2) February 1993 4-6.
808. Rave new world: librarians and electronic acquisitions, by Meta Nissley. *Library Acquisitions Practice and Theory 17* (2) Summer 1993 165-173.
809. Electronic information and acquisitions, by Richard Heseltine. *Taking Stock 2* (2) November 1993 1-6.
810. *Taming the electronic jungle: electronic information–the collection management issues*, edited by Mary Morley and Hazel Woodward. Leeds, National Acquisitions Group, 1993. ISBN 1870269101.
811. *The impact of electronic products on collection development.-a survey of academic, public and high school libraries.* New York, Association of American Publishers, 1994.
812. *Selection and evaluation of electronic resources*, by Gail K. Dickinson. Engelwood, Col., Libraries Unlimited, 1994. ISBN 1563080982.

813. From smart guesser to smart navigator: changes in collection development for research libraries in a network environment, by Yuan Zhou. *Library Trends 42* (4) Spring 1994 648-660.

814. Collection development for the electronic library: a conceptual and organizational model, by Samuel Demas. *Library Hi Tech 12* (3) 1994 71-80.

815. *Digital books? on-demand printing and publishing*, by John Akeroyd. London, South Bank University Library, Information Technology Centre, 1994.

816. Issues and experiments in electronic publishing and dissemination, by Karen Hunter. *Information Technology and Libraries 13* (2) June 1994 127-132.

817. The volatility of electronic collection development, or the care and feeding of a gopher, by Pat Ensor. *Technicalities 14* (7) July 1994 10-12.

818. New technology and publishing: six case studies in search of a theory, by Caroline Beebe, Emily Nedell, Min Song, Jeanne Sullivan, Kara Ovefelt, Jenny Schatz and Elisabeth Davenport. *Aslib Proceedings 46* (9) September 1994 217-224.

819. *Endangered species?: evolving strategies for library collection management*, edited by Hazel Woodward and Mary Morley. Leeds, National Acquisitions Group, 1995. ISBN 1870269144.

820. Electronic books '95, by Peter Stubley. *Information Management Report* May 1995 17-19.

821. *Networked scholarly publishing*, edited by F.W. Lancaster. Champaign, University of Illinois, 1995 (Library Trends vol. 43 part 4).

822. The future of electronic publishing for book publishers within Britain, by Ricky Leaver. *Aslib Proceedings 47* (7/8) July/August 1995 163-174.

823. *Public library expenditure on electronic publications in 1992-1993*, by Harry East. London, British Library, 1995 (British National Bibliography Research Fund report 76).

824. The Internet and collection development: mainstreaming selection of Internet resources, by Samuel Demas, Peter McDonald and Gregory Lawrence. *Library Resources and Technical Services 39* (3) July 1995 275-290.

CD-ROM

825. CD collection development, by B. Connolly. *Library Journal 114* (9) 15 May 1989 36-42.
826. *The multimedia library: materials selection and use,* by James Cabeceiras. Orlando, Academic Press, 1991. ISBN 0121539539.
827. Small miracle poses pricing conundrum for publishers and librarians [on networking CD-ROMs], by D. Whitaker. *Logos 3* (3) 1992 159-162.
828. Powering up for the new millennium: collection development uses of CD-ROM, by Sheila S. Intner. *Technicalities 13* (1) January 1993 2-5.
829. Acquisitions of CD ROM databases for local area networks, by Trisha L. Davis. *Journal of Academic Librarianship 19* (2) 1993 68-71.
830. *Guide to selecting and acquiring CD-ROMs, software and other electronic publications,* by Stephen Bosch, Patricia Promis and Chris Sugnet. Chicago, American Library Association, 1994. ISBN 083890629X (Acquisition guidelines, 9).
831. CD-ROM and CD; collection development issues for bibliographic databases on CD-ROM, by J.E. Rowley and R.R. Butcher. *Taking Stock 3* (1) May 1994 22-25.

Developing Countries
(See also 48, 60, 297, 367, 582, 587, 759)

832. Acquisitions from Africa: the role of SCOLMA. *Assignation 5* (2) January 1988 27-28.
833. Acquiring unpublished population documents in Africa: a personal experience, by K.O. Kwafo-Akoto. *Aslib Proceedings 40* (4) April 1988 105-110.
834. Securing Asian and African materials for library collections, by B.J. Henn. *Technical Services Quarterly 5* (4) 1988 41-48.
835. Acquisition of scientific literature in developing countries: 1. Bangladesh, by Abu Bakr Siddique. *Information Development 5* (1) January 1989 15-22.

836. Acquiring publications from the Pacific, by J.E. Traue. *New Zealand Libraries 46* (1) March 1989 3-4.
837. Publishing trends in the Spanish speaking world, by J.M. Azaola. *International Information, Communication and Education 8* (1) March 1989 75-78.
838. Acquisition of scientific literature in developing countries: Malaysia, Pakistan, Zambia, Arab Gulf countries, by R. Taib, J.J. Haider, M.C. Lundu and S.N. Ali. *Information Development 5* (2) April 1989 73-114.
839. African national bibliographies as selection sources, by G.E. Gorman. *International Library Review 21* (4) October 1989 495-508.
840. The book trade in Latin America at the end of the Age of Enlightenment, by P. Weldhaas. *Logos 1* (1) 1990 28-33.
841. Book publishing in Indonesia: issues affecting acquisitions and collections management, by G. Miller. *Library Acquisitions Practice and Theory 14* (1) 1990 61-71.
842. The acquisition of books in austere times: the Ondo State University Library experience, by W.A. Akinfolarin. *Library Review 39* (1) 1990 36-40.
843. *Collection development in African university libraries: challenges and frustrations*, by Sam E. Ifidon. Bloomington, Indiana University African Studies Program, 1990 (Monographs on African Librarianship, 1).
844. Book production and publishing in Nigeria, by J.I. Iwe. *Aslib Proceedings 42* (6) June 1990 189-197.
845. Publishing and the book trade in sub-Saharan Africa: trends and issues and their implications for American libraries, by P.B. Bischof. *Journal of Academic Librarianship 16* (6) January 1991 340-347.
846. Collections development in academic libraries: the case of Nigerian university libraries, by O.M. Okoro. *International Library Review 23* (2) June 1991 121-134.
847. Book publishing in Nigeria: problems and prospects. by L.O. Nwali. *Publishing Research Quarterly 7* (4) Winter 1991-92 65-70.

848. Acquisitions of library materials in Nigeria's university libraries: problems and prospects, by Abimola Akifarin. *Taking Stock 1* (1) May 1992 12-16.

849. Scarcity of tertiary books in Nigeria: a threat to academic excellence and suggestions for action, by A.D. Dike. *Journal of Librarianship and Information Science 24* (2) June 1992 79-85.

850. The effects of austerity on collection development in Nigerian university libraries with particular reference to Usmanu Danfodiyo University Library, Sokoto, by I.I. Ekoja. *International Information and Library Review 24* June 1992 173-187.

851. Book scarcity, law libraries and the legal profession in Nigeria, by Oluremi Jegede. *International Information and Library Review 24* (3) September 1992 229-251.

852. The effect of government policies on the acquisition of library resources in Nigeria, by D.I. Akobo. *Library Acquisitions Practice and Theory 16* (3) Fall 1992 313-320.

853. Library acquisitions and economic recovery in West Africa, by Marcel C. Obiagwu. *Collection Building 12* (1/2) 1993 60-67.

854. *Bibliography on publishing and book development in the Third World*, by Philip G. Altbach and Hyaewool Choi. Norwood, N.J., Ablex, 1993. ISBN 1567500846 (Bellagio studies in publishing, no. 3)

855. Perspectives on publishing in Africa, by Philip G. Altbach. *Publishing Research Quarterly 9* (1) Spring 1993 44-62.

856. The Nigerian book shortage: its implications for education and national development, by S.A. Ogunrombi and Gboyega Adio. *Library Review 42* (6) 1993 38-46.

857. Challenges and frustrations of an acquisitions librarian in a developing country: the case of Balme Library, by Gifty Boakye. *Taking Stock 3* (1) May 1994 26-31.

858. Focus on some unprofessional aspects of the book trade in Nigeria, by W.A. Akinfolarin. *Taking Stock 3* (1) May 1994 16-18.

859. Acquiring official publications from developing countries: a South Pacific perspective, by Stephen Innes. *Australian Academic and Research Libraries 25* (2) June 1994 89-94.

860. *Report on the project to assess the acquisitions needs of university libraries in developing countries*, by G.G. Allen and P. Katris. Odense, Denmark, Odense University Library/IFLA, 1994.
861. The academic libraries of developing countries: towards effective book provision in the face of austerity, by Gifty Boakye. *New Library World 95* (1116) 1994 12-17.
862. Indigenous publishing, 1981-1992: an IFLA pilot project, by Anne M. Galler. *IFLA Journal 20* (4) November 1994 419-427.
863. A librarian looks at the reality and the dream of book supply in Nigeria, by Ken M.C. Nweke. *Logos 6* (1) 1995 33-37.
864. Filling bare shelves [in African libraries], by Carolyn Sharples. *Library Association Record 97* (2) February 1995 96-97.
865. Collecting, publicizing and providing access to socio-economic grey literature in Southern Africa with particular reference to Botswana, by Kate Kwafo-Akoto. *Interlending and Document Supply 23* (2) 1995 10-16.
866. Supply of books from the Indian sub-continent, by Monti Bhatia. *Taking Stock 4* (1) May 1995 16-18.
867. Collection development: the experience of Kenya Polytechnic Library, by Cephas Odini. *Collection Building 14* (4) 1995 24-28.
868. Social science scholarly publishing in Africa: the CODESRIA experience, by Tade Akin Aina. *Focus on International and Comparative Librarianship 26* (2) September 1995 72-78.
869. The book chain: African Books Collective and UK book buyers, by Mary Jay. *Focus on International and Comparative Librarianship 26* (2) September 1995 90-94.
870. The book industry in Uganda during the post-Independence period (1962-1988), by J.R. Ikoja-Odongo. *Focus on International and Comparative Librarianship 26* (2) September 1995 94-108.
871. Publishing in Papua New Guinea: the National Library of Australia acquisitions trip, 1994, by Erica Ryan. *Australian*

Academic and Research Libraries 26 (3) September 1995 157-162.

872. Contemporary issues in collection development programmes of Nigerian university libraries, by Ahmed Abdu Balarabe. *International Information and Library Review 27* (4) December 1995 333-343.

873. Financing reduction of information poverty in Nigerian university libraries: a study of the IMF and World Bank credit facility, by Olu Olat Lawal. *International Information and Library Review 27* (4) December 1995 345-357.

874. Acquisition in times of financial stringency: the case study of UST Library, Kumasi, Ghana, by R.F. Creppy. *International Information and Library Review 27* (4) December 1995 375-381.

875. Collection development at the University of Agriculture Library, Abeokuta, Nigeria, by I.A. Sowole. *International Information and Library Review 27* (4) December 1995 383-391.

Library Technical Services

876. Technical services in 1984 and 1985: resources, by M. Pankake. *Library Resources and Technical Services 30* (3) July/ September 1986 218-236.

877. *Library management and technical services: the changing role of technical services in library organizations,* edited by Jennifer Cargill. New York, The Haworth Press, Inc., 1988. ISBN 0866567798 (*Journal of Library Administration,* volume 9 no. 1).

878. *Technical services today and tomorrow,* by Michael Gorman et al. Engelwood, Co, Libraries Unlimited, 1989. ISBN 087287608X.

879. *Managing technical services in the 90s,* edited by Drew Racine. New York, The Haworth Press, Inc., 1991. ISBN 1560241667 (*Journal of Library Administration* volume 15 no. 1/2).

880. *Library technical services: operations and management.* 2nd edition, by Irene P. Godden. Orlando, Academic Press, 1991. ISBN 0122870417.

881. *Technical services in libraries: systems and applications*, edited by Thomas W. Leonhardt. Greenwich, CT, JAI Press, 1992. ISBN 1559382147 (Foundations of library and information science, 25).
882. *Guide to technical services resources*, edited by Peggy Johnson. Chicago, American Library Association. 1994. ISBN 0838906249.
883. *Introduction to technical services*, 6th edition, by G. Edward Evans and Sandra M. Heft. Englewood Colorado, Libraries Unlimited, 1994. ISBN 0872879399.
884. *Technical services management 1965-1990*, edited by Linda C. Smith and Ruth C. Carter. New York, The Haworth Press, Inc., 1995. ISBN 1560249609.

Ethics

885. That's not censorship, that's selection!, by K. Atkins. *Assistant Librarian 18* (7) July 1988 102-105.
886. Libraries for all? Riposte [on selection vs censorship], by M. Atkins. *Library Association Record 90* (10) October 1988 573.
887. Impact of collection management practices on intellectual freedom, by C.B. Osborn. *Library Trends 39* (1/2) 1990 168-182.
888. *Legal and ethical issues in acquisitions*, edited by Katina Strauch and Bruce Strauch. New York, The Haworth Press, Inc., 1991. ISBN 1560240075 (*Acquisitions librarian*, 3).
889. Positive action in stock selection, by David Gunn. *Taking Stock 1* (2) November 1992 1-5.
890. A broken heart? by John Vincent. [On censorship in stock control] *Assistant Librarian 86* (7) July 1993 98-99.
891. *The code of conduct for the acquisition and supply of library materials: good practice for librarians and suppliers*. Leeds, National Acquisitions Group, 1993. ISBN 187026911X.
892. Ethical considerations in decision making, by Peggy Johnson. *Technicalities 14* (2) December 1994 24.
893. Ethics and good business practices: case studies, by Mary Devlin and Meta Nissley. *Library Acquisitions Practice and Theory 19* (1) Spring 1995 59-62.

AUTHOR INDEX

Chapter Eight:
Ownership or Access
to Electronic Information–
A Selective Bibliography

Maureen Pastine

Abel, Richard. "The Origin of the Library Approval Plan," *Publishing Research Quarterly.* 11 (1) (Spring 1995): 46-56.

Ackerman, Katherine. "An Update on Electronic Information Sources," *American Libraries.* 18 (No. 5, May 1987): 378, 380, 382-383.

"Aqueduct Action Agenda," February 7-9, 1991, Chapel Hill, North Carolina. Report–*Libadm Listserv.* (April 6, 1992).

Adalian, Paul T., Jr. and Ilene F. Rockman. "Title-by-Title Review in Reference Collection Development," *Reference Services Review.* 12 (4) (Winter 1984): 85-88.

Adams, Judith A. and Sharon C. Bonk. "Electronic Information Technologies and Resources: Use by University Faculty and Faculty Preferences for Related Services," *College & Research Libraries.* 56 (2) (March 1995): 119-131.

Aguilar, William. "The Application of Relative Use and Interlibrary Loan in Collection Development," *Collection Management.* 8 (Spring 1986): 15-24.

Maureen Pastine, AB, MLS, is University Librarian, University Libraries, Paley Library, Temple University, Philadelphia, PA 19122.

[Haworth co-indexing entry note]: "Chapter Eight: Ownership or Access to Electronic Information–A Selective Bibliography." Pastine, Maureen. Co-published simultaneously in *Collection Management* (The Haworth Press, Inc.) Vol. 22, No. 1/2, 1997, pp. 187-214; and: *Collection Development: Access in the Virtual Library* (ed: Maureen Pastine) The Haworth Press, Inc., 1997, pp. 187-214. Single or multiple copies of this article are available for a fee from The Haworth Document Delivery Service [1-800-342-9678, 9:00 a.m. - 5:00 p.m. (EST). E-mail address: getinfo@haworth.com].

Altbach, Philip C. "The Information Revolution: From the Bottom Up," *Library Issues: Briefings for Faculty and Administrators.* 12 (No. 5, May 1992): 1-3.

Anderson, Nancy D. and James L. Rovnyak. "Mathematics Research Libraries: A 1990 Snapshot," *Notices.* (December 1991): 1258-1262.

Ardis, Susan B., comp. *Library without Walls: Plug In and Go.* (Washington, D.C.: SLA, 1994).

Arms, Caroline, ed. *Campus Strategies for Libraries and Electronic Information.* (Bedford, Massachusetts: Digital Press, 1990).

Association of Research Libraries. "Monograph and Serial Costs in ARL Libraries, 1985-86–1989-90," *ARL Statistics 1989-90.* (Washington, D.C.: Association of Research Libraries, 1991). 6 p.

Association of Research Libraries. Office of Management Studies. *Qualitative Collection Analysis: The Conspectus Methodology.* SPEC Kit 151. (Washington, D.C.: ARL, OMS, 1989).

Astle, Deana. "Suicide Squeeze: The Escalating Cost of Scholarly Journals," *Academe.* 75 (July/August 1989): 13-17.

Atkins, Stephen. "Mining Automated Systems for Collection Management," *Library Administration & Management.* 10 (1) (Winter 1996): 16-19.

Atkinson, Ross. "Library Functions, Scholarly Communication, and the Foundation of the Digital Library: Laying Claim to the Control Zone," *Library Quarterly.* 66 (3) (July 1996): 239-265.

Axford, H. William. "Collection Management: A New Dimension," *Journal of Academic Librarianship.* 6 (January 1981): 325-326, 328-329.

Baensch, Robert E. "Whither Custom Textbook Publishing?" *Publishers Weekly.* (June 21, 1991): 27-28.

Baker, Nicholson. "The Author vs. The Library," *The New Yorker.* (October 14, 1996): 50-62.

Baker, Nicholson. "Demise of the Card Catalog," *New Yorker.* (April 1994): 63-66.

Baker, Shirley K. and Mary E. Jackson, eds. *The Future of Resource Sharing.* (New York: The Haworth Press, Inc., 1995). [also published as *Journal of Library Administration.* 21 (2/3)].

Baker, Shirley K. and Mary E. Jackson. "Maximizing Access,

Minimizing Cost: A First Step Toward the Information Access Future," *Public Library Quarterly.* 13 (3) (1993): 11.

Barry, Jeff, Jose-Marie Griffiths, and Peiling Wang. "Jockeying for Supremacy in a Networked World," *Library Journal.* (April 1, 1996): 40-51.

Basch, Reva, ed. *Electronic Information Delivery: Ensuring Quality and Value.* (Hampshire, England: Gower, 1995). 264 p.

Basch, Reva. "ProQuest Direct: Document Delivery [with images] to the Desktop," *Online.* 20 (2) (March/April 1996): 38-44.

Basili, Carli. "Subject Searching for Information: What Does It Mean in Today's Internet Environment," *Electronic Library.* 13 (5) (October 1995): 459-466.

Bates, John E., Ivan G. Fuchs, and Alan Greenberg. "An Alternative to Costly High Tech Contingency Plans," *CAUSE/EFFECT.* 15 (No. 3, Fall 1992): 6-11.

Battin, Patricia. "The Library: Center of the Restructured University," *College & Research Libraries.* (May 1984): 170.

Bazillion, Richard J. and Constance Braun. *American Libraries as High-Tech Gateways: A Guide to Design and Space Decisions.* (Chicago, ALA, 1995).

Bazillion, Richard J. and Connie L. Braun. "Building Virtual–and Spatial–Libraries for Distance Learning," *CAUSE/EFFECT.* 18 (4) (Winter 1995): 51-54.

Bazirjian, Rosann, ed. *New Automation Technology for Acquisitions and Collection Development.* (Binghamton, New York: The Haworth Press, Inc., 1995).

Beghtol, Clare. *The Classification of Fiction: The Development of a System Based on Theoretical Principles.* (Metuchen, New Jersey: Scarecrow Press, 1994): 366 p. [subject analysis of fiction]

Benson, Larry D. "Scholarly Research and Reference Service in the Automated Environment," *The Reference Librarian.* (48) (1995): 57-69.

Berry, John N. III. "Editorial: Copyright Must Serve Its True Purpose," *Library Journal.* (August 1992): 6.

Biddle, Stanton F. *Planning in the University Library.* (Westport, Conn.: Greenwood Press, 1992). 227 p.

Billings, Harold. "The Bionic," *Library Journal.* (October 15, 1991): 38-42.

Birdsall, William F. *The Myth of the Electronic Library: Librarianship and Social Change in America.* Westport, Conn.: Greenwood, 1994. 224 p.

Blake, Virgil L.P. and Renee Tjourmas. "The Conspectus Approach to Collection Evaluation: Panacea or False Prophet?" *Collection Management.* 18(3/4) (1994): 1-31.

Blue, Richard. "Directory of U.S. Full-Text System Vendors," *Online Review.* 3 (No. 2, 1979): 175-179.

Bosseau, Don L. "Deciphering the Character of Order," *Journal of Academic Librarianship.* (July 1995): 301-302.

Bosseau, Don L., Beth Shapiro, and Jerry Campbell. "Digitizing the Reserve Function: Steps Toward Electronic Document Delivery," *Electronic Library.* 13(3) (June 1995): 217-223.

Bosseau, Don and Susan Martin. "Visions: Taking Control of Our Destiny," *The Journal of Academic Librarianship.* (September 1992): 230-231.

Bosseau, Don. "Visions: Confronting the Influence of Technology," *Journal of Academic Librarianship.* (November 1992): 302-303.

Bordeianu, Sever and Christina E. Carter. "Tenets of Reference Selection for Academic Libraries," *Collection Management.* 20 (3/4) (1996): 39-49.

Boyce, Bert R. "Meeting the Serials Cost Problem: A Supply-Side Proposal," *American Libraries.* 24 (No. 3, March 1993): 272-273.

Braid, J. Andrew. "Electronic Document Delivery: A Reality at Last?" *ASLIB Proceedings.* 45 (1993): 161-166.

Brekon, Donald J. and Terry Snapp. "Gift Acceptance Policies: Is It the Source or Use that Matters?" *Fund Raising Management.* 26 (2) (April 1995): 14-16.

Bridge, Frank R. "Managing Technology: What Is a LAN Administrator?" *Library Journal.* (October 15, 1991): 56-57.

Brinkley, Monica and Jack O'Farrell. "Delivery of Library Services to Distance Education Students: The BIBDEL Research Project at Dublin City University Library," *Electronic Librarian.* 13 (6) (December 1995): 539-546.

Britten, William A. "A Use Statistic for Collection Management: The 80/20 Rule Revisited," *Library Acquisitions: Practice & Theory.* 14 (1990): 183-189.

Brown, David J. "An Electronic Library," *College & Research Libraries News*. 46: 533, 536-538.

Brown, David J., comp. *Electronic Publishing and Libraries: Planning for the Impact and Growth to 2003*. (East Grimstead, UK: Bowker-Sauer, 1996).

Brown University. *Library Electronic Information/Computer Files Collection Development Statement*. (September 1990).

Brunner, Theodore F. "Data Banks for the Humanities: Learning from Thesaurus Linguae Graecae," *Scholarly Communication*. 7 (Winter 1987): 1, 6-9.

Bush, Vanevar. "As We May Think," *Atlantic Monthly*. 176 (July 1945): 101-108.

Byrd, Gary. "Marketplace Challenges for Research Libraries," *College & Research Libraries News*. (November 1995): 694-695.

Byrd, Gary D., D.A. Thomas, and Katherine E. Hughes. "Collection Development Using Interlibrary Loan Borrowing and Acquisitions Statistics," *Bulletin of the Medical Library Association*. 70 (January 1982): 1-9.

Cain, Mark. "Periodical Access in an Era of Change: Characteristics and a Model," *Journal of Academic Librarianship*. (September 1995): 365-370.

Carlson, William L. "The Liberal Arts College in the Information Age: An Appropriate Response to Information Technology," *CAUSE/EFFECT*. 11 (Fall 1988): 52.

Carpenter, David and Malcolm Getz. "Evaluation of Library Resources in the Field of Economics: A Case Study," *Collection Management*. 20(1/2) (1995): 69.

Carpenter, Eric. "Adequate Representation and Numeric Equivalency: How Much is Enough," *College & Research Libraries*. 56 (2) (March 1995): 116-118.

Carrigan, Dennis P. "Collection Development-Evaluation," *Journal of Academic Librarianship*. (July 1996): 273-278.

Carrigan, Dennis P. "Data-Guided Collection Development: A Promise Unfulfilled," *College & Research Libraries*. 57 (5) (September 1996): 429-437.

Carrigan, Dennis P. "Librarians and the 'Dismal Science,'" *Library Journal*. 113 (June 15, 1988): 22.

Carrigan, Dennis P. "Toward a Theory of Collection Development," *Library Acquisitions: Practice & Theory.* 19 (1995): 97-106.

Cenzer, Pamela S. and Cynthia I. Gozzi, eds. *Evaluating Acquisitions and Collection Management.* (New York: The Haworth Press, Inc., 1991).

"The Changing Role of Suppliers: To Compete in a Digital Market, Color Houses and Printers have Extended their Services into a Whole New Business," *Publishers Weekly.* (September 14, 1992): S15-S17, S24-S25.

Christensen, Howard B. and John O. Christensen. "Application of a Sampling Method in Journal Cost Studies," *Serials Review.* 21 (Summer 1995): 17-28.

Chrzastowski, Tina E. and Karen A. Schmidt. "Surveying the Damage: Academic Library Serial Cancellations 1987-88 through 1989-90," *College & Research Libraries.* 54 (No. 2, March 1993): 93-102.

Clayton, Peter. "Japanese Management Theory and Library Administration," *Journal of Academic Librarianship.* 18 (No. 5, 1992): 298-301.

Cleveland, Gary. *Electronic Document Delivery: Converging Standards and Technologies.* (Ottawa: International Federation of Library Assns. and Institutions, International Office for Universal Dataflow and Telecommunications, 1991).

Cochenour, Donnice. "Electronic Journal Forum. Project Muse: A Partnership of Interest," *Serials Review.* 21 (3) (1995): 75-81.

Coffman, Steve and Helen Josephine. "Doing It for Money," *Library Journal.* (October 15, 1991): 32-36.

Colbert, Antoinette. "Full-Text Online Retrieval," *Online.* (March 1988): 91.

Collection Development Policies Committee of the Collection Development and Evaluation Section, RASD, "The Relevance of Collection Development Policies: Definition, Necessity, and Applications," *RQ.* 33 (Fall 1993): 65-74.

Commission on Freedom and Equality of Access to Information. "The New Technology and Access to Information," *Freedom and Equality of Access to Information: A Report to the American Library Association.* Chair, Dan M. Lacy. (Chicago: American Library Association, 1986): 29-54.

Cooper, Walter. "Integrating Information Technologies for the Library Environment," *Library Administration & Management.* 8 (3) (June 1994): 131-134.

Copler, Judith. "Full-Text and Document Delivery," *Chemical Journals Online Bulletin.* 2 (No. 4, November 1987): 3.

"Copyright Office Issues Final Regulation: Ruling May Lessen Competition in Cable Industry," *LC Information Bulletin.* (May 4, 1992): 186-187.

Cotton, F.L. "Where Full-Text is Viable," *Online Review.* 11 (No. 2, April 1987): 87-93.

Couch, Nana and Nancy Allen, eds. *The Humanities and the Library.* 2nd ed. (Chicago: ALA, 1993). 336 p.

Creth, Sheila D. "The Information Arcade: Playground for the Mind," *Journal of Academic Librarianship.* (March 1994): 22-23.

Creth, Sheila D. "Information Technology: Building a Framework for Change," *Library Issues: Briefings for Faculty and Administrators.* 12 (No. 6, July 1992): 1-2, 4.

Crump, Michele J. and LeiLani Freund. "Serials Cancellations and Interlibrary Loan: The Link and What It Reveals," *Serials Review.* 21 (29-34) (Summer 1995).

Cuadra, Carlos. "Information Technology," *Libraries and the Information Economy of California: A Conference Sponsored by the California State Library.* Editor Robert M. Hayes. (Los Angeles, California, A GSLIS/UCLA Publication, 1985): 79-123.

Culliton, Barbara J. "Harvard Tackles the Rush to Publication," *Science.* 241 (July 29, 1988): 525.

Dadlez, Eva M. "The Flip Sides of Full-Text: Superindex and the Harvard Business Review," *Online.* 8 (November 1984): 38-45.

Dearle, Tammy N. and V. Steel, comps. *Interlibrary Loan Trends: Making Access a Reality.* (SPEC Kit #184) (Washington, D.C.: ARL, OMS, 1992). 184 p.

Delaney-Lehman, Maureen J. "Assessing the Library Collection for Diversity," *Collection Management.* 20 (3/4) (1996): 29-37.

Delong, Linwood. "Valuating Library Collections," *Conference on Acquisitions, Budgets, and Collections: Proceedings.* (May 16 & 17, 1990): 89-95.

DeLoughry, Thomas J. "Crucial Role Seen for Technology in

Meeting High Education's Challenges," *The Chronicle of Higher Education.* (September 23, 1992): A21-A22.

DeLoughry, Thomas J. "Presidents Urged to Help Expand Use of Technology on Campuses," *The Chronicle of Higher Education.* (October 14, 1992): A19-A20.

DeLoughry, Thomas J. "Professors are Urged to Devise Strategies to Help Students Deal with 'Information Explosion' Spurred by Technology," *The Chronicle of Higher Education.* (March 8, 1989): A15.

Dodson, Cynthia, Jeffrey D. Kushkowski, and Kristin H. Gerhard. "Collection Evaluation for Interdisciplinary Fields: A Comprehensive Approach," *Journal of Academic Librarianship.* (July 1996): 279-283.

Dodson, Melanie. "Faculty Access to RLIN at New York University: RLG's Research Access Project," *College & Research Libraries News.* (No. 8, September 1988): 522-523.

"Dollar Watch: 1992 Year-End Update," *Library Issues: Briefings for Faculty and Administrators.* 13 (No. 4, March 1993): 3.

Dougherty, Richard M. and Carol Hughes. *Preferred Futures for Libraries: A Summary of Six Workshops with University Provosts and Library Directors.* (Research Libraries Group, Inc., 1991): 19 p.

Dowler, Lawrence and Laura Farwell. "The Gateway: A Bridge to the Library of the Future," *Reference Services Review.* 24 (2) (1996): 7-11.

Dowlin. The Electronic Library: The Promise and the Process. [Review of] *College and Research Libraries.* 45: 321-323.

Duranceau, Ellen, ed. "The Balance Point: Vendors and Librarians Speak on Outsourcing Cataloging and Acquisitions," *Serials Review.* 20 (3) (1994): 69-83.

Eaton, Nancy L. "The Director's Role in the Acquisitions Dilemma," *Journal of Library Administration.* 19 (2) (1993): 3.

Eckman, Charles. "Journal Review in an Environmental Design Library," *Collection Management.* 10 (No. 1/2, 1988): 69-84.

Elshami, Ahmed M. *Networking CD-ROMS: The Decision Maker's Guide to Local Area Network Solutions.* (Chicago: ALA, 1996). 339 p.

Ensle, Halcyon R. "Reserve On-Line: Bringing Reserve into the

Electronic Age," *Information Technology and Libraries.* 13 (3) (September 1994): 197-201.

Ensor, Pat. "Automating Document Delivery: A Conference Report," *Computers in Libraries.* 12 (December 1992): 34-37.

Ensor, Pat and S. Hardin. *CD-ROM Periodical Index: A Guide to Abstracted, Indexed, and Fulltext Periodicals on CD-ROM.* (Westport, Conn.: Meckler, 1992): 420 pp.

Epple, Margie and Ann Montanaro. "Electronic Materials Request Service for Cataloged and In-Process Books," *Resource Sharing & Information Networks.* 11 (1/2)(1996): 27-45.

Epstein, Susan Berg. "Managing Technology: Selling Automation to Your Patrons: It's Easier Than You Feared," *Library Journal.* (October 15, 1990): 63-64.

Evans, Richard I. *Resistance to Innovation in Higher Education.* (Jossey-Bass, 1968).

Euster, Joanne. "Take Charge of the Future Now," *College & Research Libraries News.* 54 (No. 2, February 1993): 89-91.

Evans, Nancy H., Denise A. Troll, Mark H. Kibbey, Thomas J. Michalsk, and William Y. Arms. *The Vision of the Electronic Library.* (Mercury Technical Report Series, No. 1) (Pittsburgh: Carnegie Mellon University, 1989).

Evans-Markuson, Barbara with Elaine W. Woods, eds. *Networks for Networkers: Critical Issues for Libraries in the National Network Environment.* (New York: Neal-Schuman Publishers, 1993).

Faber, Amy Beth and Evan I. "Lessons from DIALOG: Technology Impacts Teaching/Learning," *Library Journal.* (September 15, 1992): 26-30.

Feeney, Mary and Maureen Grieves, eds. *The Value and Impact of Information.* (London: Bowker/Saur, 1994).

Feldman, Gayle. "Modern Library Relaunch to Include Electronic Books," *Publishers Weekly.* (May 11, 1992): 10.

Feldman, Gayle. "Professional Publishing Goes Electronic," *Publishers Weekly.* (May 11, 1992): 31-33.

Ferguson, Anthony W. "Interesting Problems Encountered on My Way to Writing an Electronic Information Collection Development Statement," *Against the Grain.* 7 (2) (April 1995): 16-19.

Fidel, Raya, Trudi Bellardo Hahn, Edie M. Rasmussen, and Philip J.

Smith. *Challenges in Indexing Electronic Text and Images.* (Medford, New Jersey: Learned Information, 1994).

Floridi, Luciano. "Internet: Which Future for Organized Knowledge, Frankenstein or Pygmalion?" *The Information Society.* 12 (1) (January-March 1996): 5-16.

Frye, Billy E. "The Future of the Library: A View from the Provost's Office," *Library Issues: Briefings for Faculty and Administrators.* 12 (No. 1, September 1991): 1-2, 4.

Futas, Elizabeth and David L. Vidor. "What Constitutes a 'Good' Collection?" *Library Journal.* 112 (April 15, 1987): 45.

The Future is Now: The Changing Face of Technical Services. (Dublin, Ohio: OCLC, Inc., 1994).

Future Libraries. Ed. R. Howard Bloch and Carla Hesse. (University of California Press, 1993).

Garrett, John R. and Joseph S. Allen. *Toward a Copyright Management System for Digital Libraries.* (Washington, D.C.: ARL/ CAUSE/EDUCOM Coalition for Networked Information, March 1992). 74 p.

Geller, Marilyn, ed. & publishers. *Citations for Serials Literature.* Listserv@MITVMA.MIT.EDU

Ghikas, Mary W. "Collection Management in the 21st Century," *Journal of Library Administration.* 11 (No. 1/2, 1989): 119-135.

Gillespie, John T. and Ralph J. Folcarelli. *Guides to Library Collection Development.* (Englewood, CO: Libraries Unlimited, 1991). 441 p.

Glavash, Keith. "Full-Text Retrieval for Document Delivery–A Viable Option," *Online.* 18 (3) (May 1994): 81-84.

Goodrich, Tom. "Mining the Internet: Tools for Access and Navigation," *Syllabus.* 8 (3) (November 1994): 16-22.

Gossen, Eleanor A. and Suzanne Irving. "Ownership versus Access and Low-Use Periodical Titles," *Library Resources and Technical Services.* 39 (January 1995): 43-52.

Gotze, Dietrich. "Electronic Journals–Market and Technology," *Publishing Research Quarterly.* 11 (1) (Spring 1995): 3-20.

Gozzi, Cynthia. "Acquisitions Management Information: Do Administrators Really Care?" *Library Administration & Management.* 9 (2) (Spring 1995): 85-87.

Graham, Peter S. "Requirements for the Digital Research Library," *College & Research Libraries.* 56 (4) (July 1995): 331-339.

Graziadei, William D. and Gillian McCombs. "Wiring the Trenches: Teaching Faculty and Librarians Working Together on the Internet," *Internet Reference Services Quarterly.* 1 (1) (1996): 89-103.

Green, Kenneth C. "A Technology Agenda for the 1990s," *Change.* 23 (January/February 1991): 6-7.

Green, Kenneth C. and Skip Eastman. *Campus Computing 1990.* (Los Angeles: University of Southern California, Center for Scholarly Technology, 1990).

Green, Tim. "Online Information Services: Caught in the Web?" *Online.* 19 (4) (July/August 1995): 23-31.

Greenberg, Saul. "An Annotated Bibliography of Computer Supported Cooperative Work," *SIGCHI Bulletin.* 23 (July 1991): 29-62.

Greene, R.J. "Computer Analysis of Local Citation Information in Collection Management," *Collection Management.* 17 (4) (1993): 11-24.

Gregorian, Vartan, Brian L. Hawkins, and Merrily Taylor. "Integrating Information Technologies: A Research University Perspective," *CAUSE/EFFECT.* 15 (No. 4, Winter 1992): 5-12.

Haar, John H. "The Reference Collection Development Decision: Will New Information Technologies Influence Libraries' Collecting Patterns?" *The Reference Librarian.* (22) (1988): 114.

Hamaker, Charles A. "Management Data for Selection Decisions in Building Library Collections," *Journal of Library Administration.* 17 (2) (1992): 71.

Hamaker, Charles A. "Time Series Data for Collection Development or: You Can't Intuit That," *Library Acquisitions: Practice & Theory.* 19 (Summer 1995): 195.

Handlin, Oscar. "Libraries and Learning," *The American Scholar.* 56 (Spring 1989): 207.

Handman, Gary P., ed. *Video Collection Development in Multi-Type Libraries: A Handbook.* (Westport, Conn.: Greenwood Press, 1994): 496 p.

Hardesty, Larry. "Use of Library Materials at a Small Liberal Arts College," *Library Research.* 3 (Fall 1981): 271.

Harloe, Bart, ed. *Guide to Cooperative Collection Development.*

(No. 6, Collection Management & Development Guides). (Chicago: ALA, 1994). 35 p.

Harris, Michael A. and S.A. Hannah. *Into the Future: The Foundations of Library and Information Services in the Post-Industrial Era.* Norwood, New Jersey: Ablex, 1993. 182 p.

Harter, Stephen P. and Hak Joon Kim. "Accessing Electronic Journals and Other E-Publications: An Empirical Study," *College & Research Libraries.* 57 (5) (September 1996): 440-443, 446-456.

Harter, Stephen P. and Hak Joon Kim. "Electronic Journals and Scholarly Communication: A Citation and Reference Study," *Paper Presented at Midyear Meeting of ASIS, San Diego, CA, May 18-22, 1996.* Text of paper at URL: http://www-slis.lib.indiana.edu/PrePrints/harter-asis96midyear.html

Harter, Stephen P. "The Impact of Electronic Journals on Scholarly Communication: A Citation Analysis," *Public-Access Computer Systems Review* (1996). PACS Review is available at URL: http://info.lib.uh.edu/pacsrev.html

Hartinger, Verna J. "Justifying Non-Traditional Automation Projects," *Library Software Review.* 9 (July/August 1990): 228-230.

Harvey, Diane and L.C. Leighton, eds. *Charting the Future: Research Libraries Prepare for the 21st Century.* (Arlington, Virginia: ARL, 1993.

Hattendorf, Lynn C. "The Art of Reference Collection Development," *RQ.* 29 (2) (Winter 1989): 219-220.

Hauptman, Robert. "Publish, Purchase, Perish," *Journal of Scholarly Publishing.* 26 (4) (July 1995): 197-201.

Hawthorne, Pat and Ron G. Martin, eds. *Planning Additions to Academic Library Buildings: A Seamless Approach.* (Chicago: ALA, 1995).

Hayes, John R. "The Internet's First Victims," *Forbes.* (December 18, 1995): 200-201.

Heidenwolf, Terese. "Evaluating an Interdisciplinary Research Collection," *Collection Management.* 18(3/4) (1994): 33.

Helstien, Brian A. "Libraries: Once and Future," *Electronic Library,* 13 (3) (June 1995): 203-207.

Hernon, Peter and John A. Shuler. "Scholarly Publishers on the World Wide Web," *Journal of Academic Librarianship.* (March 1996): 142.

Hills, Paul. "Through the Electronic Copyright Maze," *Publishers Weekly.* (June 8, 1992): 35-37.

Hilton-Chalfon, Danny. "Planning for Campus Information Technology Access: What Must We Do?" *EDUCOM Review.* (Spring 1991): 51.

Hilts, Paul. "Desktop Imaging Network Beats the Clock," *Publishers Weekly.* (August 10, 1992): 24-25.

Hilts, Paul. "OnLine BookStore to Deliver Full Text Books," *Publishers Weekly.* 240 (February 1, 1993): 7, 14.

Hirshon, Arnold. "Library Strategic Alliances and the Digital Library in the 1990s: The OhioLINK Experience," *Journal of Academic Librarianship.* (September 1995): 383-386.

Hughes, Robert. "Welcome to Cyberspace," *Time.* (Spring 1995): 76-77.

Hunter, Karen. "Publishing for a Digital Library–What Did TULIP Teach Us?" *Journal of Academic Librarianship.* (May 1996): 209-211.

Imhoff, Kathleen R.T. *Making the Most of New Technology: A How-To-Do-It Manual for Librarians.* (New York: Neal-Schuman, 1996).

Intner, Sheila S. *Interfaces: Relations between Library Technical Services and Public Services.* (Englewood, CO.: Libraries Unlimited, 1993).

Intner, Sheila S. "Letters to the Editor: On Snow's Wasted Words," *Journal of Academic Librarianship.* (November 1996): 466.

Jacobsen, Kristin. "Time to Put the Internet in Perspective," *College & Research Libraries News.* (March 1995): 144-147.

Jackson, Mary E. "Integrating ILL with Document Delivery: Five Models," *Wilson Library Bulletin.* 68 (September 1993): 76-78.

Jackson, Mary E. "Library to Library: Stand and Deliver," *Wilson Library Bulletin.* 67 (April 1992): 86-88.

Jackson, Mary E. and Karen Cronlis. "Uses of Document Delivery Services," *SPEC Kit 204.* (Washington, D.C.: ARL, OMS, 1994).

Jacobsen, Robert L. "Desktop Libraries: University Researchers Strive to Make Vast Networked Collections a Reality," *The Chronicle of Higher Education.* (November 10, 1995): A25-27.

Jacobsen, Robert L. "Researchers Temper Their Ambitions for

Digital Libraries," *The Chronicle of Higher Education.* (November 24, 1995): A19.

Jaramillo, George R. and Joan C. Lamborn. "Document Delivery in Times of Shrinking Budgets," *Resource Sharing & Information Networks.* 11 (1/2) (1996): 5-15.

Jenkins, Paul O. "Working with Faculty to Build Collections," *College & Research Libraries News.* (May 1995): 322.

John, Nancy R. and Edward J. Valauskas. *The Internet Initiative: Libraries Providing Internet Services and How They Plan, Pay, and Manage.* (Chicago: ALA, 1995).

Johnson, Peggy, ed. *Guide to Technical Services Resources.* (Chicago: ALA, 1994).

Joseph, Earl C. "Twenty-First Century Information Literacies and Libraries." In *Information Literacies for the Twenty-First Century.* Ed. Virgil L.P. Blake and Renee Tjoumas. (Boston, G.K. Hall, 1990): 7-16.

"Journals Demand High Prices," *Geotimes.* (December 1991): 4.

Juergens, Bonnie. "Costs and New Technologies: The View from the Network/Broker," *Technical Services Quarterly.* 8 (No. 1, 1990): 17-28.

Kaag, Cynthia Stewart, comp. *Collection Evaluation Techniques: A Short, Selective, Practical, Current, Annotated Bibliography.* (1980-1990 RASD Occasional Papers, No. 10) (Chicago: RASD, ALA, 1991).

Kahn, Robert E. and Vinton G. Cerf. *An Open Architecture of a Digital Library System and a Plan for Its Development, The Digital Library Project, Volume 1: The World of Knowbots.* (Washington, D.C.: Corporation for National Research Initiatives, March 1988).

Kaser, Dick, ed. *Document Delivery in an Electronic Age: A Collection of Views and Viewpoints.* (Washington, D.C.: National Federation of Abstracting and Information Services, 1995).

Katz, Bill. "The Full-Text Online Magazine," *Collection Building.* (Winter 1985): 26-29.

Katz, Richard N. and Richard P. West. *Sustaining Excellence in the 21st Century: A Vision and Strategies for College and University Administration.* (Professional Paper Series, #8) (Boulder, Colorado: CAUSE, 1992).

Katzen, May, editor. *Scholarship and Technology in the Humanities: Proceedings of a Conference Held at Elvethan Hall, Hampshire, UK, 9th-12th May 1990.* (London, British Library Research/Bowker/Saur, 1991): 186 p.

Kaufman, Paula T. and Aubrey H. Mitchell, comps. *2001: A Space Reality: Strategies for Obtaining Funding for New Library Space.* (Washington, D.C.: ARL, SPEC Kit 200), February 1994.

Keese, Erich. *Survey of Micropublishers: A Report to the Commission on Preservation and Access.* (Washington, D.C.: The Commission on Preservation and Access, October 1992): 6 p.

Keller, John J. "AT & T Unveils a Chip Set That Lets PCs Be Used for Video Communication," *The Wall Street Journal.* (April 3, 1992).

Kenney, Anne R. and Lynne K. Personius. The Cornell/Xerox/Commission on Preservation and Access. *Joint Study in Digital Preservation: Report: Phase I (January 1990-December 1991): Digital Capture, Paper Facsimiles, and Network Access.* (Washington, D.C., Commission on Preservation and Access, 1992):

Khalil, Mounir. "Document Delivery: A Better Option?" *Library Journal.* (February 1, 1993): 43-44.

Kimberley, Robert. "Electronic Journal Distribution: A Prototype Study," *Electronic Library.* 13 (4) (August 1995): 313-316.

King, Kenneth M. "Letter from Kenneth M. King: Some Cheerful Thoughts" [on slow progress in realizing the potential of technology in education], *EDUCOM Review.* 27 (No. 5, September/October 1992): 56.

Kinnucan, Mart T. "Demand for Document Delivery and Interlibrary Loan in Academic Settings," *Library and Information Science Research.* 15 (1993): 355-374.

Kinsella, Bridget. "Book Groups Get Wired: The Internet is Playing a Significant Role in Bringing Bibliophiles Together," *Publishers Weekly.* (November 18, 1996): 46-51.

Klemperer, Katharina. "New Dimensions for the Online Catalog: The Dartmouth College Library Experience," *Information Technology and Libraries.* 8 (June 1989): 138-145.

Kreitz, Pat. *Electronic Formats Collection Development Bibliography.* PKREITZ@SSCVXZ.SSC.GOV

Kroll, Rebecca. "The Responsive Reference Collection: Planning for Service versus Self-Service in the Reference Area," *The Reference Librarian.* (29) (1990): 10.

Kuhlthau, Carol Collier. *Seeking Meaning: A Process Approach to Library and Information Services.* (Norwood, New Jersey: Ablex, 1993). 219 p.

Kuntz, Sandra. "Letter to the Editor, dated 8/88," *Physics Today.* (June 1989): 14.

Kurosman, Kathleen and Barbara A. Durniak. "Document Delivery: A Comparison of Commercial Document Suppliers and Interlibrary Loan Services," *College & Research Libraries.* (March 1994): 129-139.

Kuta, Janice E. "AAP Seminar Explores Document Delivery," *Publishers Weekly.* (November 30, 1992): 20-21.

LaBorie, Tim. "Computer Library Over the Campus Network," *College and Research Libraries News.* 54 (No. 2, February 1993): 70, 72-73.

LaGuardia, Cheryl. "Virtual Dreams Give Way to Digital Reality," *Library Journal.* (October 1, 1995): 42.

Lancaster, F.W. *If You Want to Evaluate Your Library* . . . (Champaign, Illinois: University of Illinois Graduate School of Library and Information Science, 1988).

Lancaster, F.W., ed. *Librarians and the Future. Essays on the Library in the Twenty-First Century.* (Binghamton, New York: The Haworth Press, Inc., 1993. 195 p.

Lancaster, F.W., ed. "Networked Scholarly Publications," *Library Trends.* 43 (4) (Spring 1995): 515-770.

Landrum, Hollis T. "The Potential of Conjoint Analysis for Measuring Value in Collection Development," *Collection Management.* 20 (1/2) (1995): 139-147.

Landrum, Margaret Cozine. "Marketing Library Services to Faculty," *Colorado Libraries.* 13 (September 1987): 15-18.

Leach, Ronald G. "Academic Library Change: The Role of Regional Accreditation," *Journal of Academic Librarianship.* 18 (No. 5): 288-291.

Leach, Ronald. "Library Materials Price Update," *Library Issues: Briefings for Faculty and Administrators.* 12 (No. 1, September 1991): 2-3 and 12 (No. 7, September 1992): 2-3. Special Issue (October 1992).

Leach, Ronald G. and Judith E. Tribble. "Electronic Document Delivery: New Options for Libraries," *Journal of Academic Librarianship*. 18 (January 1993): 359-364.

Leavitt, Michael R. *The Analyst and Technology–2000*. (Prepared for the U.S. Intelligence Research and Development Council, January 1991).

LeCompagnon, Betty and John F. Leydon. "Manage Computer Support Costs through Effective User Training," *CAUSE/EF-FECT*. 14 (No. 2, Summer 1991): 47-53.

Leonard, W. Patrick. "This Too Shall Pass, or We Will," *Journal of Academic Librarianship*. 19 (No. 5, 1992): 304-305.

Lesk, Michael. *Preservation of New Technology: A Report of the Technology Assessment Advisory Committee to the Commission on Preservation and Access*. (Washington, D.C.: The Commission on Preservation and Access, October 1992): 17.

Lewis, Peter H. "CD-ROMs to Get Better and Faster but Even So They May Not Survive," *The New York Times*. (December 13, 1994): C15.

Lewontin, Amy. "Providing Online Services to End Users Outside the Library," *College & Research Libraries News*. (No. 1, January 1991): 21-22.

Lougee, Wendy. "Beyond Access: New Concepts, New Tensions for Collection Development in a Digital Environment," *Collection Building*. 14 (3) (1995): 19-25.

Lowry, Charles B. "Putting the Pieces Together–Essential Technologies for the Virtual Library," *Journal of Academic Librarianship*. (July 1995): 297-300.

Lynch, Clifford A. "The Growth of Computer Networks: A Status Report," *Bulletin of the American Society for Information Science*. 16 (June/July 1990): 10.

Lynch, Clifford A. "Library Automation and the National Research Network," *EDUCOM Review*. 24 (Fall 1989): 22.

Manes, Stephen. "The CD-ROM in Transition: A Medium in Search of Its Message," *The New York Times*. (December 13, 1994): B10.

Manes, Stephen. "User-Friendliness: Book vs. Disk," *The New York Times*. (December 13, 1994): B10.

Markoff, John. "Building the Electronic Superhighway," *The New York Times.* (Sunday, January 24, 1993): Section 3.

Marman, Edward. "A Method for Establishing a Depreciated Monetary Value for Print Collections," *Library Administration & Management.* 9 (2) (Spring 195): 94-97.

Martin, Harry S. and Curtis L. Kendrick. "User-Centered View of Document Delivery and Interlibrary Loan," *Library Administration & Management.* 8 (Fall 1994): 223-227.

Martin, Murray S. "Acquisitions–Long Distance," *Collection Management.* 20 (1/2) (1995): 3-13.

Martin, Murray S. *Collection Development and Finance: A Guide to Strategic Library-Materials Budgeting.* (Chicago: ALA, 1995). 126 p.

Martin, Murray S., ed. *Issues in Collection Management: Librarians, Booksellers, Publishers.* (Foundations in Library and Information Science, Vol. 31). (Greenwich, Conn.: JAI Press, 1995). 193 p.

Martin, Robert Sidney, ed. *Scholarly Communication in an Electronic Environment: Issues for Research Libraries.* (Chicago & London: RBMS, ACRL, ALA, 1993). 136 p.

Martin, Susan K. "Library Management and Emerging Technology: The Immovable Force and the Irresistible Object," *Library Trends.* 37 (Winter 1989): 374-382.

Martin, Susan K. "Organizing Collections within the Internet: A Vision for Access," *Journal of Academic Librarianship.* (July 1996): 291-292.

Mathews, J.R. "The Distribution of Information: The Role for Online Public Access Catalogs," *Information Services & Use.* 14 (2) (1994): 73-78.

Massey-Burzio, Virginia. "Reference Encounters of a Different Kind: A Symposium," *Journal of Academic Librarianship.* 18 (No. 5, 1992): 276-279. Miller, William. "Breaking the Pattern of Reference Work Burnout," pp. 280-281. Whitlatch, Jo Bell. "Getting Close to the Customer," pp. 281-282. Durrance, Joan C. "Raising Expectations–Our Users' and Our Own," pp. 283-284. Ford, Barbara J. "From Discussion to Action: Changing Reference Service Patterns," pp. 284-285. Biggs, Mary. "Some Unanswered Questions," pp. 285-286.

Maxfield, Sandy. "Document Delivery Power for Faculty: An

Experiment with UnCover (at James Madison University)," *Virginia Librarian*. 39 (April/May-June 1993): 12-14.

McCarthy, Paul. "Serial Killers," *Library Journal*. (June 15, 1994): 41-44.

McClure, Charles R. and Cynthia Lopata. "Assessing the Academic Networked Environment," *Journal of Academic Librarianship*. (July 1996): 285-289.

McCombs, Gillian M. "The Internet and Technical Services: A Point Break Approach," *Library Resources & Technical Services*. 38 (2) (April 1994): 169-177.

McDonald, Joseph A. and Lynda Basney Micikas. *Academic Libraries: The Dimensions of their Effectiveness*. (Westport, Conn.: Greenwood Press, 1994).

Merimin, N. David. "What's Wrong with This Library?" *Boojums All the Way Through*. (New York, Cambridge University Press, 1990): 57.

Meyer, Richard W. "Selecting Electronic Alternatives," *Information Technology and Libraries*. 12 (June 1993): 173-180.

Michalko, James. "Costly Boundaries: Costs, New Technologies, and Bibliographic Utilities," *Technical Services Quarterly*. 8 (No. 1, 1990): 29-36.

Miller, Ruth H. and Thomas Lundstrom. "CD-ROMS in the Electronic Library: Completing the Collection Management Cycle," *Collection Management*. 20 (3/4) (1996): 51-71.

Mitchell, Eleanor and Sheila A. Walters. *Document Delivery Services: Issues and Answers*. (Medford, New Jersey: Learned Information, Inc., 1995). 333 p.

Mitchell, Steve and Margaret Mooney. "INFOMIME–A Model Web-Based Academic Virtual Library," *Information Technology and Libraries*. 15 (1) (March 1996): 20-25.

Mogge, Dru, ed. *Directory of Electronic Journals, Newsletters, and Academic Discussion Lists*. 6th ed. (Washington, D.C., ARL, 1996). 1,136 p.

Moran. "The Electronic Campus: The Impact of the Scholar's Workstation Project on the Libraries at Brown," *College & Research Libraries News*. 48: 5-16.

Moran, Barbara B., ed. "Libraries and Librarians: Meeting the Leadership Challenges of the 21st Century," *Library Trends*.

(Winter 1992). (Champaign, Illinois: University of Illinois, GSLIS, 1992): 199 p.

Morville, Peter. *The Internet Searcher's Handbook: Locating Information, People and Software.* (New York: Neal-Schuman, 1996).

Morville, Peter S. and Susan J. Wickhorst. "Building Subject-Specific Guides to Internet Resources," *Collection Building.* 14 (3) (1995): 26-31.

Nanus, Burt. *Visionary Leadership: Creating a Compelling Sense of Direction for Your Organization.* (San Francisco, Jossey-Bass, 1992): 237 p.

Negroponte, Nicholas. *Being Digital.* (New York: Knopf, 1995). 243 p.

Nelson, Nancy M., ed. *Library Technology, 1970-1990: Shaping the Library of the Future: Research Contributions from the 1990 Computers in Libraries Conference.* (Westport, Connecticut: Meckler, 1991): 139 p.

Nisonger, Thomas E. *Collection Evaluation in Academic Libraries: A Literature Guide and Annotated Bibliography.* (Englewood, Co.: Libraries Unlimited, 1992).

Nutter, Susan K. "Online Systems and the Management of Collections: Use and Implications," in *Advances in Library Automation and Networking*, ed. Joe A. Hewitt. (Greenwich, Conn.: JAI Press, 1987): 126.

Odhyzko, Andrew M. "Tragic Loss or Good Riddance? The Impending Demise of Traditional Scholarly Journals," *International Journal of Human-Computer Studies.* 42 (1995): 71-1222.

O'Donnell, Michael J. "Electronic Journals: Scholarly Invariants in a Changing Medium," *Scholarly Publishing.* 26 (3) (April 1995): 183-199.

Ogg, Harold C. "Cheap LANs: Resource Sharing on a Budget," *Library Software Review.* (May-June 1991): 179-185.

Okerson, Ann and Kendon Stubbs. "The Library 'Doomsday Machine,'" *Publishers Weekly.* 237 (February 8, 1991): 36-37.

Osburn, Charles B. "Collection Evaluation and Acquisitions Budgets: A Kaleidoscope in the Making," *Journal of Library Administration.* 17 (2) (1992): 5.

Osburn, Charles B. "The Place of the Journal in the Scholarly

Communications System," *Library Resources & Technical Services.* 28 (4) (October/December 1984): 315-324.

Osburn, Charles B. "The Structuring of the Scholarly Communication System," *College and Research Libraries.* 50 (May 1989): 277-286.

Pagell, Ruth. "Searching Full-Text Periodicals: How Full is Full?" *Database.* (October 1987): 33-36.

Pagell, Ruth. "Searching IAC's Full-Text Files: It's Awfully Confusing," *Database.* (October 1987): 39-46.

Pankake, Marcia. "Collection Bias: Eternal Vigilance the Price of Liberty," *College & Research Libraries.* 56 (2) (March 1995): 113-114.

Pankake, Marcia, Karin Wittenborg, and Eric Carpenter. "Commentaries on Collection Bias," *College & Research Libraries.* March 1995): 113-118.

Parker, Diane C. "Standards for College Libraries: Foundations," *College & Research Libraries News.* (May 1995): 330-331, 336-337.

Pastine, Maureen. "Collection Development: Past and Future Bibliography," in *Collection Development: Past and Future,* ed. Maureen Pastine. (New York & London: The Haworth Press, Inc., 1996): 179-234.

Patterson, Betsey. "People First, Technology Second: Introducing Faculty to Computer Technologies," *Library Software Review.* 10 (Winter 1980): 402-409.

Pedersen, Wayne and David Gregory. "Interlibrary Loan and Commercial Document Supply: Finding the Right Fit," *Journal of Academic Librarianship.* 20 (November 1994): 271.

Penniman, W. David. "Shaping the Future: The Council on Library Resources Helps to Fund Change," *Library Journal.* (October 15, 1992): 40-44.

Penrod, James I. and Michael G. Dolence. *Reengineering: A Process for Transforming Higher Education.* (Professional Paper Series, #9) (Boulder, CO.: CAUSE, 1992).

Peters, Paul Evan. "Digital Libraries are Much More than Digitized Collections," *Educom Review.* 30 (4) (July/August 1995): 11-15.

Pichappan, P. and N.K. Khatri. "Ioterative Approach in Finding the

'Core' of Information," *Information Services and Use.* 15 (3) (1995): 193-197.

Piontek, Sherry and Kristen Garlock. "Creating a World Wide Web Resource Collection," *Collection Building.* 14 (3) (1995): 12-18.

Pitkin, Gary M., ed. *The Impact of Emerging Technologies on Reference Service and Bibliographic Instruction.* (Westport, Conn.: Greenwood Press, 1995). 180 p.

Pitkin, Gary M., ed. *The National Electronic Library: A Guide to the Future for Library Managers.* (Westport, Conn.: Greenwood Press, 1996).

Polly, Jean Armour and Steve Cisler. "Promoting the Internet in Your Library," *Library Journal.* (June 15, 1995): 27-28.

Powell, James. Owner of *VPIEJ-L*, a discussion list for Electronic Journals. jpowell@borg.lib.vt.edu JPOWELL@VTVM1.CC.VT.EDU

Pratt, Allan D. "Are We Really Infallible at Book Selection?" *Library Journal.* (November 1, 1995): 44.

Pritchard, Sarah J. *RLG Conspectus: Supplemental Guidelines for Women's Studies.* (Mountain View, CA.: RLG, 1990).

Riggs, Donald E. "Capital Outlay–Buildings and Computers: Plans, Budgets, and Project Management," *Library Administration and Management.* 3 (Spring 1989): 87-92.

Roche, Marilyn. *ARL/RLG Interlibrary Loan Cost Study: a Joint Effort by the Association of Research Libraries and the Research Libraries Group.* (Washington, D.C.: ARL, 1993).

Rodgers, David L. "Scholarly Journals in 2020," *Serials Librarian.* 24 (3/4) (1994): 73-76.

Rogers, Michael. "Automation News: Research Libraries Group Debuts CitaDel on RLIN: Full-Text Document and Citation Delivery Service Provides Online Access to Multiple Commercial and Scholarly Databases," *Library Journal.* (June 1, 1992): 36, 38.

Rogers, Michael. National Net '92: What Now with NREN?" *Library Journal.* (May 15, 1992): 22-23.

Rogers, Michael. "Automation News: Conference Reveals Melee in Multimedia World," *Library Journal.* 117 (April 15, 1992): 22-25.

Rosenfeld, Louis B. "Guides, Clearinghouses, and Value-Added

Repackaging: Some Thoughts on How Librarians Can Improve the Internet," *Reference Services Review.* 22(4) (1994): 11-16.

Rottman, F.K. "To Buy or to Borrow: Studies of the Impact of Interlibrary Loan on Collection Development in the Academic Library," *Journal of Interlibrary Loan & Information Supply.* 1 (1991): 17-27.

Sabosik, Patricia E. "Document Delivery Services: Today's Electronic Scriptoria," *Computers in Libraries.* 12 (December 1992): 18.

Sandler, Mark. "The Changing Culture of the University," *Library Issues: Briefings for Faculty and Administrators.* 12 (No. 3, January 1991): 1-3.

Saunders, E. Stewart. "The Effect of Quality on Circulation in an Aging Collection," *Collection Management.* 20 (3/4) (1996): 149-156.

Schement, Jorge Reina. "A 21st Century Strategy for Librarians," *Library Journal.* 121 (8) (May 1, 1996): 34-36.

Schiller, Herbert I. "Public Information Goes Corporate," *Library Journal.* (October 1, 1991): 42-51.

Sellers, Minna and Joan Beam. "Subsidizing Unmediated Document Delivery: Current Models and a Case Study," *Journal of Academic Librarianship.* (November 1995): 459-466.

Senkevitch, Judith J. and Dietmar Wolfrom. "Equalizing Access to Electronic Networked Resources: A Model for Rural Libraries in the United States," *Library Trends.* 42 (4) (Spring 1994): 661-675.

"Serving the Internet Public: The Internet Public Library," *Electronic Library.* 14 (2) (April 1996): 122-126.

Sha, Vianne T. "Cataloging Internet Resources: The Library Approach," *Electronic Library.* 13 (5) (October 1995): 467-476.

Shapiro, Beth J. and John Whaley. *Selection of Library Materials in Applied and Interdisciplinary Fields.* (Chicago: ALA, 1987).

Skinder, Robert F. and Robert S. Gresehjover. "An Internet Navigation Tool for the Technical and Scientific Researcher," *Online.* 19 (4) (July/August 1995): 39-42.

Snow, Richard. "Wasted Words: The Written Collection Development Policy and the Academic Library," *Journal of Academic Librarianship.* (May 1996): 191-194.

Stohl, Clifford. *Silicon Snake Oil: Second Thoughts on the Information Highway.* (New York: Doubleday, 1995). 247 p.

Sutton, Brett, ed. *Library Texts in an Electronic Age: Scholarly Implications and Library Services.* (Urbana-Champaign, Illinois: Graduate School of Library and Information Science, University of Illinois, 1994). 207 p.

Taylor, Arlene G. "On the Subject of Subjects," *Journal of Academic Librarianship.* (November 1995): 484-491.

Taylor, Betty W., Elizabeth B. Mann, and Robert J. Munro. *The Twenty-First Century: Technology's Impact on Academic Research and Law Libraries.* (Boston: G.K. Hall, 1988).

Taylor, Sally. "Desktop Today," *Publishers Weekly.* (June 7, 1991): 19-21.

Tenopir, Carol. "Electronic Access to Periodicals," *Library Journal.* 118 (No. 4, March 1, 1992): 54-55.

Tenopir, Carol. "Flat-Fee Pricing and Other Choices," *Library Journal.* 118 (No. 2, February 1, 1993): 58, 60.

Tenopir, Carol. "Full Text Database Retrieval Performance," *Online Review.* 9 (No. 2, April 1985): 149-164.

Tenopir, Carol. "Full-Text, Downloading and Other Issues," *Library Journal.* 108 (No. 11, June 1, 1983): 1111-1113.

Tenopir, Carol. "Generations of Online Searching," *Library Journal.* (September 1, 1996): 128-131.

Tenopir, Carol and Donald W. King. "Setting the Record Straight on Journal Publishing: Myth vs. Reality," *Library Journal.* (March 15, 1996): 32-35.

Tenopir, Carol and Man Evena Shu. "Magazines in Full Text: Uses and Search Strategies," *Online Review.* 13 (April 1989): 107-118.

Tenopir, Carol. "Online Databases: File Reloads," *Library Journal.* (May 1, 1992): 57-58.

Tenopir, Carol. "Online Databases: Predicting the Future," *Library Journal.* (October 1, 1991): 70,72.

Tenopir, Carol. "Searching Full-Text Databases," *Library Journal.* (May 1, 1988): 60-61.

Tenopir, Carol. "Searching Harvard Business Review Online . . . Lessons in Searching a Full Text Database," *Online.* 9 (No. 2, March 1985): 71-78.

Teuton, Luella Bosman. "Merchandising Library Services," *College & Research Libraries News*. (No. 3, March 1989): 208-209.

Tezla, Kathy E. "Reference Collection Development Using the RLG Conspectus," *The Reference Librarian*. (29) (1990): 43-51.

Thomsen, Elizabeth. *Reference and Collection Development on the Internet: A How-To-Do-It Manual for Librarians*. (New York: Neal-Schuman, 1996). 177 p.

Tomainolo, Nicholas G. and Joan G. Packer. "An Analysis of Internet Search Engines: Assessment of Over 200 Search Queries," *Computers in Libraries*. 16 (6) (June 1996): 58-62.

Turkle, Sherry. *The Second Self*. (New York: Simon & Schuster, 1984).

Valauskas, Edward J. and Nancy R. John, eds. *The Internet Initiative: Libraries Providing Internet Services and How They Plan, Pay, and Manage*. (Chicago: ALA, 1995): 170 p.

Veaner, Allen. "1985 to 1995: The Next Decade in Academic Librarianship, Part I," *College & Research Libraries*. 46 (May 1985): 209-229.

Waggaman, John S. *Strategies and Consequences: Managing the Costs in Higher Education*. (Washington, D.C.: School of Education and Human Development, George Washington University, 1992): 130 p.

Walters, Edward M. "The Issues and Needs of Local Library Consortium," *Journal of Library Administration*. (3/4) (Fall/Winter 1987): 14.

Watkins, Beverly T. "Information Technology: Many Campuses Start Building Tomorrow's Electronic Library," *The Chronicle of Higher Education*. (September 22, 1991): A.

Watkins, Beverly T. "Virginia Tech Forms Partnership to Study an 'Electronic Village,'" *The Chronicle of Higher Education*. (May 6, 1992): A26.

Web, T.D. "The Frozen Library: A Model for Twenty-First Century Libraries," *Electronic Library*. 13 (1) (February 1995): 21-26.

Weber, Robert. "Libraries Without Walls?" *Publishers Weekly*. 237 (June 8, 1990): S20-S22.

Weber, Robert. "The Clouded Future of Electronic Publishing," *Publishers Weekly*. 237 (June 29, 1990): 76.

Weiskel, Timothy. "The Electronic Library and the Challenge of Information Planning," *Academe*. (July/August 1989): 8-12.

Wessling, Julie. "Document Delivery: A Primary Service for the Nineties," *Advances in Librarianship*. 16 (1992): 26-27.

Wessling, Julie. "Electronic ILL: The User Interface," *Document Delivery World*. 9 (April 1993): 24-26.

White, Herbert S. "Do We Want to Be Knowledge Workers?" *Library Journal*. (September 15, 1996): 41-42.

White, Herbert S. "Coalition-Building and the Image of Power," *Library Journal*. (January 1993): 69-70.

White, Herbert S. "Interlibrary Loan: An Old Idea in a New Setting," *Library Journal*. 112 (July 1987): 53-54.

White, Herbert S. "The Painful Process of Choosing Priorities," *Library Journal*. (May 15, 1992): 62-64.

White, Herbert S. "The Perilous Allure of Moral Imperativism," *Library Journal*. (September 15, 1992).

White, Howard D. *Brief Tests of Collection Strength: A Methodology for All Types of Libraries*. (Westport, Conn.: Greenwood Press, 1995). 208 p.

White, Mary Alice. "Imagery in Multimedia," *Multimedia Review*. (Fall 1990): 5-8.

White, Mary Alice. "The Third Learning Revolution," *Electronic Learning*. 7 (January 1988): 6-7.

Williams, Brian W. and Joan G. Hubbard. "Interlibrary Loan and Collection Management Applications of an ILL Database Management System," *Journal of Interlibrary Loan & Information Supply*. 1 (1991): 63-90.

Williams, James F. II, ed. *Strategic Planning in Higher Education: Implementing New Roles for the Academic Library*. (Binghamton, New York, The Haworth Press, Inc., 1991). 221 p.

Williamson, Mariyn L. "Seven Years of Cancellations at Georgia Tech," *Serials Librarian*. 9 (Spring 1985): 103-114.

Wilson, David L. "Information Technology: Huge Computer Network Quickens Pace of Academic Exchange and Collaboration," *The Chronicle of Higher Education*. (September 30, 1992): A17-A19.

Wilson, David L. "Information Technology: Major Scholarly Publisher to Test Electronic Transmission of Journals," *The Chronicle of Higher Education.* (June 3, 1992): A12, A20.

Wilson, Flo. "Article-Level Access in the Online Catalog at Vanderbilt University," *Information Technology and Libraries.* 8 (June 1989): 121-131.

Wilson, Myoung Chung and Hendrik Edelman. "Collection Development in an Interdisciplinary Context," *Journal of Academic Librarianship.* (May 1996): 195-200.

Wilson, Thomas C., ed. *Impact of Technology on Resource Sharing: Experimentation and Maturity.* (Binghamton, New York: The Haworth Press, Inc., 1993). (Also pub. In *Resource Sharing and Information Networks*, Vol 8 [1]).

Wittenborg, Karin. "Collection Bias: What's Right," *College & Research Libraries.* 56 (2) (March 1995): 114-116.

Woodsworth, Anne. "Computing Centers and Libraries as Cohorts: Exploiting Mutual Strengths." In *Computing, Electronic Publishing and Information Technology: Their Impact on Academic Libraries.* Ed. Robin Downes. (New York, The Haworth Press, Inc., 1988): 21-34.

Woodsworth, Anne and James F. Williams II. *Managing the Economics of Owning, Leasing and Contracting Out Information Services.* (Brookfield, Vermont: Ashgate Pub. Co., 1993).

Woodsworth, Anne and others. "The Model Research Library: Planning for the Future," *Journal of Academic Librarianship.* (July 1989): 132-138.

Woodward, Hazel. "The Impact of Electronic Information on Serials Collection Management," *IFLA Journal.* 20 (1) (1994): 35-45.

Woodward, Hazel and Cliff McKnight. "Electronic Journals: Issues of Access and Bibliographical Control," *Serials Review.* 21 (2) (Summer 1995): 71-78.

Woodward, Hazel and Stella Pilling, eds. *The International Serials Industry.* (Aldershot, England: Gower Pub., 1993). 275 p.

Woolfrey, Sandra. "Subscriber Interest in Electronic Copy of Printed Journals," *Scholarly Publishing.* 26 (3) (April 1995): 183-205.

Wright, Keith C. "The Power of Library Administrators Meets the Power of Technology," in *Acquisitions '91: Proceedings of the*

Conference on Acquisitions, Budgets, and Collections. Comp. and edited by David C. Genaway. (Minneapolis, Minnesota, April 10-11, 1991): 337-350.

Yavorkovsky, Jerome. "Auditing Acquisitions," *The Bottom Line.* (1986): 34-35.

Young, Peter R. "Periodical Prices 1988-1990," *Serials Librarian.* 18 (No. 3/4, 1990): 1-21.

Zemsky, Robert and William F. Massy. "Cost Containment: Committing to a New Economic Reality," *Change.* (November/December 1990): 16-22.

Conclusion

Maureen Pastine

Some might argue that the virtual library collection of the future is here now, via the information resources accessible over the Internet and the World Wide Web, as well as through CD-ROM stand-alone and networked workstations, or via the online library catalogs of the world and home pages of many of those same libraries. Others will argue that the "virtual library" is a long way off and may never truly arrive. Some point out that the emerging technologies have only served to increase the distance between the "information rich" and the "information poor."

Some perceive that much of the information available electronically is irrelevant and even largely inaccurate–a virtual mine of disconnected bits of information rather than an existing organized knowledge base. Regardless of which viewpoint anyone takes, the truth is that most academic libraries today are attempting to maintain a balance between ownership of traditional and new electronic information resources. However, most academic libraries have also experienced a loss in purchasing power for monographs and serials, a greater need to reallocate some acquisitions funds for multimedia and electronic products/access, and some have even experienced a dramatic loss in base acquisitions budgets. What that has meant for collection development has ranged from massive serials cancellations, particularly in the sciences, to a greater reliance on coopera-

Maureen Pastine, AB, MLS, is University Librarian, University Libraries, Paley Library, Temple University, Philadelphia, PA 19122.

[Haworth co-indexing entry note]: "Conclusion." Pastine, Maureen. Co-published simultaneously in *Collection Management* (The Haworth Press, Inc.) Vol. 22, No. 1/2, 1997, pp. 215-217; and: *Collection Development: Access in the Virtual Library* (ed: Maureen Pastine) The Haworth Press, Inc., 1997, pp. 215-217. Single or multiple copies of this article are available for a fee from The Haworth Document Delivery Service [1-800-342-9678, 9:00 a.m. - 5:00 p.m. (EST). E-mail address: getinfo@haworth.com].

tion and resource-sharing within a local area, a state, a region, or nationally and even internationally.

New consortial partnerships have developed, particularly within state-wide areas, to develop enhanced and improved methods of shared access to electronic information resources and expanded and enhanced document delivery methods. Many of these consortia partnerships have even provided not only for shared software costs, but also for shared hardware and networking costs. In addition, most academic libraries have provided more "global" resources through electronic means, expanding and enhancing on-site local collections.

In our planning and implementation, it is imperative that we apply the principle that technology is second, people are first. We can assume that our users want the entire world of information at their fingertips, but if we fail to include an assurance that adequate personal workstations are available, and to ensure that they will be taught how to navigate through the current maze of relevant and irrelevant information resources, then all the computing power and the information itself will not be used.

The focus should not be technology, but on quality stores of information and knowledge and provision of effective information service, along with how to integrate these resources into teaching, learning, and research.

In achieving a balance between ownership and access to electronic information, our emphasis should be on empowering the user, not just delivery of information and services. We must anticipate the needs, the problems, and what outcome we want in provision of operations, services, and resources. The client's need should be the foundation for services.

Many of our users are sophisticated in electronic access and networking, and have the technology at their desktop to do so. But, there are just as many, or more, who do not, and where needed resources in their fields are not yet available in electronic format.

Factors to consider in planning for the "virtual library" should include not only what collections mean but:

1. Constituency building with our campus users and with other area and regional libraries and consortia;

2. Developing greater visibility and participation in the campus and our larger communities, the consortia budgetary process, and the politics in setting priorities;
3. Demonstrating evidence of responsible decision-making in achieving new methods of information delivery;
4. Showing responsible reallocation of existing resources based upon surveys of user needs and demands; and
5. Assuming major roles in information policy and policy decisions.

In building the virtual library collections of the future, new funding sources must be found. In order to do that we need a greater focus on marketing what we have done and will do for our communities. They need to understand the role information has played, and will play, in the economy. We have not done that very well. We need to provide more assistance to our local communities, to form partnerships, to demonstrate the role of education and libraries in life-long learning pursuits. Over one-half of our graduates, even up to 85%, do not work in their chosen fields of study. Libraries are there to help them to educate themselves in the jobs they take outside of these fields. We must be more visible in our communities in offering our services for reciprocal financial support. Our focus on purchasing information services and building collections is important but we also need skilled and knowledgeable staff, in adequate numbers, to do coalition building off and on our campuses–to educate users, to gain widespread community support, and to gain supplemental funding. A library is not a library without adequate professional expertise to provide quality collections and services. It is only a place, or a network, in which decision-makers feel cuts and reductions can be made. People/staff are what make the difference. Currently, everyone thinks that they can operate and administer a library. We need to value our own professional expertise and demonstrate it outside of our still existent walls. We have led others to undervalue librarians and libraries. In working toward the "virtual library" we must transform our libraries into a valuable commodity, not one which others make short shrift of without adequate representation of those library personnel who make a library what it is–an intellectual study for the future.

Index

Academic Press, electronic journals of, 50,51-52
Access services, 34
   effect of electronic information technology on, 38-39
Access versus ownership issue, 5, 16-17,30-33,215
   collection development and, 39-40
   definition of, 30
   interlibrary loan and, 46-48,49
   selective bibliography about, 187-214
   users' empowerment and, 216
   users' expectations regarding, 31-32
Acquisition
   budgets for, 215
   selective bibliography about, 101-186
Administrators
   expectations about electronic information technology, 35
   perceptions of librarians' role, 1
Advertising, on the World Wide Web/Internet, 16,19
Aggregator services, 49-50
Alfred P. Sloan Foundation, 76
Alta Vista, 19-20
Amazon (book seller), 16
American Library Directory, 57
America Online, 34,76,77
Approval plans, 92-93
Ariel, 39
ARL Statistics, 57
Association for Higher Education, 59
Association of Research Libraries
   collection analysis by, 65-67

collection development
   conspectus of, 48-49
Audio-video delivery systems, 77

Babson College, 79
Bibliographers, role in virtual libraries, 53-55
Bibliographic databases, "common," 84
Bibliographies
   library acquisitions (1986-1995), 101-186
   ownership versus access issue, 187-214
Books
   digitization of, 18
   electronic technology versus, 22-23
Borders Books, 16
Browsing, 53
Budgets
   for acquisition, 215
   for cooperative collection development, 93-95
"Build versus buy" issue, 86,87-88

Catalogs, online. *See* Online catalogs
CD-ROM
   full-text books on, 22
   indexes and abstracts on, 26
Circulation services, 33,34,38
CMU Universal Library Repository, 18
Collection analysis, 57-69
   national collecting studies, 61-62, 64-68
   non-electronic approaches to, 57, 58,60

Distributed education, 71-80
  asynchronous, 5-6,72-79
  comparison with distance
     learning, 71-72
  definition of, 80n.
  electronic conferencing use in, 71,
     72
     application to libraries, 77-79
     chats, 74,76
     e-mail, 73,75
     FirstClass, 75-76
     Lotus, 76
     mailing lists, 73-74
     online services, 76-77
     tutor-facilitator model of, 6,73
     Usenet, 74
     World Wide Web, 74-75,76
  synchronous, 72
Document delivery services, 4-5,
     45-46,77-78
  cost of, 39
  users' direct access to, 46
Drexel University, 76
DVD, 22,26

Electronic conferencing, use in
     distributed education. *See*
     Distributed education;
     electronic conferencing use
     in
Electronic information resources,
     costs of, 35
Electronic mail
  costs of, 15
  use in distributed learning, 73,75
  libraries' use of, 78
Evans, Glyn, 60
Excite, 19-20
Expertise, as political resource,
     82-83
Extranets, definition of, 17

FirstClass, 75-76,79

Hardware
  maintenance and upgrading of, 35
  reference librarians' responsibility
     for, 37
Hypertext, 21

IDC, 13,14
Indexes and abstracts, on CD-ROM,
     26
Information, forms of, 10-11
Information management, as
     librarians' role, 10-11
Information superhighway, 12,14-15,
     22-23,34
Integrated library systems, 33-34
Interlibrary loan
  as circulation, 46-48,49
  comparison with document
     delivery services, 45-46
  consortial approach to, 47-48,49
  cost of, 46,47
  effect of electronic information
     technology on, 2-3,4-5,39
  implication of electronic journals
     for, 50-51
  inadequacy of, 46-47
  as public service, 33
Internet, 12. *See also* World Wide
     Web
  user costs of, 15
Intranets
  definitions of, 17
  of special libraries, 23

Journals
  cancellations of, 215-216
  electronic, 49-52
     cost of, 49-50
     interlibrary loan implications
        of, 50-51
  "fee versus free" issue of, 6-7
  price information about, 79
  subscriptions to, 44-45
     article delivery versus, 45-46

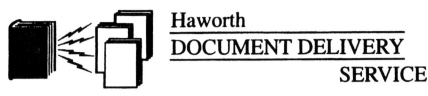

Haworth
DOCUMENT DELIVERY
SERVICE

This valuable service provides a single-article order form for any article from a Haworth journal.

- *Time Saving:* No running around from library to library to find a specific article.
- *Cost Effective:* All costs are kept down to a minimum.
- *Fast Delivery:* Choose from several options, including same-day FAX.
- *No Copyright Hassles:* You will be supplied by the original publisher.
- *Easy Payment:* Choose from several easy payment methods.

> *Open Accounts Welcome for...*
> - Library Interlibrary Loan Departments
> - Library Network/Consortia Wishing to Provide Single-Article Services
> - Indexing/Abstracting Services with Single Article Provision Services
> - Document Provision Brokers and Freelance Information Service Providers

MAIL or *FAX* THIS ENTIRE ORDER FORM TO:

Haworth Document Delivery Service
The Haworth Press, Inc.
10 Alice Street
Binghamton, NY 13904-1580

or FAX: 1-800-895-0582
or CALL: 1-800-342-9678
9am-5pm EST

PLEASE SEND ME PHOTOCOPIES OF THE FOLLOWING SINGLE ARTICLES:
1) Journal Title: _____
   Vol/Issue/Year:_____Starting & Ending Pages:_____
   Article Title:_____
   _____

2) Journal Title: _____
   Vol/Issue/Year:_____Starting & Ending Pages:_____
   Article Title:_____
   _____

3) Journal Title: _____
   Vol/Issue/Year:_____Starting & Ending Pages:_____
   Article Title:_____
   _____

4) Journal Title: _____
   Vol/Issue/Year:_____Starting & Ending Pages:_____
   Article Title:_____
   _____

(See other side for Costs and Payment Information)

COSTS: Please figure your cost to order quality copies of an article.

1. Set-up charge per article: $8.00

            ($8.00 × number of separate articles)   _____

2. Photocopying charge for each article:

            1-10 pages: $1.00   _____

            11-19 pages: $3.00   _____

            20-29 pages: $5.00   _____

            30+ pages: $2.00/10 pages   _____

3. Flexicover (optional): $2.00/article   _____

4. Postage & Handling: US: $1.00 for the first article/

            $.50 each additional article   _____

            Federal Express: $25.00   _____

            Outside US: $2.00 for first article/

            $.50 each additional article_____

5. Same-day FAX service: $.35 per page   _____

                    GRAND TOTAL: _____

METHOD OF PAYMENT: (please check one)

❑ Check enclosed   ❑ Please ship and bill. PO # _____

             (sorry we can ship and bill to bookstores only! All others must pre-pay)

❑ Charge to my credit card: ❑ Visa; ❑ MasterCard; ❑ Discover;

             ❑ American Express;

Account Number:_____ Expiration date:_____

Signature: ✗_____

Name: _____ Institution: _____

Address: _____

_____

City: _____ State:_____ Zip:_____

Phone Number: _____ FAX Number: _____

MAIL or *FAX* THIS ENTIRE ORDER FORM TO:

Haworth Document Delivery Service	**or FAX:** 1-800-895-0582
The Haworth Press, Inc.	**or CALL:** 1-800-342-9678
10 Alice Street	9am-5pm EST)
Binghamton, NY 13904-1580	